D1525185

GENESIS – REVELATION
DAILY DEVOTIONAL

WISDOM
FOR TODAY

Chuck
Smith

Wisdom For Today
Genesis – Revelation Daily Devotional
by Chuck Smith

© 2007 The Word For Today
Published by The Word For Today
P.O. Box 8000, Costa Mesa, CA 92628
(800) 272-WORD (9673)

Web Site: www.twft.com
E-mail: info@twft.com

ISBN: 978-1-59751-031-8

Unless otherwise indicated, Scripture quotations in this book are taken from the New King James Version, Copyright © 1979, 1980, 1984 by Thomas Nelson, Inc., Publishers. Used by permission. Translational emendations, amplifications, and paraphrases are by the author.

Edited by Shannon Woodward
Interior design by Bob Bubnis

All Rights Reserved. No part of this publication may be reproduced, stored in a retrieval system, or transmitted in any form or by any means without the express written consent of The Word For Today Publishers.

Printed in the United States of America

INTRODUCTION

The world in which we live places great value on knowledge. But people don't always strive to know the most important things. The truth is you may be extremely knowledgeable about insects, or stars, or the sciences. You may be very wise about those sorts of things and people might really admire you for that knowledge. That's all well and good, but if you don't have the wisdom of God, you're missing the most important knowledge a man can ever hope to attain.

How do you gain the wisdom of God? Proverbs tells us that, "The fear of the LORD is the beginning of wisdom, and the knowledge of the Holy One is understanding" (9:10). Wisdom starts when we begin to reverence God above all other things. And when that reverence moves us to seek God through His Word, we gain understanding.

But in the quest for wisdom, God has not left us to our own devices. He made a provision for us. He is such a good Father like that—always helping us in our weaknesses, always providing where we lack. And He so desires that we attain wisdom that He sent a special blessing to help us in that quest.

In looking toward His own death, Jesus prepared His disciples by promising them that He would not leave them as orphans in this world, but would send them a Comforter and a Guide. "And I will pray the Father, and He will give you another Helper, that He may abide with you forever—the Spirit of truth, whom the world cannot receive, because it neither sees Him nor knows Him; but you know Him, for He dwells with you and will be in you" (John 14:16-17). And then Jesus named the Comforter and promised this concerning Him: "But the Helper, the Holy Spirit, whom the Father will send in My name, He will teach you all things, and bring to your remembrance all things that I said to you" (John 14:26).

What a marvelous promise we have been given! God has put His Holy Spirit within us. He will dwell in us forever—and will teach us all that we need to know. In fact, John writes elsewhere that, "You have an anointing from the Holy One, and you know all things" (1 John 2:20). The Holy Spirit, abiding within us, reveals God's truths to our hearts. As we are reading God's Word, He makes it come alive. It might be a verse you have read dozens of times before, but at the time when you most need it, the Holy Spirit brings it to life and makes it jump off the page.

What a blessing the Holy Spirit is to us. How He ministers to us! His work in our individual lives and in the church is so very important. But tragically, men have tried to substitute the wisdom of the Holy Spirit with the wisdom of man. We have convinced ourselves that spiritual wisdom can be attained only after studying Greek and Hebrew. We think that what qualifies a man to instruct people in the Word of truth is a seminary degree. But I have to disagree with that theory. It's not a degree on the wall that qualifies a man—it's the Holy Spirit in the heart. I would rather listen to an uneducated man who is filled with the Holy Spirit than some doctor of theology who is not filled with the Spirit, and who approaches the Bible as just an interesting piece of literature on the subject of moral values.

Over the years, I have met many people whom the world would consider to be simple, or even ignorant, but who in reality possessed great wisdom in the Lord. I think of one woman that Kay and I met years ago when we were vacationing up at Bass Lake. The town closest to the lake was called North Fork, and when Sunday came around and we wanted to find a church to attend, we drove to that little town. As it turned out, the pastor was away on vacation that Sunday and had asked a woman from the hills of Kentucky to be the guest speaker. I have to tell you, when that woman spoke, it sounded like she had a mouthful of gravel. She really butchered the English language with her hillbilly talk. But the Holy Spirit in her moved with such dynamic power that Kay and I were blessed tremendously that Sunday morning.

And then there was one particular dear saint of God that we knew when I pastored the church in Huntington Beach. She was a little grandmotherly woman who always seemed to know when I was discouraged about something. Sometimes I looked too hard at the condition of the world and all the bad things that were happening, and I would let it upset me. God would send this little woman my way, and she would say, "Remember, Charles, the Lord is still on the throne." Just that simple line, but oh, the wisdom it contained! No matter how dark the world became or how hopeless things looked, that one sentence had the power to clear my vision and chase my discouragement. "The Lord is on the throne."

I pray that you become wise in all the things that matter most. And I pray that you remember the anointing you have from God. Cherish that anointing. Cherish the ministry of the Holy Spirit in your heart as you study the Word and as you draw close to the Lord.

Wisdom is yours for the taking. God desires to give it to you. Honor Him, meditate on His Word, and obey whatever He asks you to do. And as you open the pages of this book, invite the Holy Spirit to guide you daily into all truth. That's the *Wisdom For Today*.

JANUARY 1

CREATED IN HIS IMAGE

Then God said, "Let Us make man in Our image, according to Our likeness ..." So God created man in His own image, in the image of God He created him; male and female He created them.

— GENESIS 1:26-27

Why would God want to create us in His image?

He did so because He desired a loving, meaningful relationship with us. Because God is love, He gave us the capacity to love. Because He is self-determinate, He gave us the capacity to choose. He made us able to love and choose, so that we could bring Him pleasure—not only receiving His love, but choosing to love Him in return.

Many people choose not to love God. In doing so, they fail to respond to the very purpose of their existence and should not be surprised when life feels empty, frustrating, and worthless.

> CHOICE IS A WONDERFUL THING, BUT IT CAN ALSO BRING DEVASTATING CONSEQUENCES.

The exercise of man's free choice in the garden brought about a fall from God's image. It brought spiritual death, and caused man to live like an animal—absorbed only in satisfying his physical appetites. But man can never be satisfied relating to the animal kingdom. He can find real contentment only when he has a relationship with God.

Jesus came for that purpose. He took our sin and died in our place. He now offers another choice—we can live a life in the Spirit in fellowship with Him, or continue the life of the flesh, which leads to death and alienation.

Choose carefully, for God honors our choices.

Father, thank You that as we behold Your glory, we are being changed into Your image by the Holy Spirit who works within us.

AMEN.

BREAKING AWAY

And God said to Noah, "The end of all flesh has come before Me,
for the earth is filled with violence through them; and behold
I will destroy them with the earth."

— GENESIS 6:13

In the days before the flood, mankind turned from God and lived as though He did not exist. Morals failed. Men's minds were corrupted and they embraced abnormal sexual activity. Violence covered the face of the earth and men began living like animals. And it was upon these conditions that God looked and said, "My Spirit will not always strive with man" (Genesis 6:3).

You see, the time eventually comes when God's patience is exhausted.

We, too, live in a world filled with violence and corruption. It is only a matter of time before God again says, "That's it." Matthew 24:37 tells us, "As it was in the days of Noah, so shall it be at the coming of the Son of God." As He did the first time, God will tell His people, "Come on into the ark." Thank God He has provided that place of refuge for us. That ark today is Jesus Christ.

> YOU ARE EITHER A PART OF THE SYSTEM THAT IS CORRUPTING THE WORLD AND DRAGGING IT UNDER, OR YOU ARE A PART OF THE SYSTEM THAT WILL FLOAT OVER IT WHEN IT FALLS.

God has established absolute standards of righteousness, and we must submit ourselves to His authority, because Jesus is coming very soon to judge the world in righteousness.

Father, may we heed those things which we have heard, lest we
drift away from them. Help us make a definite, decisive break
with this corrupt world, that we might stand and be numbered
with those who love and serve You.

IN JESUS' NAME, AMEN.

ALL GOD'S PROMISES

*While the earth remains, seedtime and harvest, cold and heat,
winter and summer, and day and night shall not cease.*

— GENESIS 8:22

"While the earth remains...." The inference here is that the earth won't last forever, but in the words that follow, God promises that as long as the earth remains, there will be certain constants: seedtime and harvest, cold and heat, winter and summer, day and night. We have confidence in these promises of God. I don't lose any sleep at night worried that it might not dawn a new day tomorrow.

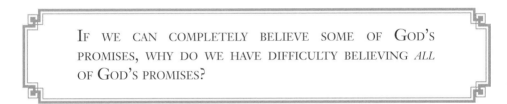

IF WE CAN COMPLETELY BELIEVE SOME OF GOD'S PROMISES, WHY DO WE HAVE DIFFICULTY BELIEVING *ALL* OF GOD'S PROMISES?

Jesus said, "I will never leave you nor forsake you," but sometimes we worry that He just might do so. Just as I have great confidence that God will keep the earth spinning, I should also have confidence that God will supply all of my needs.

I think God intended these promises to remind us daily of His faithfulness. Every morning when we wake up and see it is getting light outside, we should say, "Boy, is God ever faithful to His promise!" Every evening as the sun sets we ought to say, "Wow, God sure keeps His Word, doesn't He?"

God will keep His promises whether we believe them or not. When troubled, we can become anxious and fearful, or we can have a victorious, happy attitude. We can have victory because God is going to take care of us. He promised.

God is faithful—you can bet your life upon it.

---

*Thank You, Father, for Your steadfast promises. May we begin to
live in glorious confidence because You're on the throne.*

IN JESUS' NAME, AMEN.

No Compromise

And Terah took his son Abram and his grandson Lot ... and Abram's wife; and they went out with them from Ur of the Chaldeans to go to the land of Canaan; and they came to Haran and dwelt there.... Now the LORD had said to Abram: "Get out of your country, from your family and from your father's house, to a land that I will show you."

— GENESIS 11:31, 12:1

Desiring an intimate relationship with Abram, God called him to do three things: leave the place of idolatry, leave his family, and go to the land God would show him. But Abram did not fully obey. He left Ur with both his father and his nephew and failed to go directly to Canaan. Also, they stayed within the border of the Babylonian plain—still within the land he was to leave.

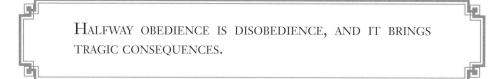

HALFWAY OBEDIENCE IS DISOBEDIENCE, AND IT BRINGS TRAGIC CONSEQUENCES.

God remained silent while Abram dwelt in Haran and didn't speak again until Abram reached Canaan. In his disobedience, Abram lost the privilege of close communion with God.

What about you? Are you living in Haran? Have you stopped short of full obedience? Have you compromised? Are you holding on to old habits? God is calling you today to deny yourself, shun evil, take up your cross, and follow Jesus. He is calling you to a place of blessing, a place of promise, a place of communion and intimate relationship—because He loves you.

Father, we pray that as Your Holy Spirit leads us along Your path, we wouldn't stop short of that which You desire for us. In obedience, Lord, may we take up our cross—no matter what the cost.

AMEN.

WHEN GOD WAITS

When Abram was ninety-nine years old, the LORD appeared to
Abram and said to him, "I am Almighty God; walk before Me
and be blameless. And I will make My covenant between Me and
you, and will multiply you exceedingly."

— GENESIS 17:1-2

God spoke to Abraham when he was eighty-six years old … and then waited thirteen more years before He spoke again. Why do you suppose God waited so long?

God often chooses to wait until we have exhausted every possible resource before us. He waits until we reach a point of hopelessness. That is where Abram was, finally. Had God spoken any earlier, Abram probably would have tried to help God perform His promise.

While training to be a lifeguard, I learned that when someone is drowning, you don't approach them directly. If you come too close while they are still strong and flailing, they might take you down with them. You have to wait until they are exhausted. I think God works on this same principle. As long as we are flailing about, God waits.

> WHEN WE FINALLY GIVE UP, GOD CAN BEGIN TO WORK OUT HIS GLORIOUS PLAN.

"Oh, that men would praise the Lord for His marvelous works!" Many times we are prone to give some rationalistic explanation or say how lucky we are when things work out. We don't give God credit for the work He has done.

Maybe you are in a situation that looks impossible. You did your best and failed. Hey, are you ever in good shape! For man's impossibilities are God's opportunities. God will do for you what you can't do for yourself!

Father, thank You for Your patience. We give You all our
impossible situations. Bring glory to Your name, Lord,
that men would praise You.

AMEN.

No Complaints

*Then Rebekah and her maids arose, and they rode on the camels
and followed the man.*

— Genesis 24:61

Rebekah made a commitment of faith when she got on that camel and agreed to a 400-mile journey. She had to depend completely upon Isaac's servant, and take his word for the wealth and glory of the kingdom awaiting her.

Riding a camel is a real experience. The camel does not move smoothly. If you don't relax and move with him, he will bump you to death.

The Christian life isn't easy, either. "Beloved, do not think it strange concerning the fiery trial which is to try you, as though some strange thing happened to you" (1 Peter 4:12). As you ride that awkward beast, you'll be tested, jostled, and placed in uncomfortable positions. Along the desert ride, you may even get discouraged.

After Rebekah reached her destination, do you suppose she yelled, "You rotten beast!" and kicked the camel? I don't think so. She probably patted him and said, "It was miserable trying to ride you, but you have done your job. You've brought me to my master and my lord."

LIFE'S TRIALS ARE GOD'S INSTRUMENTS TO BRING US TO HIM.

One day the journey will be over. The camels are there to bring us into a full reliance on Jesus. Very soon we're going to look up and see our Lord coming. And when I jump off my camel, I'm not going to kick it. It has brought me along to my Lord, and I will thank God that I have arrived.

*Father, thank You for the difficulties that draw us to You. Help
us to look upon our trials as Your instruments. And may we not
become weary of the journey.*

In Jesus' name, amen.

JANUARY 7

Sweetening a Sour Relationship

*[Jacob] crossed over before them and bowed himself to the ground
seven times, until he came near to his brother. But Esau ran to meet
him, and embraced him … and kissed him, and they wept.*

— Genesis 33:3-4

For twenty years, these brothers had been estranged. But Esau's hatred changed suddenly. Though he intended to meet Jacob with a sword, he ended up embracing him. Close relationships can sometimes sour. Perhaps you have been estranged from a loved one.

> When love has grown cold, can it be restored? The Scriptures say "yes."

The first thing that Jacob did was pray. The first thing you should do is pray and ask God to change the heart of that person who is estranged from you. When we do that, God often shows us where *we* need to change.

Jacob's nature was to take, not to give. But after praying, he decided to send ahead presents to Esau. Find ways to bless that person you're estranged from.

Next, he edified his brother, referring to him as "lord." Too often, our relationships sour because we tear down instead of build up.

Then Jacob shared with Esau the things that transpired during their absence. Openness—sharing your thoughts and feelings—heals relationships. And then Jacob and Esau touched. They embraced one another.

Can God heal your relationships? Yes. If you follow Jacob's example—praying, blessing, edifying, sharing, and touching the one you are estranged from, God can take that sour relationship and make it sweet again.

---

*Father, help us to learn through Your Word how to love each
other, that we may see a glorious fragrance filling our lives.*

In Jesus' name, amen.

OVERCOMING TEMPTATION

She caught him by his garment, saying, "Lie with me." But he
left his garment in her hand, and fled …
— GENESIS 39:12

We each face daily temptations—temptations to lie, cheat, and steal. Joseph faced powerful temptation, yet he resisted. What were the keys to his success?

First, Joseph knew that someone trusted him implicitly. He did not want to violate the trust Potiphar had placed in him.

Second, Joseph knew he was different from the rest of the world. Because God had called him as a chosen race, Joseph said the obvious: "How can I…?"

Third, Joseph knew that the temptation was wicked. One of our problems today is our lax attitude towards sin. We have learned to be very tolerant towards sin.

Finally, Joseph knew that if he succumbed, the sin would ultimately be against God, not against Potiphar. And then Joseph took the wisest possible action—he ran. If all else fails, run. Paul told Timothy, "Flee from youthful lusts." Stay away from places where you know that you are weak and where you will be tempted to fall.

WE CAN LIVE A PURE LIFE. WE CAN OVERCOME TEMPTATION. GOD HAS GIVEN US ALL THE RULES WE NEED TO LIVE IN VICTORY.

Like Joseph, recognize four important points: (1) People have put their trust in you. (2) You're special because you're a child of God and you can't do what other people can do. (3) Temptation is wicked, and when you give in, you're sinning against God Himself. (4) If everything else fails—run. Flee to Jesus.

Father, may we resolve to live a righteous, holy life. Help us, Lord,
to resist the temptations placed in our pathway day after day.
IN JESUS' NAME, AMEN.

GUILT

And Reuben answered them, saying, "Did I not speak to you,
saying, 'Do not sin against the boy'; and you would not listen?
Therefore behold, his blood is now required of us."

— GENESIS 42:22

Twenty years have passed since Joseph's brothers sold him as a slave, but his cries are still buried in the recesses of their minds. Guilt! How it lingers in our memories, only to surface again and remind us of our deeds. The brothers had successfully hidden their guilt from their dad, but it wasn't gone. Getting rid of guilt is almost an impossible task. But it is an important task.

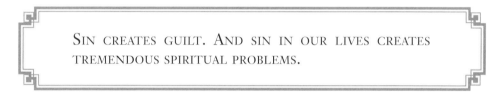

SIN CREATES GUILT. AND SIN IN OUR LIVES CREATES TREMENDOUS SPIRITUAL PROBLEMS.

David described what happened when he tried to hide his sin. "For day and night Your hand was heavy upon me; my vitality was turned into the drought of summer" (Psalm 32:4).

God said, "The wages of sin is death." Sin that goes unforgiven causes us to become dead to God. We no longer see Him, feel Him, or touch Him. That is why we must get rid of guilt. It separates us from God and destroys our lives.

But how? If I've done something wrong, how can I undo it?

You don't have to be punished for your sins; someone else has taken your punishment. God has made a way by sending His Son. And if you will just believe in Him, God will forgive you and make you new. He will give you a fresh start.

Father, thank You for the glorious removal of our guilt
through Jesus Christ, Who has washed us and cleansed us
from all of our unrighteousness.

IN JESUS' NAME, AMEN.

SEEKING GOD FOR DIRECTION

Then God spoke to Israel in the visions of the night, and said,
"Jacob, Jacob!... do not fear to go down to Egypt, for I will make
of you a great nation there. I will go down with you to Egypt, and
I will also surely bring you up again."

— GENESIS 46:2-4

For years, Jacob had thought his son Joseph was dead. Now his eldest sons give Jacob the startling news that Joseph is alive and wants him to come to Egypt. And so they begin their journey. But when they reach Beersheba, fear suddenly grips Jacob.

Fear is a powerful motivator. Jacob's fear caused him to seek God. It is better to be motivated by love, but if you won't seek God for that reason, He may put you in a place of necessity so you will seek Him out of need. If that doesn't work, He may put you in a fearful situation so you will seek Him out of fear. Because God loves you so much and enjoys fellowship with you, He will use whatever it takes to get you to Him.

> WE OFTEN PUT OURSELVES IN SOME PRETTY MISERABLE POSITIONS BECAUSE WE MOVE AHEAD WITHOUT SEEKING GOD.

When God—who knows all things and loves you supremely—has offered to guide your life, it seems rather ridiculous to ignore that help and move in your own limited wisdom. When we reach a crossroad and don't know which way to turn, it is wise to seek God.

Teach us, O Lord, to seek Your will, to walk in Your path,
and to be led by Your Spirit.

IN JESUS' NAME, AMEN.

God Knows

I have surely seen the oppression of My people who are in Egypt,
and have heard their cry because of their taskmasters, for I know
their sorrows. So I have come down to deliver them …

— Exodus 3:7-8

God's people had been treated cruelly by the Egyptians for years. They could see no escape from their bondage. They cried unto God, but feared that He wasn't listening.

> When going through trials, we often feel alone. We think nobody sees or understands. But God knows.

The Israelites didn't know that God was already at work, that He had a plan. But He did.

God first told Moses, "I know what is going on." Then He added, "For I know their sorrows." A lot of times all I really need to know is that somebody knows, understands, and cares.

But God takes it one step further. He says, "Moses, I see, I've heard their cries, I know their sorrows, and I have come to deliver them."

I am so glad that the God I serve is a God who can see, a God who can hear, a God who knows, and a God who is able to do exceedingly above all I ask or all I need. He is able to take the impossible situation and turn it around.

You may be in a pretty tough situation. You have been crying unto the Lord, but you wonder if He hears. God is saying to you, "I have seen your affliction. I've heard your cry. I know your sorrow. And I have come this day to deliver."

Father, we thank You that You are a living, powerful God, able to do exceedingly abundantly above what we need, ask, or imagine.

Amen.

WHO IS THE LORD?

Afterward Moses and Aaron went in and told Pharaoh, "Thus says the LORD God of Israel: 'Let my people go, that they may hold a feast to Me in the wilderness.'" And Pharaoh said, "Who is the Lord, that I should obey His voice to let Israel go? I do not know the Lord, nor will I let Israel go."

— EXODUS 5:1-2

Moses and Aaron came to Pharaoh with the demands of the Lord to let their people go. But he answered, "Who is the Lord that I should obey Him? I do not know the Lord, neither will I obey." Who is the Lord? Pharaoh was about to get the answer to his question.

The Egyptians had chosen to worship the forces of nature. They made a mistake that many people make even today—worshiping and serving the creation more than the Creator. Jehovah, the only true and living God, made His demand upon Pharaoh, but Pharaoh professed ignorance of Him and an unwillingness to obey.

What was God's response? He revealed Himself to Pharaoh through the plagues He brought upon Egypt—darkness, boils, flies, and frogs, water turned to blood, death; plagues that tormented the Egyptians, but spared God's own people.

WHO IS THE LORD THAT YOU SHOULD OBEY HIM? THERE IS NO EXCUSE FOR NOT KNOWING HIM.

He is the God who has revealed Himself through nature, through His Word, and through His Son. He is the God over all the universe, the Creator of all things, the King of kings and the Lord of lords, the eternal Almighty, all powerful, loving God who invites you to know Him better today.

We thank You, Father, that we have come to know You. We want to know You even more.

AMEN.

The Passover

Now the blood shall be a sign for you on the houses where you are.
And when I see the blood, I will pass over you; and the plague shall
not be on you to destroy you when I strike the land of Egypt.

— Exodus 12:13

God has been so patient with the Egyptians. They had afflicted His people for at least eighty years. But He didn't just wipe them out. He gave them preliminary notices that the day of judgment was arriving. He gave them the opportunity to change and to escape His judgment.

In proclaiming His coming judgment, God also provided a way of escape for the children of Israel. As long as they remained in the house with the lamb's blood on the door, God said, "When I pass through the land, they will be safe."

The chief characteristic of God is love—love that is beyond our capacity to fully comprehend. But God is also righteous, so the wicked must be judged. Ultimately, the righteousness of God must prevail. It has been a long time coming, but already we are beginning to see a foreshadowing of the judgment that is to come. Are you in a place of safety today?

> GOD HAS MADE ONLY ONE PROVISION FOR YOUR SAFETY WHEN THE DAY OF JUDGMENT COMES, AND THAT IS IN JESUS CHRIST.

Jesus is the Lamb of God who takes away the sins of the world. We must rely fully on Him. There is no other refuge.

Father, thank You for the marvelous provisions You have made for
us through Jesus Christ—that He bore our sin, He took our guilt,
He died in our place, and His blood was shed for us. Thank You
for Your patience, long-suffering, mercy, and love.

Amen.

TRAPPED

Moses said to the people, "Do not be afraid. Stand still, and see the salvation of the LORD.... For the Egyptians whom you see today, you shall see again no more forever. The LORD will fight for you, and you shall hold your peace.

— EXODUS 14:13-14

The children of Israel had left the bondage in Egypt, their miserable life of slavery, and were determined now to serve the Lord. But the very first place that God leads them is into a trap. There is no way out of this valley but to turn around. They can't cross over the mountains on either side, and they can't go through the Red Sea.

Why would God lead His people into a trap?

GOD WANTS US TO LEARN TO TRUST IN HIM COMPLETELY— EVEN WHEN WE CANNOT SEE ANY POSSIBLE SOLUTIONS.

He wants us to realize that He is able to make a way even when there is no way; that He is not limited by man's resources or by man's capacities; and what He has promised, He is able to perform.

God's plan of deliverance requires faith. When you find yourself trapped and you can't see any way out, the natural tendency is to run. But if we step out in faith, God will go before us and make a path through the sea.

You may be feeling trapped. Maybe you are in circumstances where you can't see any way out. But maybe God has led you into a trap just so that you would turn to Him today.

Oh, Lord, how we thank You for Your deliverance. So often You have parted that sea of difficulty or removed the mountains for us. Help us not to fear but to trust.

IN JESUS' NAME, AMEN.

ON EAGLES' WINGS

Thus you shall say to the house of Jacob, and tell the children of Israel; "You have seen what I did to the Egyptians, and how I bore you on eagles' wings and brought you to Myself. Now therefore, if you will indeed obey My voice and keep My covenant, then you shall be a special treasure to Me above all people; for all the earth is Mine. And you shall be to Me a kingdom of priests and a holy nation."

— EXODUS 19:3-6

An eagle builds its nest high up on the wall of a cliff. When the time comes for an eaglet to learn to fly, the mother flutters over the nest, flaps her wings, and pushes the young eagle out. That little eaglet begins spinning and tumbling toward the rocks below. Just when you think that poor bird is going to be destroyed, the mother swoops underneath, picks it up on her wings, and carries it back to the nest. Lesson one is over. But the lesson will be repeated over and over, until the eaglet learns to fly.

We feel very comfortable and secure in the nest. We don't like it when God kicks us out and we begin tumbling. We think, "Surely I'm going to be destroyed."

BUT THEN GOD LIFTS US UP AND HE SHOWS US HIS FAITHFULNESS.

God delivered you and me from the bondage of living a life after the flesh. He bore us up on eagles' wings, bringing us to Himself, and He has made us His special treasure.

Father, how grateful we are that we are Your children, that You have brought us on eagles' wings to Yourself. We want to be Your special treasure, bringing forth good works for Your glory.

AMEN.

LITTLE BY LITTLE

*I will not drive them out from before you in one year, lest the land
become desolate and the beasts of the field become too numerous for
you. Little by little I will drive them out ...*

— EXODUS 23:29-30

The Israelites faced a formidable enemy. We face a daily enemy, too, as we battle against our flesh. The flesh has real strongholds in our lives—fortresses surrounded by high walls. Giants dwell in our land. But God wants us to enter in and possess all of His promises. He wants us to live a life of blessedness and victory. To do so, we have to battle the flesh.

How do we do that? We can learn to battle our flesh by observing the principles God set forth for Israel. Notice that He didn't give Israel victory in one year. Instead, He conquered their foes little by little.

GOD WILL NOT GIVE YOU VICTORY OVER THE FLESH IN ONE YEAR. SUCCESS HAS NO SHORTCUTS—IT IS A LIFE-LONG BATTLE.

As long as you live in this body you are going to be troubled with the things of the flesh. God doesn't show us the whole battle at once, because He knows that would discourage us. So He shows us one territory at a time.

Just as Israel never completely took all the territory that God promised to them, we will never have complete victory over our flesh until we stand before His throne. But we can rejoice in the territory that we have conquered so far, and rest in the knowledge that He will continue that work—little by little.

*Lord, help us not to be satisfied with a partial conquering of the
land, but may we press on until we have taken all that You
have promised.*

AMEN.

Not a Far-Off God

I will dwell among the children of Israel and will be their God.
And they shall know that I am the LORD their God …
— EXODUS 29:45-46

Where does God dwell?

You might say He dwells in the universe, but whenever you start talking about the universe, you are describing something so vast and so distant that it can make God seem very far removed.

But God is not remote or far-removed. Paul said that we should not think of God as way-off somewhere in the heaven where we cannot reach Him. The truth is, He is as close as our mouths. "If you confess with your mouth the Lord Jesus and believe in your heart that God has raised Him from the dead, you will be saved" (Romans 10:9).

God is very near. He surrounds us. And we are told in this Scripture that He was near to His people Israel. The tabernacle was to be located in the very center of their camp and the tribes were to camp all around it. The first thing they would see each morning was the ascending smoke of the morning sacrifice—and they would remember that God dwells right in the midst of His people.

> GOD WANTS YOU TO KNOW THAT HE IS NEAR ENOUGH
> THAT YOU CAN REACH OUT AT ANY TIME AND FELLOWSHIP
> WITH HIM.

No matter what your situation or problem, He is close enough. You can reach out today and pray to God, and by that prayer—be healed, helped, and strengthened.

Father, we thank You that You are a God who is near. Manifest Yourself in our lives, Lord, that we would be filled with Your infinite grace and love.

AMEN.

WHAT IS GOD LIKE?

And the LORD passed before him and proclaimed, "The LORD, the Lord God, merciful and gracious, longsuffering, and abounding in goodness and truth ..."

— EXODUS 34:6

What do you believe God is like?

In the Hebrew language, God's name is *"Yahweh, Yahweh El."* The word *Yahweh* means the self-existent God. Some have also translated it "all-becoming." That is, He is to you whatever your particular need might be. If you need strength, He is your strength. If you need salvation, He is your Savior. If you need healing, or righteousness, or peace, He becomes those things for you. Whatever man's need might be, God is all-sufficient. So, God reveals Himself in His name.

But He goes on from there. God describes His nature as being merciful, or full of mercy. This means that God doesn't give us what we deserve. He then says He is full of grace. Where mercy is a negative quality (not getting what you deserve), grace is a positive quality. It is getting what you don't deserve—the goodness and the blessing of God.

God also declares that He is longsuffering and patient. And then He describes Himself as abounding in goodness and in truth.

IN THE NEW TESTAMENT, WE SEE GOD'S FINAL REVELATION OF HIMSELF THROUGH JESUS CHRIST—SHOWING US THE FULL EXTENT OF GOD'S MERCY, PATIENCE, AND GRACE.

This is the God we serve; the God who is at work maturing and perfecting us—and making us into His own image.

—————

Thank You, Father, for revealing the truth of Yourself to us. Help us to embrace the truth and surrender ourselves, that we may be like You.

AMEN.

Unintentional Sin

*If anyone of the common people sins unintentionally ... then he
shall bring as his offering a kid of the goats ... for his sin which
he has committed. And he shall lay his hand on the head of the sin
offering, and kill the sin offering at the place of the burnt offering.*

— Leviticus 4:27-29

The word *sin* means to "miss the mark." Missing the mark isn't always intentional. If I deliberately, willfully do what I know is wrong, that is a transgression. But when I, through weakness, inability, or ignorance do things unintentionally that aren't right, then that is sin. And even sin needs atonement.

WHAT IS THE MARK? IT IS PERFECTION. AND WE HAVE ALL
COME SHORT OF THAT.

Sin causes spiritual death, and thus, alienation from God. Because sinful man cannot have communion with a holy God, God provided the sin offering so we could have fellowship with Him.

But looking at the Scripture, goat sacrifices could not take away sins, only cover them. The people could only enjoy this glorious fellowship with God until they blew it again, which, unfortunately, didn't take too long. And, of course, it wasn't long before the common people ran out of goats.

So God provided another sin offering: Jesus Christ, who took my guilt and punishment. By dying in my place, He enabled me to have fellowship with God and experience the joy, the blessing, the thrill, the glory, and the richness of knowing Him.

*Father, we thank You that Jesus has become the sin offering for us
so we might know the joy of living in fellowship with You.*

AMEN.

STRANGE FIRE

Then Nadab and Abihu, the sons of Aaron, each took his censer
and put fire in it, put incense on it, and offered profane fire before
the LORD, which He had not commanded them. So fire went out
from the Lord and devoured them, and they died before the Lord.

— LEVITICUS 10:1-2

These two men offered strange fire to God. And their service came to a sudden end as the fire of God consumed them. What was the strange fire they offered? Their fire came from a source other than fire that was kindled spontaneously by God.

It could be that they were just excited and caught up in the emotion of the moment. It is quite possible that they had disobeyed verse 9 of chapter 10 where the Lord commanded, "Do not drink wine or intoxicating drink, you, nor your sons, when you go into the tabernacle of meeting, lest you die." It could be that these boys were a little tipsy and not in full control of their faculties. Or maybe they were motivated by the desire of bringing attention to themselves and to their ministry rather than bringing glory to God.

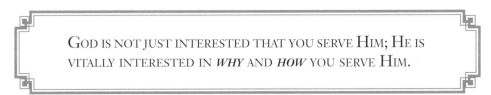

GOD IS NOT JUST INTERESTED THAT YOU SERVE HIM; HE IS VITALLY INTERESTED IN *WHY* AND *HOW* YOU SERVE HIM.

We may earn our living by doing other things, but the real call upon each of us is to serve the Lord.

The question is: what *motivates* you? From whence is that fire kindled in your heart?

God, help us to serve You with the true fire of Your Spirit burning
in our hearts. May we know the joy, the privilege, and the blessing
of being an instrument that You have used to minister to others.

AMEN.

CLEANSED AND RESTORED

*Then the LORD spoke to Moses, saying, "This shall be the law of
the leper for the day of his cleansing …"*
— LEVITICUS 14:1-2

Despite all of our advancements in science and medicine, there is no known human cure for leprosy. It can now be arrested, but not cured. The disease spreads through the body by a rotting process—first it destroys the nerves; gradually it spreads until it hits a vital part of the body and kills. And so it is with sin—it attacks the spirit's nerve system so that you are being destroyed without even realizing it. One tolerated area of sin will spread until it blights your whole life—yet you're unconscious of what it is doing to you.

Why would God establish a law for the leper in the day of his cleansing when leprosy is incurable? It indicates that God has left the door open that He might do a sovereign work of grace which lepers could never do for themselves.

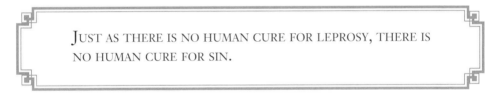

JUST AS THERE IS NO HUMAN CURE FOR LEPROSY, THERE IS
NO HUMAN CURE FOR SIN.

But God has provided cleansing through Jesus Christ. The blood of Jesus, God's Son, cleanses a man from all sin.

"For sin shall not have dominion over you" (Romans 6:14). I don't need to be ruled by it anymore. I am no longer subject to sin because of the power given to me through Jesus Christ—I have been cleansed, washed, and restored. And now I can have fellowship with God.

*Father, we thank You that the coming of Your Son has brought
the power of the Spirit, which enables us to live a life freed from
the bondage of sin and corruption. Lord, we rejoice and we agree
with David: "Oh how blessed is the man whose transgressions are
forgiven, whose sins are covered!"*

AMEN.

THE ATONING BLOOD

*For the life of the flesh is in the blood, and I have given it to you
upon the altar to make atonement for your souls; for it is the blood
that makes atonement for the soul.*

— LEVITICUS 17:11

God's Word declares that atonement for the soul comes through the blood. God's penalty for sin was death. Thus, in that we have all sinned, we have all been condemned to death. And that death is spiritual death. Alienated and separated from God, man loses the consciousness of the presence of God in his life.

Our attitude toward sin is very casual. Today, we have a total misunderstanding of sin and the holiness of God. Man asks God to become a part of his sinful life. But we are told that God is so holy and pure that He cannot look upon sin. And surely the cross of Jesus Christ should convince you that God will not accept sin. God forsook His own Son when Jesus took your sins upon Himself.

> IF GOD FORSOOK HIS OWN SON BECAUSE OF SIN, HOW CAN YOU EVER EXPECT GOD TO BE IN FELLOWSHIP WITH YOU AS LONG AS YOU HAVE SIN PERMEATING YOUR LIFE?

Thanks be to God that when we look at Jesus Christ, we see God's plan of redemption completed. Rather than trying to bring our own righteousness before God, we can come to Him through the righteousness of Christ.

---

*Thank You, Father, that the blood of Jesus Christ brought
atonement for our sins. Lord, we receive that cleansing this
day, that we might live with You in newness of life.*

IN JESUS' NAME, AMEN.

PERFECTION REQUIRED

*And whoever offers a sacrifice of a peace offering to the Lord,
to fulfill his vow, or a freewill offering from the cattle or the sheep,
it must be perfect to be accepted; there shall be no defect in it.*

— LEVITICUS 22:21

When it came to sacrifices, God demanded perfection because He knew man's tendency to offer the castoffs to Him. "I'll just offer God my old, blind cow … or that lamb that broke its leg last week. It is not going to survive. Let's sacrifice it to God."

> IN YOUR DESIRE TO HAVE FELLOWSHIP WITH GOD, HOW
> DO YOU APPROACH HIM?

Do you think that you can just approach God as you are?

Some people seek to approach God on the basis of their good works. But are your works perfect? Not only must the works be perfect, but the motivation *behind* the works must be perfect. That immediately eliminates me. And it surely eliminates my works.

Some try to seek God through the church. They believe the church will save them. But the church is filled with imperfections, and the rites of the church are administered by imperfect men.

Our only hope for fellowship with God is through a perfect sacrifice. Jesus is that perfect sacrifice, and outside of Him, there is no way for us to have fellowship with God. "I am the way, the truth, and the life," Jesus said. "No one comes to the Father except through Me" (John 14:6).

---

*Help us, Lord, not to be so foolish approaching You with our
imperfect efforts. May we come by the way of Jesus Christ into
that life of fellowship—loving You, walking with You, and being
one with You through Him.*

IN JESUS' NAME, AMEN.

REPRESENTING GOD

*And the LORD spoke to Moses, saying: "Speak to Aaron and his sons,
saying, 'This is the way you shall bless the children of Israel. Say to
them: "The Lord bless you and keep you; the Lord make His face
shine upon you, and be gracious to you; the Lord lift up His countenance upon you, and give you peace."' So they shall put My name
on the children of Israel, and I will bless them."*

— NUMBERS 6:22-27

A priest of God had a twofold duty. First, he was to go in before God to represent the people. Secondly, he would represent God to the people as he declared God's Word to the people.

WHAT AN AWESOME RESPONSIBILITY IT IS TO REPRESENT
GOD TO OTHER PEOPLE.

Those watching God's representatives develop their concepts of Him by what they see in the priest. This is why God is so concerned in how He is represented before the people.

In this passage, first we see that God desired to bless the people. Secondly, the idea of God's face shining upon us indicates that God Himself is the source of that grace. Finally, God wants His name associated with peace.

People long to see the reality of God. They are watching you. Do you represent Him as being upset and angry over small annoyances? May His love, compassion, tenderness, and goodness flow forth from your life, that people might get a true concept of God as they see that work of His Spirit through you.

*Father, may we reflect You to this world. Help us, Lord, and
forgive us where we have misrepresented You and given to people
a false concept of our God.*

AMEN.

GRAVES OF LUST

*Now the mixed multitude who were among them yielded to
intense craving; so the children of Israel also wept again and said:
"Who will give us meat to eat?"*

— NUMBERS 11:4

Recalling their old life, the mixed multitude that had come out of Egypt with the children of Israel began to lust for that old life. God was displeased that they had fondly looked back at Egypt, nevertheless He provided for them despite their murmuring against Him.

"But while the meat was still between their teeth, before it was chewed, the wrath of the Lord was aroused against the people, and the LORD struck the people with a very great plague. So he called the name of that place Kibroth Hattaavah [which means graves of lust], because there they buried the people who had yielded to craving" (11:33-34).

It could be they were so hungry for meat that they swallowed without chewing, the bones lodged in their throats, and they choked to death. Or it is possible that after more than a year's time of this bland diet of manna, their bodies could not suddenly assimilate all of this meat and they gorged themselves, filling their stomachs until they bloated. Whatever it was, their lust brought them death.

GOD WANTS US TO HAVE VICTORY OVER THE FLESH, AND THAT VICTORY COMES ONLY WHEN WE WALK AFTER AND LIVE AFTER THE SPIRIT.

Paul said, "The flesh lusts against the Spirit, and the Spirit against the flesh" (Galatians 5:17). Yielding to the flesh only brings spiritual suffering. God never intended that we be enslaved by the desires of our flesh.

*Father, we see the destructive power of the flesh. Help us to
exercise good wisdom and judgment—that we might live and
walk after the Spirit.*

AMEN.

STAND BETWEEN THE DEAD AND THE LIVING

*Then Aaron took it as Moses commanded, and ran into the midst of
the assembly; and already the plague had begun among the people.
So he put in the incense and made atonement for the people. And he
stood between the dead and the living; so the plague was stopped.*

— NUMBERS 16:47-48

Because they rebelled against Moses' authority, the entire congregation was guilty before God. The only thing separating the dead and the living was Aaron—who stood offering incense and making atonement.

Incense is associated with the prayers of the saints. In Psalm 141, the psalmist refers to our prayers as incense set before God.

TO GOD, THE PRAYERS OF HIS PEOPLE ARE A PLEASANT ODOR.

Just as Aaron interceded between the dead and the living, we can stand between the dead and the living through the power of prayer. I believe many people are sustained today only because someone is praying for them.

Because God is just, He must punish the guilty or He would no longer be just. But God is also merciful and loving; and therefore, He is slow to wrath. Because God does not *want* to punish, He seeks to exercise His mercy and looks for people to stand in the gap.

Our world is in great rebellion against God. How important that we stand in the gap offering the incense of prayer between the dead and the living—that by our prayers we might sustain those who deserve to die, and stop the plague of God in our nation.

*Father, challenge our hearts with the spiritual imperatives
brought to us through the Scripture. May we stand in the gap and
make a difference by our prayers.*

AMEN.

THE BATTLE OF THE FLESH

The utterance of Balaam the son of Beor, and the utterance of the man whose eyes are opened; the utterance of him who hears the words of God, and has the knowledge of the Most High, who sees the vision of the Almighty, who falls down, with eyes wide open: "I see Him, but not now; I behold Him, but not near; a Star shall come out of Jacob; a Scepter shall rise out of Israel, and batter the brow of Moab, and destroy all of the sons of tumult."

— NUMBERS 24:15-17

Balak, the king of Moab, was distressed because the children of Israel wanted to pass through his land. So he sent for Balaam to bring a curse against them. But instead of cursing them, he began to prophesy a blessing.

Balaam's declaration confirms that he did indeed hear the Word of God, but he was still a false prophet. Although he initially spoke only blessings, he ultimately told the king how to tempt and stumble Israel.

Balaam said, "In the Spirit, I can do nothing. Get them in the flesh. Send the gals down there with their little idols. Get them excited in their flesh and they will stumble and fall—and then God will deal with them."

Using that advice, Moab caused the children of Israel to go after the flesh. Balaam knew that was their weakest point. Satan knows that too.

SATAN APPEALS TO OUR FLESH IN ORDER TO DESTROY US.

When the Scepter of Israel comes, He will deliver us from the flesh. What a glorious day that will be!

Awaken us, Lord, to the perils of the life in the flesh. Cause this message to sink in deeply that we might walk after the Spirit.

AMEN.

The Good Shepherd

*Then Moses spoke to the LORD, saying, "Let the Lord, the God of
the spirits of all flesh, set a man over the congregation, who may
go out before them and go in before them, who may lead them out
and bring them in, that the congregation of the Lord may not be
like sheep which have no shepherd."*

— NUMBERS 27:15-17

God has just declared to Moses that his leadership is over and he will not be able to lead the children of Israel into the Promised Land.

Moses knew that sheep without a shepherd would scatter. They would wander away from the herd and starve, or be devoured by wolves. Moses, who was a true shepherd, loved these people that he led through the wilderness for the last forty years.

There is a big difference between a shepherd and a hireling. The hireling is not all that concerned about the sheep. He will run from the danger rather than stay and defend the sheep. But a true shepherd has a heart for the sheep.

JESUS SAID, "I AM THE GOOD SHEPHERD. THE GOOD SHEP-HERD GIVES HIS LIFE FOR THE SHEEP" (JOHN 10:11).

Jesus also said that His sheep would hear His voice and follow, but they would not follow a stranger. Someone can try to imitate the shepherd's call, but the sheep will not even look up. They know the whistle or the call of their shepherd.

How glorious to have heard the call of our Good Shepherd and to have followed!

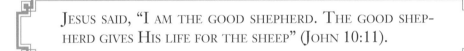

*Father, how grateful we are that Jesus Christ is our Shepherd
who watches over His flock, who cares for His own, who gave His
life for the sheep. Thank You for leading us on the right path.*

AMEN.

No Secret Sin

But if you do not do so, then take note, you have sinned against the LORD; and be sure your sin will find you out.

— NUMBERS 32:23

Forty years of wandering have ended. Israel is now at the border ready to go into the land. But the elders from Reuben and Gad don't want to go across; they are content to remain on this side of the Jordan. "We promise to send troops to fight until you take the whole land," they told Moses. "Then we will return and dwell on this side."

Moses warned them that if they didn't do as promised, they would sin against the Lord—and their sin would find them out.

What sin? He's talking about the sin of omission, the sin of doing nothing. And I suggest that this is the sin of the silent majority. Evil will prevail in our land if we just stand back and do nothing.

THERE IS NO SUCH THING AS SECRET SIN.

The Bible tells us that everything is naked and open before God. He so surrounds your life that nothing can be done secretly.

You can be sure your sin will find you out in your conscience and your countenance. And it will find you out in the end. One day you will stand before God where all secrets will be revealed.

I am so thankful for Jesus. The Bible tells us, "If we confess our sins He is faithful and just to forgive us our sins and to cleanse us from all unrighteousness" (1 John 1:9).

Father, plant Your Word deep in our hearts. Help us, Lord, to confess our sins and receive Your abundant pardon.

AMEN.

BACKSLIDDEN

But from there you will seek the LORD your God, and you will find Him if you seek Him with all your heart and with all your soul. When you are in distress, and all these things come upon you in the latter days, when you turn to the Lord your God and obey His voice (for the Lord your God is a merciful God), He will not forsake you nor destroy you, nor forget the covenant of your fathers which He swore to them.

— DEUTERONOMY 4:29-31

Sometimes God's children backslide and find themselves captive again in the enemy's territory. To the church of Ephesus Jesus said, "I have this against you: you have left your first love."

If you can point to any time in your Christian experience when you walked closer to the Lord than you are walking today, when you experienced His presence and power in your life in a greater measure, then you are in a backslidden state.

> BACKSLIDING HAPPENS WHEN YOU ALLOW ANY OTHER DESIRE, AMBITION, OR PREFERENCE TO TAKE FIRST PLACE IN YOUR HEART AND IN YOUR LIFE.

God needs to be first, above everything else. And when anything else takes His place, you are on the road towards backsliding.

But there is hope for the backslider. Even if you have wandered far, you can find God again if you will seek Him with your whole heart and soul. God is patient and will work in your life again. He will not forsake you. He will not destroy you. He will remember His covenant, for He is a merciful God.

Father, may Your Holy Spirit challenge our hearts with the truth of Your Word. Help us to cast down every idol and put Christ upon the throne of our lives.

AMEN.

PROVEN THROUGH TESTING

*And you shall remember that the LORD your God led you all the
way these forty years in the wilderness, to humble you and test
you, to know what was in your heart, whether you would keep His
commandments or not. So He humbled you, allowed you to hunger, and fed you with manna … Your garments did not wear out
on you, nor did your foot swell these forty years. You should know
in your heart that as a man chastens his son, so the Lord your God
chastens you.*

— DEUTERONOMY 8:2-5

I n his final instructions, just as the children of Israel are about to enter the
Promised Land, Moses reminds them that God permitted a bitter testing to
teach them three things.

First, God wanted the children of Israel to see what was in their hearts.
When tested, would they obey Him? Trust Him? Praise Him?

> GOD USES TRIALS TO SHOW US OUR HEARTS, THAT WE MIGHT
> BE CLEANSED AND THEN BROUGHT INTO THE LAND OF
> BLESSING—PHYSICALLY AND SPIRITUALLY.

Secondly, the Israelites needed to know that life is more than just a physical
experience. God wants us to live in the spiritual realm, walking in the Spirit and
being led by the Spirit.

Thirdly, they needed to know that God chastens His own, to keep us from
those things that would destroy us.

God uses testings in the same way today. He uses trials to show us our hearts,
that we might be cleansed and then brought into the land of blessing.

———⋙⋘———

*Father, reveal what is in our hearts, that we might surrender it
to the cross.*

AMEN.

The Lord's Requirements

*And now, Israel, what does the LORD your God require of you,
but to fear the Lord your God, to walk in all His ways and to love
Him, to serve the Lord your God with all your heart and with
all your soul, and to keep the commandments of the Lord and His
statutes which I command you today for your good?*
— DEUTERONOMY 10:12-13

What does God require of us? This passage makes God's requirement pretty clear. We are to fear Him (have respect for Him), walk in all His ways, love Him, serve Him, and obey Him.

It sounds simple, but there is a problem. I have failed God in all these areas. Though the desire to obey Him is present, so is the desire to disobey.

> ONE DAY SOME MEN ASKED JESUS, "WHAT MUST WE DO TO DO THE WORKS OF THE FATHER?" JESUS ANSWERED, "THIS IS THE WORK OF GOD, THAT YOU BELIEVE IN HIM WHOM HE SENT" (JOHN 6:29).

You mean all I have to do is believe in Jesus Christ? That is within my grasp. I can handle that. I may not be able to keep all the commandments, walk in all of His ways, or serve Him with all my heart and soul, but I can believe in Jesus Christ.

The truth is, God hasn't given up on the ideal requirements, but He recognizes the weakness of my flesh. Through Jesus, God did for me what I could not do. And as I put my faith in Jesus, I find He gives me the power to do the rest.

---

*Father, thank You for the power we have through Jesus Christ.
Help us, Lord, by Your Spirit, to become the men and the women
You would have us to be.*

IN JESUS' NAME, AMEN.

THE PROMISED PROPHET

*I will raise up for them a Prophet like you from among their
brethren, and will put My words in His mouth, and He shall
speak to them all that I command Him. And it shall be that
whoever will not hear My words, which He speaks in My name,
I will require it of him.*

— DEUTERONOMY 18:18-19

To the present day, Jews recognize this as a prophecy concerning the
Messiah. Just as Moses was a mediator who brought the Word of God to
the people, so the promised Prophet would be the Mediator who would
bring God's Word to the people. A mediator is necessary because of the fact
that God is infinite and man is finite. Man cannot understand or comprehend
the infinite God.

> BECAUSE I AM FILLED WITH SIN AND INIQUITY, I CANNOT
> APPROACH GOD WHO IS ABSOLUTELY HOLY AND PURE. SO
> I NEED A MEDIATOR.

This prophecy in Deuteronomy was fulfilled in Jesus Christ. Paul tells us in
1 Timothy that there is only one God and one Mediator between God and man,
and that is the man Christ Jesus. He can touch God because He is God. He can
touch me because He became man. And now through Him I can touch God.

God kept His promise. Jesus Christ is that Prophet, that Mediator. He is our
comfort. He is The Word through whom we have life, strength, love, forgiveness, hope, and peace.

*Father, thank You for sending Your Son to provide the forgiveness
we need. May we walk in the light even as Jesus is in the light
that we might have fellowship with You.*

IN HIS NAME WE PRAY, AMEN.

MORTIFY THE FLESH

*Remember what Amalek did to you on the way as you were
coming out of Egypt, how he met you on the way and attacked
your rear ranks, all the stragglers at your rear, when you were
tired and weary; and he did not fear God. Therefore it shall be,
when the LORD your God has given you rest from your enemies all
around, in the land which the Lord your God is giving you to
possess as an inheritance, that you will blot out the remembrance
of Amalek from under heaven. You shall not forget.*

— DEUTERONOMY 25:17-19

In biblical typology Amalek is a type of the flesh. Just as Amalek sought to destroy Israel, the flesh seeks to destroy the people of God. When we are born again by the Spirit of God, the enemy, our flesh, comes to do battle. The flesh wars against the Spirit and the Spirit against the flesh.

> ATTACKS AGAINST OUR FLESH ALWAYS COME IN THE MOST
> VULNERABLE AREAS.

In Colossians 3:5, God tells us to mortify our flesh. We are to put it to death. Those are harsh terms. But you need to remember what the flesh life did to you, how it took advantage of you. Wipe it out! Utterly destroy it! It is a life and death battle. If you yield to the flesh, the flesh will destroy you.

Maybe you are struggling against the flesh and have become weary and tired. The battle is fierce, but God wants to deliver you. The Spirit of God can give you victory over your flesh. Ask God for His help.

*Help us, Lord, to reckon the old life dead, that we might live a life
that is pleasing and acceptable to You.*

IN JESUS' NAME, AMEN.

SERVE THE LORD WITH GLADNESS

Because you did not serve the LORD your God with joy and gladness of heart, for the abundance of everything, therefore you shall serve your enemies …

— DEUTERONOMY 28:47-48

What an honor it is to be chosen by God to be His special people! And yet with this honor comes an awesome responsibility. We are to be God's witness to the world. We are to show them the joy that comes to those who follow and serve the Lord, that they might also be drawn to Him and submit their lives to His lordship.

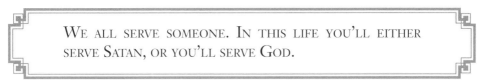

WE ALL SERVE SOMEONE. IN THIS LIFE YOU'LL EITHER SERVE SATAN, OR YOU'LL SERVE GOD.

Those who serve Satan are at home in this world. They are comfortable because they blend right in. But the end result of serving Satan is death.

Those who serve God are aliens in this world. That is because the closer you draw to God, the more out of step you will feel with this world. But ours is a loving Master who is concerned about you and desires the very best for your life. And He will prepare you emotionally, physically, and spiritually to do whatever work He's called you to do for His good pleasure.

Serving the Lord is a privilege and a blessing. If the work you are doing is what God has called you to do, then you won't find it unbearable, intolerable, or heavy. He said, "My yoke is easy, My burden is light." Instead, you will find yourself serving with joy.

Lord, help us to undertake the work You've created us to do with gladness. May we discover the joy, contentment, and satisfaction of serving You.

IN JESUS' NAME, AMEN.

GOD'S SECRETS

The secret things belong to the LORD our God, but those things
which are revealed belong to us and to our children forever, that
we may do all the words of this law.

— DEUTERONOMY 29:29

Two realms exist—those secret things that belong to God, and those things that He has chosen to reveal to us.

Science has made many discoveries, but there are still vast mysteries and secrets of the universe that we haven't yet tapped. God knows them all. And as He chooses to reveal them to us, we continue to learn. The same is true in our personal lives.

WE DON'T ALWAYS KNOW WHY CERTAIN THINGS HAPPEN TO US, BUT GOD KNOWS.

We want answers. We want to know why. But sometimes God's response is simply, "Trust Me."

Just as God has established laws that govern our physical universe, such as the laws of electricity, aerodynamics, and gravity, He has also established spiritual laws. And just as the discovery of those physical laws benefited our lives, God's spiritual laws—the secret of His love, His faithfulness, His grace and mercy—can be used to benefit and bless us as well.

You won't always understand what God is doing. But He is faithful. He will reveal His secrets as you wait upon Him. And one day you will thank Him for the trial you are enduring now, because the secrets of God were revealed through it.

Father, we're so grateful for the revelation of Your love and Your
law. Help us to keep Your law and use it for our benefit, for the
enrichment and the enhancement of our lives.

IN JESUS' NAME, AMEN.

FEBRUARY 6

GOD'S EVERLASTING ARMS

*The eternal God is your refuge, and underneath are the
everlasting arms …*
— DEUTERONOMY 33:27

Because the future is unknown and unsure, man has a tendency to fear it. But this short verse contains three facts that have the power to cure that fear:

(1) God is eternal. Before you arrive at a situation or an experience, God has already preceded you there.

(2) God is your refuge. A refuge is a shelter, a secure place where you can be safe from the storm. And oh, how safe are those who have made their shelter in God. The Scriptures tell us that the name Yahweh is a strong tower; the righteous run into it and are safe (Proverbs 18:10).

(3) Underneath are the everlasting arms. That means that I cannot fall. Though I may think I am going to fall, the truth is that God is holding me up.

NO MATTER WHAT TOMORROW BRINGS, GOD IS READY TO
HOLD AND PROTECT US.

Someone might say, "Hey, I really hit bottom this week." That is fantastic. That means you are resting now directly on God, because when you get to the bottom, underneath you are His everlasting arms.

We have no need to fear. The eternal God has gone before us and knows all things that are ahead. He is our dwelling place, our place of safety and security. His arms are ever beneath us, holding us firmly.

*Thank You, Father, that You're always there when we need You,
and that Your everlasting arms are always beneath us. Hold us
tight today. For those who are fearful, give them the faith to
believe that You will not let them fall.*

IN JESUS' NAME, AMEN.

LORD OF HEAVEN AND EARTH

*And as soon as we heard these things, our hearts melted; neither
did there remain any more courage in anyone because of you,
for the LORD your God, He is God in heaven above
and on earth beneath.*

— JOSHUA 2:11

Rahab only knew of God by hearsay, and yet she had a clear perception of Him. "He is the God of heaven above," she said. But because the heavens above are so vast, some people think that God seems far away and impersonal. Though they believe in God as a power or force, they don't think they can know Him.

But then Rahab went on to say, "He is the God of the earth beneath." And there is where we come close to Him and begin to understand that He is not just a God of awesome power, but also a God of intricate detail.

Looking at the heavens, God seems remote. Who am I that God should think about me? Yet the psalmist writes, "How precious also are Your thoughts to me, O God! How great is the sum of them! If I should count them, they would be more in number than the sand" (Psalm 139:17-18).

> IF YOU WANT A POWERFUL SPIRITUAL EXPERIENCE, GO TO THE BEACH AND PICK UP A HANDFUL OF SAND. EVERY GRAIN OF SAND REPRESENTS GOD'S THOUGHTS CONCERNING YOU.

Rahab came to believe in God just by hearsay, but you have more than hearsay. You have God's clear revelation of Himself in His Word.

*Father, we know that You are not just some ethereal energy out in
the universe. May we come to know You as a personal, loving God.*

IN JESUS' NAME, AMEN.

The Uncertainty of Tomorrow

And Joshua said to the people, "Sanctify yourselves, for tomorrow
the LORD will do wonders among you."

— JOSHUA 3:5

With the wilderness journey behind them, the children of Israel are about to begin an entirely new experience with the Lord. Forty years of wandering had taught them a lot about themselves and God. But now they faced an uncertain future.

Unknown, uncharted territory often brings fear. Perhaps I am going into a new job—will I be able to handle it? What does tomorrow hold?

Standing before the people, Joshua assured them with these comforting words, "Sanctify yourselves, for tomorrow God...." And that is the thing that I need to hold in my mind, too. "Tomorrow God." You see, God has already gone before me. God is already there.

Although there are uncertainties about the future, there are also some certainties—one of which is yesterday. The past gives me assurance for the future. The past deliverance of God predicts the future deliverance of God.

> THOUGH THE FUTURE IS UNCLEAR, YOU CAN FACE IT WITH CONFIDENCE IN GOD.

God is not going to leave you. He is not going to let you down. The God who brought you through the wilderness is going to take you in until you have conquered the land and possessed the promises.

Father, thank You for the hope that springs out of Your past faithfulness. May we find security and peace in Jesus who has promised never to leave us nor forsake us.

IN HIS NAME WE PRAY, AMEN.

GOD IS FOR US

*Joshua ... lifted his eyes and looked, and behold, a Man stood
opposite him with His sword drawn in His hand. And Joshua
went to Him and said to Him, "Are You for us or for our
adversaries?" So He said, "No, but as Commander of the army
of the LORD I have now come." And Joshua fell on his face to
the earth and worshiped ...*

— JOSHUA 5:13-14

Joshua's load is heavy and frightening. God has made him responsible for leading the people. As he stands looking over Jericho—probably developing a strategy for assaulting the walls—he sees a Man with a drawn sword. Joshua asks, "Are You for us or are You for our adversaries?"

When he learns the Man has come from God, Joshua worships Him. By this action, we can conclude that this Commander was none other than Jesus Christ. An angel would not have accepted worship.

It was a long time before I realized that God was for me rather than for my adversaries. I used to believe God was just waiting for me to make a mistake so He could punish me. I thought He was going to chastise me because I was not always what I should be.

> WHEN YOU HAVE A TRUE ENCOUNTER WITH GOD, YOU COME AWAY WITH THE REALIZATION THAT GOD IS FOR YOU.

As Paul said, "If God is for us, who can be against us?" (Romans 8:31). With God on our side, how can we lose?

*Father, we thank You for assuring us that You are on our side.
Lord, in Your name we go to face our problems. In Your name,
we go to claim the territory that You have promised to us.*

AMEN.

GLORIOUS VICTORY

And the LORD said to Joshua: "See! I have given Jericho into your hand …"

— JOSHUA 6:2

If you want victory over the strongholds of the old nature, look at Israel's conquest of the land. The principles of victory are found right here. First of all, notice that God spoke to Joshua in the past tense. "I have done it. It is finished." In the same way, your victory is a finished work of Jesus Christ. The Lord has already provided you with victory over your flesh life—all you have to do is believe it.

The second principle is to follow God's plan for victory even when we don't understand it. God's plan for conquering Jericho was interesting, to say the least. As Joshua called his generals together to explain the battle strategy of marching around the city, they probably began to have second thoughts about their allegiance to follow this guy.

> GOD'S PLAN FOR YOUR SITUATION MAY SEEM PECULIAR. AND YOU MAY EVEN BE RELUCTANT TO TRY IT. OBEY THE IMPRESSIONS OF GOD UPON YOUR HEART.

The third principle is that the people were to give a great shout of victory—even though the walls were still standing. This was an expression of faith and anticipation.

We can trust God's Word. He promises that He is going to work. Praise Him for those promises of victory. God doesn't want you to go on in defeat, being mastered by your flesh and the strongholds of the flesh-life. Turn your life over to Him and trust Him. He will bring the walls down.

Father, thank You for the glorious victory that we can experience through the power of Jesus Christ. Thank You for setting us free from our past sins.

AMEN.

UNGODLY ALLIANCES

*Then the men of Israel took some of their provisions; but they did
not ask counsel of the LORD. So Joshua made peace with them, and
made a covenant with them to let them live; and the rulers of the
congregation swore to them.*

— JOSHUA 9:14-15

God specifically told the Israelites that they were not to make any covenant
with the people in the land, but were to utterly drive them out. God knew
that if the inhabitants remained, their practices would ultimately destroy His
people. The Gibeonites realized they couldn't stand against the armies of Israel,
so they devised a scheme to make it appear that they had traveled from a far
country in order to make a covenant with Israel.

Joshua's mistake was that he examined the evidence but didn't inquire of
the Lord. God would have warned him about this ungodly alliance, but Joshua
didn't seek God's counsel. He just sized up the situation by what was before him.
Some things seem so obvious. You shouldn't have to bother God about those
things; right? You can just go ahead and use your common sense.

Wrong. The Scriptures tell us, "Trust in the Lord with all your heart,
and lean not on your own understanding; in all your ways acknowledge Him,
and He shall direct your paths" (Proverbs 3:5-6).

WE CAN AVOID TRAGIC MISTAKES BY: (1) ALWAYS ALLOW-
ING GOD'S WORD TO GUIDE OUR DECISIONS. (2) NEVER
MAKING A DECISION UNTIL YOU HAVE FIRST SOUGHT GOD'S
GUIDANCE THROUGH PRAYER.

Isn't it rather foolish to trust my own judgment when I have the advantage
of going to God for counsel?

*Lord, help us to pay attention to the warnings in Your Word. May
we seek You to help us in making every decision.*

AMEN.

THE POWER OF GOD

Then Joshua spoke to the LORD in the day when the Lord delivered
up the Amorites before the children of Israel, and he said in the
sight of Israel: "Sun, stand still over Gibeon; and Moon, in the
Valley of Aijalon." So the sun stood still, and the moon stopped,
till the people had revenge upon their enemies.

— JOSHUA 10:12-13

The Israelites had fought hard, and victory was near—but night was coming. Joshua realized that when it got dark, the Amorites would be able to escape. They needed more time. So in front of all of his troops, he commanded, "Sun, stand still, and moon, you hold there in the valley of Aijalon. Don't move!" And the sun stood still, and the moon held its position.

The same resources that were available to Joshua—the resources that brought the universe into existence, the resources that began the earth on its axis and put it in its rotation around the sun—are available to you as a child of God.

We often make the mistake of thinking that God will do it all and that there's nothing for us to do. But the Bible tells us that faith without works is dead.

> GOD EXPECTS US TO DO OUR BEST, AND THEN COMMIT THE REST.

When we reach our own limitations, we discover infinite resources that are available to us to accomplish and to finish the work of God.

Father, we are so grateful that we serve You—an unlimited,
infinite God who is able to do exceedingly, abundantly above
all that we ask or think. Lord, we are weak and we need Your
strength. Take over our lives, Lord, and guide and direct us.

AMEN.

THE FAITHFULNESS OF GOD

So the LORD gave to Israel all the land of which He had sworn to give to their fathers, and they took possession of it and dwelt in it. The Lord gave them rest all around, according to all that He had sworn to their fathers. And not a man of all their enemies stood against them; the Lord delivered all their enemies into their hand. Not a word failed of any good thing which the Lord had spoken to the house of Israel. All came to pass.

— JOSHUA 21:43-45

What a powerful witness this is to the faithfulness of God—for God was faithful to His Word even though the people were not. They had broken their covenant with God on many occasions. At one point they were even trying to persuade someone to lead them back to Egypt. But God kept His Word.

NOT A SINGLE WORD OF GOD HAS FAILED.

We need to realize the certainty of God's Word. He promised to send His Son to be born of a virgin, and to die for the sins of man. As God has promised, so God has fulfilled. He promised to gather Israel again and birth a nation in one day. On May 14, 1948, Israel became a nation. God has fulfilled His Word.

And He has promised to come again and receive us to Himself.

If God has been faithful up to this point, you can be sure He is going to continue to be faithful. Though heaven and earth may pass away, His Word shall stand forever. You can bet your life on that!

Father, thank You that what You have said, You have done. Lord, help us today to have that assurance that we can trust Your Word.

AMEN.

SINCERELY YOURS

Now therefore, fear the LORD, serve Him in sincerity and in truth, and put away the gods which your fathers served on the other side of the River and in Egypt. Serve the Lord!

— JOSHUA 24:14

The children of Israel had begun serving other gods. They still acknowledged God's existence, but their time and energy were absorbed in other pursuits. They shoved God into a secondary place.

Joshua saw how the hearts of God's children were turning away from Him. So he issued a challenge. When Joshua stood before the people, he gave them a choice. They could continue serving themselves—their intellect and their pleasures—or they could serve the Lord.

> GOD ISN'T INTERESTED IN MERE LIP SERVICE, THOUGH THAT'S WHAT MOST PEOPLE OFFER TO HIM. WE CAN SERVE GOD WITH SINCERITY AND TRUTH WHEN WE REMEMBER HIS GOODNESS AND FAITHFULNESS TO US.

In Deuteronomy, Moses asked, "What does the Lord require of you?" The first two requirements listed were that we fear God and serve Him with all of our hearts. So Joshua reminded the people of God's requirements: fear God (reverence Him), and then serve Him in sincerity and truth—serve genuinely.

God had brought the Israelites into the land, driven out their enemies, and delivered them from bondage. Because God had been so good to them, they should have *wanted* to serve Him!

The glorious thing about choosing to serve the Lord is that it brings you everything else. When you choose to make Him first in your life, He then blesses you with the desires of your heart.

———⟶⬥⟵———

Father, we are so grateful for the opportunities You have given to us. Teach us to serve You with sincerity and truth.

IN JESUS' NAME, AMEN.

THE ONLY WISE CHOICE

*... choose for yourselves this day whom you will serve, whether the
gods which your fathers served that were on the other side of the
River, or the gods of the Amorites, in whose land you dwell. But as
for me and my house, we will serve the LORD.*

— JOSHUA 24:15

In prosperous times, it is easy to take your eyes off God. That's what was
happening with Israel. Settled in the land, they were beginning to prosper—
and beginning to turn to the gods of their fathers again. A choice awaited
them—the same choice that awaits every man.

> WHATEVER IT IS YOU ARE LIVING FOR, WHATEVER PASSION
> RULES YOUR LIFE, WHATEVER IT IS THAT GETS YOU OUT
> OF BED IN THE MORNING AND DRIVES YOU—THAT IS YOUR
> GOD.

Whom will you serve? Whom are you serving? To discover that, just finish this sentence: "For me to live is...." Ultimately, when you reach the hour
of death and you are facing eternity, money can't save you. Pleasure can't save
you. Intellect can't save you. If you have made those things your god, you're in
trouble. Only Jesus has the power to save you, so Jesus is the only wise choice
you can make.

The fact is, you've already bowed your knee to something. If you've chosen
to serve a false god, choose this day to serve the true and the living God—the
God who is faithful, the God who is powerful, the God who is able to deliver
His people.

*Father, we choose to serve You, crown You as King of our lives,
bow our knee before Your throne, kiss Your scepter, and submit as
obedient servants through Jesus Christ.*

AMEN.

An Inescapable Law

*And Adoni-Bezek said, "Seventy kings with their thumbs and big
toes cut off used to gather scraps under my table; as I have done,
so God has repaid me." Then they brought him to Jerusalem,
and there he died.*

— Judges 1:7

Adoni-Bezek was a powerful king. He had conquered seventy other kingdoms, and cut off the thumbs and big toes of each defeated king. When he was finally conquered by the men of Judah, what did they do? They cut off his thumbs and big toes. And he said, "As I have done to others, so God has requited me."

In the New Testament we read, "Do not be deceived, God is not mocked; for whatever a man sows, that he will also reap" (Galatians 6:7).

> We often get upset because we think someone is getting by with evil deeds. But sooner or later, their sins will catch up with them.

The law of reaping what you sow is an inescapable law. But it is also a beautiful law. If you sow love, kindness, and forgiveness, you will reap love, kindness, and forgiveness. If you sow mercy, you will reap mercy.

Maybe your past is dark and dismal, and you have sown a lot of bad seed. Take heart. God has made a way that you don't have to reap what you have sown. He took the guilt of your iniquity and laid it all upon His Son. Jesus Christ reaped the consequences for you—that you might reap the glory of God's love and eternal kingdom.

*Help us, Lord, that we might sow good seeds in the hearts and
lives of those around us; that we might reap, Lord, the beautiful
fruit of that harvest.*

In Jesus' name, amen.

THE SIN OF DOING NOTHING

"Curse Meroz," said the angel of the LORD, "Curse its inhabitants bitterly, because they did not come to the help of the Lord, to the help of the Lord against the mighty."

— JUDGES 5:23

The angel of the Lord pronounced a bitter curse upon Meroz because they didn't help in the time of crisis and need. In the day of the battle, they did nothing to come to the help of the Lord.

God has called His people to action. You have been saved to serve. "Be doers of the word," James tells us, "and not hearers only, deceiving yourselves" (James 1:22). So many times when we hear the Word of God, we say, "Right on, man, that's so true. Yes, we ought to do more for God." But then we do nothing.

LOVE IS DEMONSTRATED BY OUR ACTIONS.

Jesus said, "He who has My commandments and keeps them, it is he who loves Me" (John 14:21). You may leave church on Sunday morning saying, "Wow, I really enjoyed that sermon." But what are you doing about it? You see, if it doesn't bring you into action, you are building on sand. You are resting on a false security. When the storms come, your house will fall because you haven't been doing—only hearing.

I wonder how many of us belong to the clan of Meroz. We are so busy doing our own thing that we don't respond to the call of God. There is no evidence in our lives that we're doing the work of God. Instead, we are engaged in the sin of doing nothing.

Father, we pray that Your Holy Spirit will challenge us to action. Help us to volunteer ourselves willingly, Lord, to obey Your Word and keep Your commandments.

IN JESUS' NAME, AMEN.

GOD'S ARMY

Then the LORD said to Gideon, "By the three hundred men who
lapped I will save you, and deliver the Midianites into
your hand."

— JUDGES 7:7

God thinned the troops in order to get men He could use for His glory. Eventually, from the 32,000 men who answered Gideon's call, only 300 remained. God disqualified the majority in two ways: He eliminated those who were fearful, and those who were careless.

Fearful men run in the midst of the battle, and they can infect others with their fear.

> GOD KNOWS THAT FEAR IS BORN WHEN WE FOCUS ON THE PROBLEM OR ON THE POWER OF THE ENEMY.

Two-thirds of Gideon's army went home after this first cut, leaving 10,000 men. So God said, "Gideon, the men with you are still too many. Take them to the stream and observe how they drink. All who get down on their knees and put their face in the water are disqualified." Only 300 cupped the water with their hands, as they kept a watchful eye. God had found His army.

Today, God seeks men who are fearless and alert. Fearlessness that is borne of faith results in keeping your eyes upon God. He is also looking for men who are aware and alert to the war around them. Men who, even when involved in the necessities of life—whether it be drinking water or working on the job—are always aware of the larger issues, the spiritual battle in which we are all engaged.

Father, help us to go forth in faith without concern, knowing that
if You are for us, no man can stand against us. May we be used in
the accomplishing of Your purposes and Your will.

AMEN.

TURN AND SERVE

*And the children of Israel said to the LORD, "We have sinned!
Do to us whatever seems best to You; only deliver us this day, we
pray." So they put away the foreign gods from among them and
served the Lord. And His soul could no longer endure the misery
of Israel.*

— JUDGES 10:15-16

Israel had forsaken God. Once again, they began worshiping false gods. And once again, they ended up in bondage—crying out to God.

God responded by saying, "I have helped you in the past, but I will deliver you no more." In Genesis 6:3, God warned, "My Spirit shall not strive with man forever." There comes a time when God says, "Enough." To the children of Israel, He said, "Go and cry unto the gods you have chosen."

They knew those gods couldn't help them. It is interesting that whenever someone is in real trouble, they know instinctively that the only One who can help is the true and the living God. When trouble comes, even the rebellious cry out, "Oh, God, help me!"

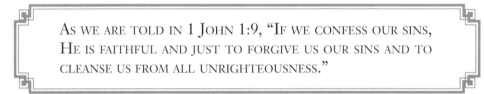

AS WE ARE TOLD IN 1 JOHN 1:9, "IF WE CONFESS OUR SINS, HE IS FAITHFUL AND JUST TO FORGIVE US OUR SINS AND TO CLEANSE US FROM ALL UNRIGHTEOUSNESS."

These people did a wise thing. They cast themselves on the mercies of God. And because they did so, God delivered them again from the hands of their enemies. God is so merciful! And that same mercy is available to us today.

God doesn't owe us anything. But He has promised to be merciful to any who forsake their wicked ways and turn to Him.

*Lord, thank You for continuing to strive with men and women
today. Help us to surrender our hearts to You.*

IN JESUS' NAME, AMEN.

VOWS

And Jephthah made a vow to the LORD, and said, "If You will indeed deliver the people of Ammon into my hands, then it will be that whatever comes out of the doors of my house to meet me, when I return in peace from the people of Ammon, shall surely be the Lord's, and I will offer it up as a burnt offering ... for I have given my word to the Lord, and I cannot go back on it."

— JUDGES 11:30-31, 35

Jephthah had made a terrible vow.

Sometimes when we are in trouble we do that. "God, if You will just get me out of this, I'll do such and such." When a person has made a foolish vow it is really better to confess the sin of the foolish vow than to carry the vow through. In Jephthah's case, to carry the vow through was a greater sin than breaking the vow.

> SOME VOWS SIMPLY SHOULD NOT BE KEPT. BUT THERE ARE OTHER VOWS YOU CANNOT GO BACK ON.

I have opened my mouth before the Lord and confessed that Jesus Christ is my Savior; that I am depending solely upon Him for my salvation; and that He is the Lord of my life.

And because of this, there are certain things I cannot do. Number one: I cannot go back into that old life of sin and self-centeredness. With the apostles, I must declare, "Lord, only You have the words to eternal life. To whom can I go?" Number two: I cannot deny the love and the peace that Jesus has brought into my life.

Lord, if we have strayed from that first love, help us listen to Your Holy Spirit and return again, until we love You with all we have.

AMEN.

THE SECRET OF STRENGTH

So Delilah said to Samson, "Please tell me where your great
strength lies, and with what you may be bound to afflict you."
— JUDGES 16:6

Samson's strength had become legendary. When the Spirit of God came upon him, he would do feats of astounding strength. His enemies sought to find the secret of his strength. When they saw he had fallen in love with the Philistine girl, Delilah, they approached her and said, "Look, each of us will give you fifteen hundred pieces of silver if you will find for us the secret of that fellow's strength."

So Delilah said unto Samson, "Samson, tell me, honey, what makes you so strong? What is the secret of your strength?"

Unfortunately, one of Samson's weaknesses was a sense of invincibility. He seemed to enjoy flirting with danger, and was forever venturing into the territory of the enemy.

Samson finally told Delilah his secret. He explained the vow he had taken—a vow of consecration to God. No razor had touched his head. "If my hair were shaved, I would be weak just like any other man." But Samson's long hair was only a symbol. The secret of his strength was his commitment to God. As long as he kept that commitment, he really was invincible. When the commitment was broken, however, he was weak like any other man.

THE SECRET OF YOUR STRENGTH LIES IN YOUR COMMITMENT TO JESUS CHRIST.

If you commit yourself fully to Jesus, you will be invincible. Even the gates of hell cannot prevail against you. But if you break that commitment to Jesus Christ, you will become weak just like any other man.

Lord, help us not to flirt with danger, but may we give ourselves
fully and completely over to You.
AMEN.

THE REDEEMER

*And Boaz said to the elders and all the people, "You are witnesses this
day that I have bought all that was Elimelech's.... Moreover, Ruth
the Moabitess, the widow of Mahlon, I have acquired as my wife, to
perpetuate the name of the dead through his inheritance ... "*

— RUTH 4:9-10

Under Jewish law, if a married man died before he had children, the man's brother became obligated to marry his wife. The firstborn child would then be named for the dead brother so that his inheritance might continue in Israel.

Boaz—a relative of Elimelech's—redeemed the field because he was in love with Ruth. He purchased the field in order that he might get a bride whom he loved.

JESUS SAID, "THE KINGDOM OF HEAVEN IS LIKE TREASURE HIDDEN IN A FIELD, WHICH A MAN FOUND AND HID; AND FOR JOY OVER IT HE GOES AND SELLS ALL THAT HE HAS AND BUYS THAT FIELD" (MATTHEW 13:44).

The field, in this parable, is the world, and Jesus is the One who gave all to purchase the world. Who then is the treasure? Amazing as it seems, the treasure is you and me—we who trust Him as Lord and Savior. We are the bride of Christ. Just as Boaz was willing to buy the field in order to gain the bride, so, too, Jesus willingly paid the price of redemption to purchase the world. He did that because He loved you and wanted you for His own.

---

*Thank You, Lord, that You place such a high value upon us that
You willingly gave Yourself to purchase us out of the bondage and
slavery of sin, that we might become Your bride.*

AMEN.

DELAYED ANSWERS

*Then she made a vow and said, "O LORD of hosts, if You will
indeed look on the affliction of Your maidservant and remember
me, and not forget Your maidservant, but will give Your maidservant a male child, then I will give him to the Lord all the days of
his life, and no razor shall come upon his head."*

— 1 SAMUEL 1:11

Hannah wanted a son in order that she might be delivered from the incessant vexing of Peninnah, her husband's other wife. Day after day she begged for release from this woman's torment. But God wanted more. He wanted a man to deliver His whole nation from their moral corruption. So He allowed the daily agony to mold and shape Hannah, and withheld the answer to her prayers until He brought her into harmony with His desire. And through her son, Samuel, spiritual revival came.

Maybe God has delayed the answers to some of your prayers. Maybe you have waited so long you feel desperate. If that is where you are, it's time to begin interceding before the Lord. As you do, God may astound you by the changes He brings in your attitudes as He shapes and moves you to that place of harmony with Him.

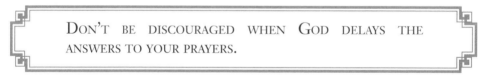

DON'T BE DISCOURAGED WHEN GOD DELAYS THE
ANSWERS TO YOUR PRAYERS.

Usually God has so much more that He wants to do and you just haven't been brought to that understanding yet. The moment you realize that, you will see God's hand at work.

*Father, bring us into perfect harmony with Your purpose and Your
desires. Work in us, Lord, those changes that are necessary until
You bring us to that place where You can work and accomplish
Your will.*

IN JESUS' NAME, AMEN.

TOUCHED BY GOD

*And Saul also went home to Gibeah; and valiant men went with
him, whose hearts God had touched.*
— 1 SAMUEL 10:26

What does it mean to have your heart touched by God? It means that
God is now at the center of your will and your being. It means that
you have surrendered your life in totality unto Him.

How does God touch your heart? He does so by the gentle influence of
His Holy Spirit. The Holy Spirit leads us to the Word of God, and through
the Scriptures, God touches our hearts. Once the Holy Spirit begins to illu-
mine your mind, it is amazing how glorious and exciting and wonderful the
Bible becomes.

When God touches your heart, bitterness, anxiety and fears have to go.
They can't stay in a heart that has been touched by God. Habits and vices
that were destroying your life fall away. Things you used to cherish, you now
despise. Things you used to despise, you now cherish.

> WHEN GOD TOUCHES YOUR HEART, IT FILLS WITH LOVE
> AND PEACE. THOUGH THE STORMS MAY RAGE, YOU HAVE
> A GLORIOUS CONFIDENCE IN GOD'S ABILITY TO CONTROL
> LIFE'S CIRCUMSTANCES.

Jesus surrounded Himself with a group of men whose hearts He had
touched—men who went out and turned a world upside down. When God
touches your heart, you will receive a whole new perspective. You stop living
just for today and you begin living for eternity.

*Thank You, Father, for Your Holy Spirit who touches our hearts
and challenges us through the Word. Touch the hearts of Your
people today.*
AMEN.

Show No Mercy

Thus says the Lord of hosts: "I will punish Amalek for what he did to Israel, how he ambushed him on the way when he came up from Egypt. Now go and attack Amalek, and utterly destroy all that they have, and do not spare them."

— 1 Samuel 15:2-3

The Amaleks were probably the most vicious, vile people who ever lived on the face of the earth. For the sake of humanity, God ordered the extermination of these people, and chose the children of Israel to be His instrument of judgment.

In the story of Esther, we read of Haman, the guy who plotted the destruction of the Jews. Haman was an Amalekite, a descendant of King Agag whom Saul had kept alive. God had told Saul to "utterly destroy" the Amalekites, but Saul did not obey. And because of that, Amalek came back and almost destroyed all of Israel.

The Bible says the flesh wars against the Spirit, and the Spirit against the flesh. Even as Amalek sought to attack Israel at their weakest place, so your flesh will be attacked at that weakest place. The battle is for supremacy.

GOD HAS DETERMINED THAT OUR FLESH MUST BE PUT TO DEATH.

Though we want to reform it, God says no. His edict for your flesh is utter destruction.

Which will rule your life? Will you yield to the Spirit, or to the flesh? Will you enjoy fellowship with God, or will you show mercy to your flesh and thereby become a slave to its appetites, alienating yourself from God? Choose wisely.

Father, strengthen us by Your Spirit that we might live after the Spirit, walk after the Spirit, and have the mind of the Spirit, which is life and peace and joy.

Amen.

DEFEATING GIANTS

*Then David said to the Philistine, "You come to me with a
sword, with a spear, and with a javelin. But I come to you in
the name of the LORD of hosts, the God of the armies of Israel,
whom you have defied."*

— 1 SAMUEL 17:45

Every day, this giant named Goliath would come out into the battlefield and challenge the armies of Israel to a winner-take-all contest. Using his words, his armor, and his size, Goliath sought to intimidate Israel.

And it worked. Saul's army faced the giant with great fear and dismay. But then along came David, who expressed great confidence before Goliath.

David's confidence wasn't in himself, but in the Lord. He saw more power in the ability of God to deliver him than in this giant to destroy him. "It is not really a contest between the giant and me. It is a contest between the giant and the Lord. And though I wouldn't stand a chance against the giant, he doesn't stand a chance against the Lord." David saw the conflict as an opportunity to bring glory to God.

WE NEED A PROPER PERSPECTIVE OF THE GIANTS IN OUR LIVES.

We need to take our eyes off of those problems and look instead on the Lord.

We need to remember that God is for us, and He has made all the resources of heaven available to us. Through the power of the Lord, every giant in your life can fall. But you've got to trust Him.

*Father, we thank You that You are bigger than any giant we may
face. Help us to remember that the battle is not won with swords
and spears and the wisdom of man,
but with the power of the eternal God.*

ONE STEP

*David took an oath again, and said, "Your father certainly knows
that I have found favor in your eyes, and he has said, 'Do not let
Jonathan know this, lest he be grieved.' But truly, as the LORD
lives and as your soul lives, there is but a step between me and
death."*

— 1 SAMUEL 20:3

David just had a close encounter with death. Saul had tried to kill him, and David realized he could lose his life at any time.

Close calls make us aware of just how close death is. No matter how healthy or strong I may be, there is just one step between me and death.

If death is so inevitable, and so close, how should I live? First, I shouldn't live for this life only.

I SHOULD LIVE IN CONSTANT PREPAREDNESS FOR ETERNITY.

The Bible teaches that the real me is spirit, not body. The body is only a tent. But one day I will move out of this tent and into a mansion. If I live in fellowship with God through Jesus Christ, I won't take that step between life and death. According to the word of Jesus, if I live and believe in Him I will never die—but I will move. I'll move out of this tent into that building of God. So there is one step between me and eternity.

I look forward to that move. For you see, even though I have not yet seen Him, I love Him and rejoice with a joy unspeakable, full of glory in the anticipation of that day when I shall stand beside my Lord, in that new body, in His eternal kingdom.

*Thank You, Father, for the gift of eternal life through
Jesus Christ.*

AMEN.

FEBRUARY 28

GOOD DISCONTENTMENT

*And everyone who was in distress, everyone who was in debt, and
everyone who was discontented gathered to him. So he became captain
over them. And there were about four hundred men with him.*

— 1 SAMUEL 22:2

God has anointed David as king. However, Saul is still on the throne. And because Saul wants to hold onto that which is no longer his, and tries to kill David, David has become a fugitive.

Those who gathered with David were a ragtag band of misfits—unlikely candidates to be David's mighty men. Yet God raised them up and used them with David to establish the kingdom of Israel.

There is an interesting parallel here. God has ordained His Son, Jesus Christ, to reign as King over the earth; however, Satan is still on the throne. And Satan is doing his best to hold onto the kingdom. Jesus is gathering together men unto Himself—unlikely candidates, to be sure—but men through whom He plans to establish His kingdom and bring to pass His reign over the earth.

> GOD IS LOOKING FOR MEN AND WOMEN WITH OPEN, WILLING HEARTS, THOSE WHO WOULD SAY, "HERE I AM, LORD. I AM NOT CONTENT WITH MY LIFE THE WAY IT IS, LORD. I WANT TO GIVE IT ALL TO YOU."

When discontentment brings you to a total commitment to Jesus Christ, that's good discontentment because it leads to progress.

*Father, we thank You that You gather unto Yourself those of
Your choosing. Mold and shape us into those persons
You want us to be that we might one day reign with
You in the glory of Your kingdom.*

IN JESUS' NAME, AMEN.

THE FOOL

Then Saul said, "I have sinned.... Indeed I have played the fool
and erred exceedingly."
— 1 SAMUEL 26:21

Jealous of David's popularity, Saul sought to kill him. One night, David snuck into Saul's camp when he was asleep. But instead of killing him, David said, "That man has been anointed of God. Don't touch him. If God wants to deal with him, that is God's business." Instead, he grabbed his cruse of water and his spear.

When he got a safe distance away, David called out to Saul's bodyguard. Saul woke up and said, "Is that the voice of you, my son David?" David answered, "Why are you chasing me? Look, I've got your spear. The men who were with me wanted to kill you, but I wouldn't let them." It is then that Saul said, "I have played the fool, and have erred exceedingly."

Saul had many natural advantages in life, but that did not guarantee him success. Saul's life teaches us that it's possible to squander God's blessings. We learn that a man plays the fool when, like Saul, he tries to hide from the call of God upon his life, or takes credit for another man's victories, or makes rash promises. A man plays the fool when he does not completely obey God, or offers outrageous excuses for his failure, or becomes jealous of godly, loyal friends, or seeks guidance from spirit beings.

THE REAL FOLLY OF SAUL'S LIFE WAS HIS FAILURE TO TOTALLY SURRENDER HIS LIFE TO GOD.

When you fail to surrender, you're really saying, "I know better than God." And only a fool would think that.

Father, we pray that You would help us surrender completely to You.
IN JESUS' NAME, AMEN.

BOW PRACTICE

Also [David] bade them teach the children of Judah the use of the bow ...
— 2 SAMUEL 1:18 (KJV)

When David received word of the death of his dear friend Jonathan and of King Saul whom he admired so greatly, he grieved. But he did not just sit by weeping. One of the ways David dealt with his grief was to order all of the dads in the tribe of Judah to train their children how to use a bow.

It was an extremely fitting memorial to Jonathan. David took one of the assets of Jonathan's life and ordered everyone to teach it to their children. In this way, Jonathan's influence continued on. We can spiritualize the text by thinking of the bow as being a spiritual weapon in the form of prayer.

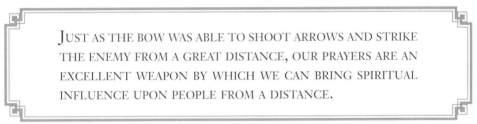

JUST AS THE BOW WAS ABLE TO SHOOT ARROWS AND STRIKE THE ENEMY FROM A GREAT DISTANCE, OUR PRAYERS ARE AN EXCELLENT WEAPON BY WHICH WE CAN BRING SPIRITUAL INFLUENCE UPON PEOPLE FROM A DISTANCE.

Sometimes when we have witnessed to loved ones so much that they begin to resent it (and us), we can shoot arrows from a distance. The Spirit begins to work in their hearts as we, through prayer, bind the work of the enemy.

Just as David ordered them to teach the children the use of the bow, we need to learn the use of the bow of prayer that we might be effective for God in the spiritual battle in which we are engaged.

———⟶⟶⟶———

Father, help us to become adept at using
the weapons of warfare You have given us,
that we might do battle on behalf of our loved ones.
AMEN.

Who Am I?

*Then King David went in and sat before the Lord; and he said:
"Who am I, O Lord GOD? And what is my house, that You
have brought me this far?"*
— 2 SAMUEL 7:18

It was Nathan the prophet who brought God's word to David. "David, you can't build a house for Me, but I will build a house for you. Your son who will sit upon the throne after you will build the house for Me. And I will establish your throne forever." David rightly understood this to mean that the Messiah would be his descendant.

David was so overwhelmed by this, he excused himself from Nathan, and sat down before God. He recognized his total unworthiness and realized it was God's grace that had been showered upon him in such abundance.

Like David, you may be saying, "Who am I? I've done something wrong. I have messed up." Take a look at David's life. This guy was no angel. He did a lot worse than you have; yet look what God did for him.

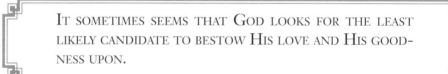

IT SOMETIMES SEEMS THAT GOD LOOKS FOR THE LEAST LIKELY CANDIDATE TO BESTOW HIS LOVE AND HIS GOODNESS UPON.

God so often goes to the gutter to find the recipient for His grace. He lifts him out, washes him, and transforms him—making him into a child of God fit for His kingdom. That is God's grace.

---

*Thank You, Father, for Your abundant grace. Despite all of our
failings, You loved us and began to heap upon us rich blessings.
But if that were not enough, You have spoken of the eternal age to
come and the glory that shall be revealed to us.*

IN JESUS' NAME, AMEN.

THE GOD WHO SEEKS

So David said to him, "Do not fear, for I will surely show you kindness for Jonathan your father's sake, and will restore to you all the land of Saul your grandfather; and you shall eat bread at my table continually."

— 2 SAMUEL 9:7

Several years earlier, David made a covenant with Jonathan, Saul's son. David promised, for Jonathan's sake, that when he came to the throne, he would treat the family of Saul with great kindness. So once David was on the throne and had been blessed and prospered by God, David sought to find one of Saul's descendants that he might show kindness.

In the same way that David sought a descendant to show kindness, God is seeking the lost that He might show the exceeding richness of His love and kindness towards them through Jesus Christ. This is what makes Christianity different from religion. In religion, men seek God. In Christianity, God seeks lost men.

Mephibosheth was actually frightened when he was brought to David, because he didn't know David's intent. So often we misunderstand God and imagine Him as being angry or disgusted with us. We think He's seeking us that He might come down on us with a heavy hand. But we're wrong.

David wanted to bless Mephibosheth for Jonathan's sake. God wants to bless us for Christ's sake.

> IT'S NOT BECAUSE WE DESERVE IT—IT'S BECAUSE JESUS WANTS US AS HIS INHERITANCE.

Just as Mephibosheth dined at the king's table as part of the king's family, we too have been brought into the family of God and invited to come and sit at His table.

Thank You, Father, for the joy, the blessing, the richness that we experience at Your table because of Jesus.

AMEN.

CONFESSION AND FORGIVENESS

So David said to Nathan, "I have sinned against the LORD." And Nathan said to David, "The Lord also has put away your sin; you shall not die.

— 2 SAMUEL 12:13

David's confession of sin was a true confession. He had indeed sinned against the Lord. His endeavor to hide his sin had only compounded things.

But notice that with David's confession came immediate forgiveness. Oh, that we would cease trying to cover or justify our sins! Forgiveness can only come with confession. It is not until you acknowledge and confess your guilt before God that you can receive the cleansing God wants to give to you.

GOD DELIGHTS IN MERCY.

He wants to forgive. But until there is the confession, God doesn't have the opportunity to exercise His mercy and grace.

What a relief it is when that heavy load of sin is gone. The Hebrew word for "blessed" means "Oh, how happy." This is what David describes in Psalm 32. "How blessed (how happy) is the man whose sins are forgiven." How happy is the man who's been restored into fellowship with God.

It should be noted that though God forgave David, sin still left its mark. Don't think that you can sin without it taking a toll upon your life. God forgives, and the penalty of sin is removed. Nails driven into a board can be removed, too, but the board will still be scarred by holes. Your sin may be removed, but it leaves its mark.

Father, we pray that Your Holy Spirit will speak to us who are weighed down by guilt. May there be confession, that there might also be that flowing forth of Your grace and forgiveness.

AMEN.

No Longer Banished

*For we will surely die and become like water spilled on the ground,
which cannot be gathered up again. Yet God does not take away
a life; but He devises means, so that His banished ones are not
expelled from Him.*

— 2 Samuel 14:14

The woman speaking to David has come to beg the king to reconcile with his son, Absalom, whom he had banished. And through this word picture, she reminds David of the finality of death. We all must die. When we do, we are as water that has been spilled on the ground and can't be gathered up again.

She warns the king that if the bitterness continues, and either he or his son should die, they will never be able to rectify their relationship. Death ends all opportunities for reconciliation.

Families often divide over very small issues. And oftentimes, we deal more harshly with those we love than those we don't even know.

Isn't it interesting how we feel that some people are more forgivable than others? But God will forgive even the worst of crimes. God offers His forgiveness and His pardon freely.

> The gate of forgiveness is open to all who will call upon Him.

God has indeed devised a means by which His banished be not expelled from Him. That's what the gospel is all about—restoration. Through His Son, who took our guilt and shame upon Himself, God restored those who had been banished as the result of sin.

---

*Lord, I pray for those who have been alienated from Your love
and fellowship through their actions and sins. May they turn and
receive mercy, pardon, grace, and forgiveness.*

In Jesus' name, amen.

COMMITMENT

But Ittai answered the king and said, "As the LORD lives,
and as my lord the king lives, surely in whatever place my lord
the king shall be, whether in death or life,
even there also your servant will be."
— 2 SAMUEL 15:21

ttai made a total commitment to David, although he had just arrived from Gath the day before. Many of David's loyal friends were jumping ship and joining Absalom, yet here comes this stranger pledging undying loyalty to David. David wasn't making any kind of enticing offers to Ittai, but this fellow figured that the worst David had to offer was better than the best that Absalom had to offer.

One of the tragedies of our age is the lack of true commitment.

> PEOPLE ARE UNWILLING TO MAKE A TOTAL COMMITMENT TO ANYTHING.

In marriage, we may say "for better or for worse," but as soon as things start getting worse, people want to bail out. The commitment they made was not a total commitment.

There is a great weakness in the church today. People accept the Lord, but then they vacillate. They show there is not a true, deep commitment to Jesus.

The kind of commitment Ittai made to David is the kind that Jesus desires from us today. He did not offer a cheap gospel or an easy path. But if you commit yourself completely to Him, your life will be full, joyous, and satisfying—because you'll know you are right where God wants you to be.

Father, we realize we were at one time strangers in this world,
alienated from You. How thankful we are that You chose us to be
Your disciples and brought us to that place of commitment, where
we said, "Lord, I'm Yours."
IN JESUS' NAME, AMEN.

JUST REST

*Then the king said to Zadok, "Carry the ark of God back into the
city. If I find favor in the eyes of the LORD, He will bring me back
and show me both it and His dwelling place. But if He says thus:
'I have no delight in you,' here I am, let Him do to me as seems
good to Him."*

— 2 SAMUEL 15:25-26

David is fleeing Jerusalem from Absalom and his army. As David's loyal friends are gathering with him, Zadok, the high priest, comes out of the city gates with some of the Levites who are carrying the sacred ark of the covenant.

David said, "I'm not going to depend upon a religious relic to save me. I'm going to depend completely upon God. If God saves me, fine. I will come back. I will see the ark again. But if God doesn't see fit to save me, then here I am and whatever seems good to Him, let Him do it."

David's life is completely committed to the purpose and the plan that God may have for him.

> I CANNOT CHANGE WHAT GOD HAS ORDAINED. IF I SEEK TO
> FIGHT AGAINST THE PLAN OF GOD, THEN I AM DESTINED TO
> LOSE.

If I fight against God, all I will experience is anxiety, futility, and frustration. But when I finally realize there's nothing left for me to do, I find the place of rest.

Knowing that God's ways are better than mine, knowing that God loves me and is totally aware of the circumstances I'm facing, and acknowledging that I really don't know the way out, I place it in His hands.

*Father, may we cease from our fretting and worrying, and may
we just rest knowing that You love us and will do what is best.*

AMEN.

THE PROMISES OF GOD

*Blessed be the LORD, who has given rest to His people Israel,
according to all that He promised. There has not failed one word
of all His good promise, which He promised through
His servant Moses.*

— 1 KINGS 8:56

In Leviticus 26, God promised Moses He would give the people the land and peace within it.

In Leviticus 26:11, God also said, "And I will establish My tabernacle in the midst of the people." Here, in 1 Kings, Solomon is dedicating that very temple, and he takes the opportunity to remind the people of God's promise. Though it took Him 490 years, not a single word failed of all that God promised to do.

GOD KEEPS HIS PROMISE; NOT A SINGLE WORD HAS FAILED.

You had better really pay attention to what God says. The fact that God is so exacting in keeping His word will either bring great encouragement to your heart, or it will bring terror. It all depends on where you are in relationship to Him.

I am so thrilled that God keeps His word faithfully, for He has promised that if I confess with my mouth that Jesus is Lord, and believe in my heart that God raised Him from the dead, I am going to be saved. God has promised if I will confess Jesus before men, He will confess me before His Father. God has promised that if I receive Him, I will have eternal life.

---

*Father, even as Solomon could testify of Your faithfulness, so we,
some three thousand years later, can give the same witness and the
same testimony of Your faithfulness.*

IN JESUS' NAME, AMEN.

MORE THAN WE ASK

And the LORD said to him: "I have heard your prayer and your supplication that you have made before Me; I have consecrated this house which you have built to put My name there forever, and My eyes and My heart will be there perpetually."

— 1 KINGS 9:3

The God who created this universe loves me. He thinks about me, and He hears me when I pray. Not only does He hear me, but amazingly, God answers me.

He doesn't always answer when I want Him to, however. And I get impatient. I want God to answer me and act on my behalf immediately. But often God waits because He desires to give more than what I am asking. So He waits for me to get in perfect sync with His plan.

Solomon had prayed that this house would be a place where God's people could gather to meet God, and he asked that the eyes of the Lord be upon this place. God said, "Not only My eyes, but My heart is going to be there too."

GOD DESIRES TO GIVE MORE THAN WHAT WE ASK. TOO OFTEN, PEOPLE SEEK THE EYES OF GOD INSTEAD OF THE HEART OF GOD, BUT IT IS IN THE HEART OF GOD TO BLESS US.

May God draw you into a more intimate fellowship than you've ever experienced, where not just His eyes will be upon you but His heart as well, as you seek after Him and as He reaches out to you. May you experience the touch of God's love, power, and presence in a greater measure.

Father, we thank You for hearing us when we call. Draw us unto Yourself. May we find that place of quiet rest near to Your heart.

AMEN.

Easy Religion

The king ... made two calves of gold, and said to the people, "It is
too much for you to go up to Jerusalem. Here are your gods,
O Israel, which brought you up from the land of Egypt!" And he
set up one in Bethel, and the other he put in Dan. Now this
thing became a sin ...
— 1 Kings 12:28-30

King Jeroboam sought to create an easy religion for the people. His reasoning was, "It is too hard for you to go up to Jerusalem to worship the Lord. That takes too much of a sacrifice. So we will make it easy on you. We will put gods right here in your own community."

Easy religions always appeal to the flesh because they don't require a denial of self. Yet what did Jesus give as the first requirement for someone who wanted to follow Him? "Deny yourself." I cannot live after the Spirit and after the flesh. These two things are contrary.

> EASY RELIGIONS WILL NEVER BRING YOU TO THE TRUE
> AND LIVING, ETERNAL CREATOR.

Easy religions might please my flesh, but they do not please God. In seeking my own pleasure, I lose His. If you follow these easy religions, you will find yourself alienated from the true God as you seek to make a god out of yourself.

The path into eternal life begins at the cross; you can't escape it. It is a straight path. It is a narrow path. But it leads to eternal life.

Father, if our passion or the motivating center of our lives is some-
thing other than You, help us deny ourselves and bring it to the
cross, that we might follow You wholeheartedly.

Amen.

Heavy Tidings

And so it was, when Ahijah heard the sound of her footsteps as she came through the door, he said, "Come in, wife of Jeroboam. Why do you pretend to be another person? For I have been sent to you with bad news."

— 1 Kings 14:6

Jeroboam had once created false gods for the people to worship. But when his son became deathly ill, Jeroboam didn't seek help from those false gods. Instead, he disguised his wife as a peasant and sent her to seek help from God's prophet, Ahijah.

> How foolish it is to think that we can hide the truth from God.

He knows the truth. God sees right through all of the disguises, because He sees our hearts.

The prophet was blind, but he certainly wasn't deaf. He could hear the voice of the Lord, and he passed on God's message to Jeroboam's wife. He said to her, "I am come to you with heavy tidings."

Knowing that God is gracious and full of compassion, I cannot help but believe that had Jeroboam truly repented and sought the Lord with sincerity, God would have touched and healed his son and established his throne forever. But such was not to be.

Hypocrisy only leads to destruction. If your heart isn't honest before God, you are headed down a dangerous path. But if you drop your disguise and come to God with complete sincerity, He will be quick to lift that heavy burden from you, because He loves you and wants to bless your life.

Father, thank You for Your faithfulness in dealing with us. Lord, we want to hear what You have to say concerning the future. Help us to hear and obey.

Amen.

INDECISION

And Elijah came to all the people, and said, "How long will you falter between two opinions? If the LORD is God, follow Him; but if Baal, follow him." But the people answered him not a word.

— 1 KINGS 18:21

When Elijah issued his challenge to the prophets of Baal and Ashtoreth, two groups joined that faithful servant on Mount Carmel: the 850 "prophets" of those two false gods, and the halting multitude—the crowd Elijah cried out to in this passage.

Times have changed, but people haven't. Today we have the same three categories of people. There are those who, like Elijah, have committed their lives to the Lord and serve Him actively. Then there are those who have given their lives over to evil. They work hard to remove God out of the public sector and march for causes such as abortion and homosexuality. These are the people who seek to bury our nation in the slime pits of immorality.

THE UNCOMMITTED STAND BY AND WATCH AS THE FORCES OF DARKNESS TAKE OVER.

And then there is that final group—the halting multitude. These are people who haven't yet made a commitment either way. Jesus described these people as being lukewarm, which is a nauseating condition. They do nothing at all to stem the tide of evil. Because they stand for nothing, they allow anything.

If you have been on the fence, today is a good day to choose sides. Let your choice be Jesus—that your life might be a positive influence for good.

Help us, Father, to stand up for righteousness. Give us the same determination, the same enthusiasm, that the workers of iniquity have—that we might stand up for Jesus and bring Him glory.

IN JESUS' NAME WE PRAY, AMEN.

WHAT ARE YOU DOING?

And there he went into a cave, and spent the night in that place;
and behold, the word of the LORD came to him, and He said to
him, "What are you doing here, Elijah?"

— 1 KINGS 19:9

We tend to think of the great men of God as being super saints, men that are out of our league. We think, "I could never do the things Elijah did." But he was just a man. Though he had the same flaws and weaknesses we have, God used him in a mighty way. And that is encouraging. That means God can use me too.

At this particular time, Elijah was so discouraged that he wanted to die. Knowing this, God came to him and, with a still small voice, asked Elijah what he was doing. But instead of telling Him honestly, "I'm hiding," Elijah offered excuses to God.

We do the same thing. God sees us hiding and asks us what we're doing. Rather than confessing, "I'm doing nothing," we begin to make excuses. And when you get good at making excuses, you're usually good for nothing else.

Are you discouraged? If so, let me ask: What are you doing for God that really counts? How much time and energy have you invested in eternal things?

> THE GREATEST CURE FOR DISCOURAGEMENT IS TO GET BUSY DOING GOD'S WORK.

As you get busy for Him, you'll forget about your own problems and you'll begin to experience a sense of fulfillment. If you will listen today for that still small voice, you might be surprised what God will call you to do.

Father, we thank You for being patient with us. May we hear Your still small voice and answer You honestly.

IN JESUS' NAME WE PRAY, AMEN.

CRAVINGS

But Jezebel his wife came to him, and said to him, "Why is your
spirit so sullen that you eat no food?" He said to her, "Because I spoke
to Naboth the Jezreelite, and said to him, 'Give me your vineyard for
money; or else, if it pleases you, I will give you another vineyard for it.'
And he answered, 'I will not give you my vineyard.'"

— 1 KINGS 21:5-6

Ahab coveted Naboth's vineyard. And because he coveted it, he allowed Jezebel to sway him. He allowed Naboth to be condemned under perjury and stoned to death ... and then he stole Naboth's vineyard. Ahab's coveting led to lying, murder, and theft.

There is a vast difference between admiring and coveting. I can admire what you have. I can say, "My, that's great. That's really beautiful. I'm glad you have that." But when I start craving what you have, and I start thinking, "I wish that thing belonged to me," then I have become guilty of covetousness.

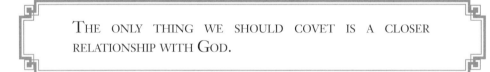

THE ONLY THING WE SHOULD COVET IS A CLOSER RELATIONSHIP WITH GOD.

The Bible tells us that covetousness is idolatry. That's because the thing you desire becomes the central focus of your heart and mind. All your waking hours are spent scheming ways to get that thing for yourself.

The Bible says we are to covet just one thing. "But covet earnestly the best gifts (of the Spirit)" (1 Corinthians 12:31 KJV). The only thing we should covet is a closer relationship with God. If you are going to crave anything at all, crave the power of God's Spirit working freely and fully in your life.

Father, create in us a heart that longs after You, that we might
know the joy and contentment of living in fellowship with You.

IN JESUS' NAME WE PRAY, AMEN.

Where is the God of Elijah?

*Then he took the mantle of Elijah that had fallen from him, and
struck the water, and said, "Where is the LORD God of Elijah?"
And when he also had struck the water, it was divided this way
and that; and Elisha crossed over.*

— 2 KINGS 2:14

Elisha had seen the power of God on Elijah's life. In fact, he saw a chariot of fire take the prophet into heaven. Now the responsibility of being a prophet to the people rested upon Elisha, and he knew he could not serve apart from the empowering of God. So he cried out for help.

"Where is the God of Elijah?" Elisha sought help from the God who revealed His power on Mount Carmel. He wanted Him to reveal that same power before the people so they would know that Jehovah is alive and He is God.

GOD DOESN'T CHANGE. HE WANTS TO SHOW HIS POWER TO THIS GENERATION.

Living in this age of skepticism, I also cry out, "Oh God, show Yourself. Prove Yourself, Lord." My cry is with Elisha: Where is the God of Elijah who can demonstrate His power as proof unto the people that He still lives?

We are not seeing the demonstration of God's power in our world, but the fault lies with us. God is alive and in control. May we be a people who cry out to Him; a people through whom He is revealed to the world.

*Father, we seek the power of Your Spirit at work among Your
people, to see Your name glorified on our lips. May we be the
instruments through which Your power and love are revealed.*

AMEN.

EYES TO SEE

And Elisha prayed, and said, "Lord, I pray, open his eyes that he may see." Then the Lord opened the eyes of the young man, and he saw. And behold, the mountain was full of horses and chariots of fire all around Elisha.

— 2 Kings 6:17

When Gehazi, the servant of Elisha, woke up and looked out, he saw the chariots of the Syrian army surrounding the city of Dothan. Running back inside, he said to Elisha, "There's no way out. We're surrounded."

Elisha said, "Don't be afraid. There are more with us than are with them." Then he prayed that his servant's eyes would be opened so that he might catch a glimpse of the spiritual realm. And when Gehazi's eyes were opened, he saw chariots of fire surrounding the enemy.

> How different things look when our spiritual eyes are opened!

When we just look at our physical circumstances, we despair. But if you can look at the spiritual truth, you will gain a whole new perspective. Rather than certain defeat, you see certain victory. With my spiritual eyes and the Word of God as my guide into spiritual things, I can see what God is doing, and I can rejoice because I know that Christ has already won the battle over the forces of darkness and evil.

May God open up our eyes to see the power that is available to us through Jesus Christ and by the Holy Spirit, that we can know and have God's complete and full victory in our lives.

Father, we thank You that we need not be defeated in any areas of our lives. God, open our eyes that we might see the truth and the reality of the spiritual realm.

In Jesus' name, amen.

MORE THAN RESPECT

Elisha had become sick with the illness of which he would die.
Then Joash the king of Israel came down to him, and wept over
his face, and said, "O my father, my father, the chariots of Israel
and their horsemen!"

— 2 KINGS 13:14

Though King Joash walked in idolatry, he respected God's prophet. Elisha had altered Israel's history. Through him, God wrought more miracles than through any other man of the Old Testament period. And thus, when the king heard that Elisha was dying, he came down to visit him, and began to weep over him. In this passage, Joash acknowledged that this man was the true strength of Israel, for he referred to him as, "The chariot of Israel, and the horsemen thereof."

In those days the chariot was the most formidable weapon that a nation could put into the battlefield. It was the deciding factor in a war. So that term represented strength and power. And looking at this prophet, he recognized that this man in fellowship with God was the true strength and the power of the nation, the chariot of Israel.

Down deep Joash knew that the only hope for the nation was in God. And yet he persisted in his evil ways. He is like so many people today who respect and acknowledge God, yet refuse to serve Him. They live as though He does not exist.

HALF-HEARTED COMMITMENT WILL NEVER RESULT IN TOTAL VICTORY.

Respect for God is not enough. Even the demons respect Him. But respect doesn't bring salvation. Total victory comes only through total commitment.

Father, we surrender our lives to You. Make us Your servants and Your instruments, that through us You might accomplish Your purposes.

IN JESUS' NAME, AMEN.

MEDDLING

You have indeed defeated Edom, and your heart has lifted you up.
Glory in that, and stay at home; for why should you meddle with
trouble so that you fall—you and Judah with you?
— 2 KINGS 14:10

Amaziah had just defeated Edom. Feeling prideful, he challenged Joash, the king of Israel, to come out and fight. Joash's advice to the younger king was, "Why should you meddle to your own hurt?"

But Amaziah continued his challenge until Joash brought his troops, defeated Amaziah's army, and came to the city of Jerusalem, where he broke through a section of wall and took the gold and silver he found there. He then took hostages and returned to Israel.

MEDDLING WILL ONLY BRING DEFEAT.

Great spiritual victories can leave us vulnerable, because we walk away from those victories feeling like we can conquer the world. The truth is, apart from Christ, we are helpless in this spiritual battle.

Like Amaziah, some of you are meddling where you have no business meddling. Perhaps it is with drugs and alcohol. Maybe you are married but flirting with someone, or maybe you're unmarried and have begun to meddle with sex. Don't fool yourself. Meddling breaks walls and destroys defenses, which makes it easier for the enemy to attack you in that same place later. And meddling brings the loss of innocence and purity.

But God is a restorer. If you turn to Him today, He can rebuild your defenses and restore your purity.

Thank You, Lord, for lifting us up when we have fallen. Thank
You for restoring the treasures that had been ripped off
by our encounter with the world.
IN JESUS' NAME, AMEN.

WHY NATIONS FALL

*Therefore the L*ORD *was very angry with Israel, and removed them from His sight; there was none left but the tribe of Judah alone.*

— 2 KINGS 17:18

In this brief sentence, we find the record of the death of the nation of Israel. After expending the patience of God, Israel is removed as a nation from the face of the earth.

When He brought them out of Egypt, God made a covenant with Israel. He promised that if they kept His laws, He would be their God and they would be His people. He further promised that if they kept His commandments, He would bless, protect, and prosper them as a nation.

The people agreed to the covenant—but they didn't keep it. Instead, they turned from God and worshiped idols. And for this cause, God removed them.

FOLLOWING AFTER EMPTINESS ONLY MAKES YOU EMPTY.

It amazes me when I consider the patience of God. He dwelt with this people for 240 years, and sent prophet after prophet to warn them of their folly. How longsuffering our God is!

And how foolish man is when he turns from the living God. You see, when you turn from God, you create a void in your life. Nature abhors a void. Inevitably, you will reach out for something to fill that inner emptiness. That is exactly what happened with Israel. They turned to pagan gods to fill the void, and in return, they received absolutely nothing.

That is because nothing else can fill the spot intended for God.

Father, we thank You for Your patience and Your mercy. We acknowledge that You alone can fill the void in our lives.

IN JESUS' NAME, AMEN.

BREAKING IDOLS

*He removed the high places and broke the sacred pillars, cut down
the wooden image and broke in pieces the bronze serpent that
Moses had made; for until those days the children of Israel burned
incense to it, and called it Nehushtan.*

— 2 Kings 18:4

While journeying through the wilderness, Israel complained against God and Moses. So God sent fiery serpents which began to bite and kill. Realizing they had sinned against God, the people asked Moses to pray for them. The Lord told Moses to make a brass serpent and put it on a pole in the midst of the camp. When the people were bitten, they were to look in faith upon the serpent on the pole. If they did so, they would live.

Faith in God's promise healed those bitten. But later, Israel began to worship the serpent Moses had made. When Hezekiah saw that, he broke the snake in pieces and called it *Nehushtan*, which in Hebrew means, "A thing of brass." He wanted to remind the people that the snake was not a thing to be worshiped; it was simply a thing of brass.

When man makes an idol out of a religious relic, it means he has lost the consciousness of the presence of God in his life. It means he is trying to recapture what has been lost.

OUR WALK WITH GOD SHOULD ALWAYS BE PROGRESSING.

If you can remember a time when you were closer to God than you are today, then you are backslidden. It's time to break those brass serpents and put your faith in Jesus again.

*Father, help us to have a closer relationship with You, where Jesus
means more to us than anything in the world.*

IN JESUS' NAME, AMEN.

Setting our House in Order

In those days Hezekiah was sick and near death. And Isaiah the prophet, the son of Amoz, went to him and said to him, "Thus says the LORD: 'Set your house in order, for you shall die, and not live.'"

— 2 KINGS 20:1

There are so many things I intend to do before I die. There are people I intend to call, cards I intend to write, words I intend to say. And I know that if I were to receive the same message from the Lord as did Hezekiah, my initial reaction would be much like Hezekiah's, "Lord, can You wait a little while?"

I WANT MY HOUSE TO BE IN ORDER BEFORE THE LORD CALLS ME HOME.

When I stand before God, I want to be able to say with Paul, "I have fought the good fight, I have finished the race, I have kept the faith" (2 Timothy 4:7).

Before long, all of us will stand before the Lord. When that happens, you will either stand guilty in your sins, or innocent in Christ. Is your spiritual house in order? Are you ready? If not, you can set your house in order by establishing the right relationship with God and, through God, the right relationship with your family and friends.

Remember: there is no guarantee of tomorrow. I pray that when God calls us, we will not leave unfinished business behind.

*Father, help us adjust our lives and our schedules so that we will accomplish those things most important to You.
May we speak that word of love, or that word of apology that someone else needs to hear.*

IN JESUS' NAME, AMEN.

The Prayer of Jabez

And Jabez called on the God of Israel saying, "Oh, that You would bless me indeed, and enlarge my territory, that Your hand would be with me, and that You would keep me from evil, that I may not cause pain!" So God granted him what he requested.

— 1 Chronicles 4:10

Jabez's prayer is misunderstood by many people. They think prayer is a way to get what we want. But that is wrong. God doesn't exist for our pleasure, nor does He exist to do our bidding. When my heart is aligned with God's, my prayers won't be about my desires, but about His.

> Prayer is about getting God's will done, not ours.

Jabez understood that God wanted to bless him. God wants to bless you too, but there are things you must do to receive those blessings. You must hearken diligently to the will of God. You must walk in the ways of God. You must do the things God has commanded you to do.

If, like Israel, you ignore the voice of God, walk in your own ways, and disobey His commandments, you put yourself outside the place of blessing. But if you will just listen to His voice, if you will walk in His ways, if you will observe to do the things that He has commanded, then the blessings will be yours.

Father, help us to truly understand the purpose of prayer, and may we not seek to use it as a means to gratify our own desires. We pray that we will walk in Your ways, and that we will observe the things that You have commanded so that we might know Your blessings upon our life.

In Jesus' name, amen.

An Undivided Heart

*… there were fifty thousand who went out to battle, expert in war
with all weapons of war, stouthearted men who could keep ranks …*
— 1 Chronicles 12:33

The men who gathered to David were skillful warriors, but their real strength was the fact that they had undivided hearts.

David prayed, "Unite my heart" (Psalm 86:11). He knew the heart's tendency. "Yes, I love the Lord. But I also have this attraction for the worldly things." When only part of my heart wants to serve the Lord, that means part of my heart wants to serve the flesh.

A DOUBLE HEART HINDERS OUR SERVICE TO THE LORD.

Many people want to be counted with God's servants, but they also have a heart for worldly things. They're caught up in worldly activities. They have given the Lord a place in their hearts, but they haven't given their hearts completely to the Lord. They are being drawn by the Spirit after the things of the Lord, but they're also being drawn by their flesh after the things of the world.

You will find them in church most Sunday mornings, unless it's Super Bowl Sunday. The rest of the week there is very little place for God in their lives, and they seldom communicate with Him.

Is your heart divided or torn? Are you fervently following after Jesus, or things of the world? Is He truly the Lord and Master of your life? If He isn't, ask for help. Ask God to give you a single-hearted devotion to Him.

*Lord, challenge our hearts today to a true commitment, that we
would not love in word alone but in deed and in truth. Help us to
give You Your rightful place in our hearts.*
In Jesus' name, amen.

CALL UPON THE LORD

Call upon His name …
— 1 CHRONICLES 16:8

What is the name of our Creator? "God" is not His name; it is His title. When the Hebrew name for God was translated into our English text, it was translated L-O-R-D with all capitals. But "Lord" is also a title, so people have become confused. They think that "Lord" is His title, and "God" is His name. But His name is actually *Yahweh*, or *Jehovah*.

The name *Jehovah* is a verb in Hebrew meaning "to be" or literally "the becoming one." It is the name by which God chose to reveal Himself to us, the I Am, the Becoming One, as God becomes to you whatever you might need. I am your healer—*Jehovah-rapha*. I am your provider—*Jehovah-jireh*. I am your peace—*Jehovah-shalom*. I am your salvation—*Jehovah-shua*.

The name *Jehovah-shua* was shortened to *Jehoshua*, then shortened further to *Yashua*. In the Greek, *Yashua* is Jesus. So Jesus is the name of our God. He is *Jehovah-shua*. He is the One who has saved us from our sins. He has become our Savior.

> GOD HAS GIVEN TO HIM A NAME THAT IS ABOVE EVERY NAME, THAT AT THE NAME OF JESUS, *YASHUA*, EVERY KNEE SHOULD BOW AND EVERY TONGUE SHOULD CONFESS THAT HE IS LORD.

Call upon His name—but not just in the time of need. Call upon Him continually, day by day, because He is the Lord of your life, and because you want to do His will, and above all else, because you love Him.

Father, we are so thankful that You have called us into this covenant relationship with You. May we bring glory to Your precious name.
AMEN.

Do Your Best and Commit the Rest

Be of good courage, and let us be strong for our people and for the cities of our God. And may the Lord do what is good in His sight.
— 1 Chronicles 19:13

As Joab and the armies of Israel prepared to fight the Ammonites, the Syrians came up behind them. Joab realized they had fallen into a trap. With enemies before them and enemies behind them, Joab decided that he and his brother, Abishai, would divide the army into two regiments.

Then Joab gave this exhortation to Abishai. In essence, he was saying, "Be courageous, and we will leave the consequences with the Lord. We will do our best and then commit the rest."

> God doesn't require that I do *the* very best, only *my* very best.

We often excuse ourselves from serving the Lord because of our inadequacies. We leave the battle because we know that others are more qualified or more talented and could do the job better. But God doesn't always call the most qualified person to do His work. He is not always looking for ability, just availability.

When faced with overwhelming odds, we need to remember the words Joab spoke to his young brother, "Be of good courage, behave yourself valiantly for the people and for the cities of our God; and then let the Lord do that which is good in His sight."

Do your best and commit the rest.

———

Lord, forgive us for the many times we have surrendered without even engaging in battle. May we respond to your love by doing our best for You.

The Lord be with You

Now, my son, may the LORD be with you; and may you prosper,
and build the house of the Lord your God, as He has said to you.
— 1 Chronicles 22:11

As Solomon begins the task of building this magnificent temple for the Lord, his father encourages him. And the first thing David says is, "The Lord be with you." That is significant.

Over the years, the church has endeavored to do the work of God with the wisdom of man. Man's desire to be independent of God is a common desire but should never be exercised within the church. We need the Lord to be with us in every undertaking. It isn't enough just to know *what* God wants done. It is important that we know *how* God wants it done.

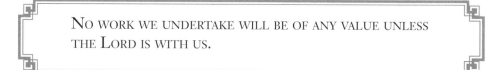

No work we undertake will be of any value unless the Lord is with us.

I don't know what God is calling you to do. But as you look at that ministry or that task, you may feel dismayed. You may be saying, "I could never do that, Lord. Surely You've got the wrong person."

Remember Moses, who said, "Lord, I can't talk very well. I stutter and stammer and the people won't pay attention to what I have to say." What was the Lord's answer? "I'll be with you." That's all it takes.

God's answer is always, "I will be with you." His presence will go before you. And when God guides, God provides all the wisdom, all the direction, all that you need to fulfill the calling He places upon your heart.

Lord, how thankful we are that Your presence is with us.
We depend upon that. We know, Lord, that without You,
we can do nothing.
In Jesus' name, amen.

GIVING TO GOD

*Then the people rejoiced, for they had offered willingly, because
with a loyal heart they had offered willingly to the LORD; and
King David also rejoiced greatly.*

— 1 CHRONICLES 29:9

The people offered willingly and they gave willingly. As they gave, they began rejoicing and praising God. And that is the way it should be, whether you are giving of your time, your energy, your money, or your possessions. Whatever you give to God should be offered willingly, from the heart.

Giving to the Lord should be the greatest joy and the greatest happiness that you know. Anything I offer to God must come from a willing heart if it's to have any value.

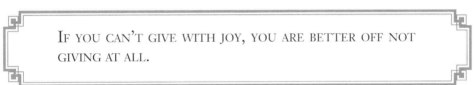

IF YOU CAN'T GIVE WITH JOY, YOU ARE BETTER OFF NOT GIVING AT ALL.

Before his visit to the Corinthian church, Paul wrote ahead and asked them to take up an offering for the saints in Jerusalem, who were suffering real poverty. And then he added, "So let each one give as he purposes in his heart, not grudgingly or of necessity; for God loves a cheerful giver" (2 Corinthians 9:7). In the Greek, the word for "cheerful" means "hilarious." In other words, God loves a hilarious giver. He is blessed when we give hilariously, out of a heart of rejoicing.

May we never forget that all that we have has come from God. All that we have is actually His; it belongs to Him. But we have the privilege of giving back to Him willingly—from the heart—as an expression of our love and gratitude.

*Father, thank You for the privilege, the blessing, and the joy of
giving to You. Take our lives, Lord. We offer them to You to use as
You see fit.*

IN JESUS' NAME, AMEN.

GREATER THAN ALL OTHER GODS

And the temple which I build will be great, for our God is greater than all gods. But who is able to build Him a temple, since heaven and the heaven of heavens cannot contain Him? Who am I then, that I should build Him a temple?

— 2 CHRONICLES 2:5-6

How big is the universe? Does space just continue on and on into infinity, or is there a sign somewhere that reads, "You've reached the end"?

As we consider the vastness of our universe, we begin to see the greatness of the God we serve. If our finite minds cannot comprehend even the greatness of a finite universe, how can we comprehend the infinite God who created that universe?

David recognized that the heathens made little gods for themselves out of wood, stone, silver or gold—gods with eyes that couldn't see, ears that couldn't hear, mouths that couldn't speak, and feet that couldn't walk. But ours is a great God. He is a loving God—a living God.

> WHEN WE CONSIDER WHO GOD IS AND WHAT HE HAS DONE FOR US, HOW CAN WE DO LESS THAN OFFER HIM OUR BEST?

For this reason, whatever we do for God has to be our best. How can we not live completely for Him?

From the simple cell to the magnificent universe, our great God rules and reigns over all. The question is, does He rule and reign in your life—or are you worshiping one of these lesser gods?

We thank You, Lord, for the blessing and the privilege of knowing and serving You.

Choose Your Path Carefully

*Nevertheless they will be his servants, that they may distinguish
My service from the service of the kingdoms of the nations.*

— 2 Chronicles 12:8

When Rehoboam led the people to forsake the Lord and serve other gods, God's response was, "You don't want to serve Me? Okay, I will let you see what it is like to serve the kingdoms of the countries around you. I'll let you experience the heavy bondage of serving other gods."

Many today live solely to serve their own pleasure.

People haven't changed. Living for the moment, they have become slaves to the passions of their flesh. If these people only knew where their chosen path would lead, I believe they'd choose another path. When Jesus called us to follow Him, He said, "My yoke is easy, and My burden is light." That cannot be said concerning the yoke that comes upon the person who has chosen to live after his own flesh.

God has never asked me to do a single thing that would harm me. He has never asked me to give up anything that was beneficial to me. The only things that God has asked me to give up were those things that would ultimately destroy me. And in serving God, He never requires anything of me except that which He has given me the power and capacity to fulfill.

You choose the god you will serve. Take a look at the end of the path that you are walking on. Does it lead to life or death?

*Father, give us that wisdom that will cause us to look down the road
and see where the path is leading before we embark upon our journey.*

In Jesus' name, amen.

God's Victory

*You will not need to fight in this battle. Position yourselves, stand
still and see the salvation of the LORD, who is with you, O Judah
and Jerusalem! Do not fear or be dismayed; tomorrow go out
against them, for the Lord is with you.*

— 2 CHRONICLES 20:17

The three nations to the east joined forces and sent their army to destroy Judah. Jehoshaphat knows that Judah is no match for these combined forces. Humanly speaking, they are as good as gone.

Sooner or later, we all encounter situations that are beyond our own abilities. The Bible tells us that as Christians, we have three formidable foes: the forces of the world, the flesh, and the devil. Any one of them constitutes a real problem for us, but combined, there is no human way that we can know victory.

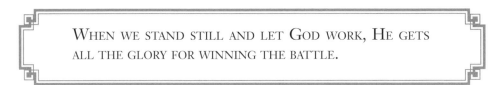

WHEN WE STAND STILL AND LET GOD WORK, HE GETS
ALL THE GLORY FOR WINNING THE BATTLE.

When those monumental problems appear, we often wish God would give us a formula that would take care of the problem. But if we had a formula, then we would want to market it. Then we'd go around bragging about how well we did.

God has so many interesting ways to work out our problems. How important it is when we are faced with those dilemmas that we remember to reach out to Him. We need to pray to the true and living God, the Creator of heaven and earth. He is able to do exceeding abundantly above all that we ask or think. The battle, after all, is His.

*Father, help us today to recognize and confess our limitations,
in order that we might rely upon You. We rejoice, Lord, in Your
promise of help.*

IN JESUS' NAME, AMEN.

A GODLY INFLUENCE

And he walked in the way of the kings of Israel, just as the house
of Ahab had done, for he had the daughter of Ahab as a wife; and
he did evil in the sight of the LORD.

— 2 CHRONICLES 21:6

Jehoshaphat was a good king and led the people to serve the Lord. But his son, Jehoram, was one of the most wicked kings in the history of Judah. How could such a godly man have such a wicked son?

Though Jehoshaphat was a godly man, he had a curious fascination with evil. That curiosity drew him north again and again, until eventually he aligned with King Ahab. Although Jehoshaphat himself did not become personally involved with the wicked practices of King Ahab, he made the mistake of exposing his son to those practices. And Jehoram, who did not have a strong commitment to God, fell to that wickedness.

MANY PROFESSING CHRISTIANS TODAY SEEM TO HAVE THE SAME CURIOUS FASCINATION WITH EVIL.

Though they would never think to do those things themselves, they love to read about others doing evil and watch others doing evil in movies and on television. The rationale seems to be, "It doesn't hurt to just watch."

You may argue that your watching the filth of the world doesn't affect your relationship with God. I doubt that. But think about this: What effect is it having upon your children?

When I stand before God I want to stand there in the holiness, purity, and righteousness of Jesus Christ. And I want my children to be standing there with me, complete in Him.

God, let our lives be the light of this world as we reflect
Your holiness, Your beauty, Your grace, and Your love.

IN JESUS' NAME, AMEN.

MARCH

THE SECRET TO SUCCESS

[King Uzziah] sought God in the days of Zechariah, who had understanding in the visions of God; and as long as he sought the Lord, God made him prosper.

— 2 CHRONICLES 26:5

The secret to a good life is seeking the Lord. Jesus said, "Seek first the kingdom of God and His righteousness, and all these things shall be added to you" (Matthew 6:33). In other words, you take care of your relationship with God and He will take care of everything else.

King Uzziah focused upon his relationship with God, and he sought the Lord in the days of Zechariah who had understanding in the visions of God. This would indicate that Zechariah acted as a spiritual model for him. And indeed, as long as Zechariah was living, Uzziah sought the Lord. And as long as he sought the Lord, God made him to prosper.

THE MOMENT I QUIT SEEKING GOD, I AM AS WEAK AS OTHER MEN.

However, prosperity often brings danger. Sometimes you begin to think your success is due to your own skill and genius, and leave God out of your life. As Uzziah looked at the strength and wealth of his kingdom, his heart became lifted up. We read in verse 16, "But when he was strong his heart was lifted up, to his destruction."

I must always remember that the secret of my strength is my relationship with God.

Lord, help us not to fight with You. Help us to be sensitive and open to the voice of Your Spirit.

IN JESUS' NAME WE PRAY, AMEN.

FINAL CALL

Then the runners went throughout all Israel and Judah with the
letters from the king and his leaders, and spoke according to the
command of the king: Children of Israel, return to the LORD God
of Abraham, Isaac, and Israel; then He will return
to the remnant of you who have escaped from the
hand of the kings of Assyria.

— 2 CHRONICLES 30:6

When Hezekiah became king, he sought to bring the people back to a spiritual renewal, back to the acknowledgment that Jehovah was God over the nation. So he sent notice throughout the land for the people to return to the Lord and observe the Passover Feast.

The Assyrians had conquered the northern kingdom and taken captives, but many had evaded capture. Hezekiah's invitation went out to those who remained. They had forsaken God, but He was calling them back. As it turned out, this was God's final call to Israel. The northern kingdom mocked the invitation, and within three years, they were gone.

> IT IS FRIGHTENING TO REALIZE THAT IF A MAN PERSISTS IN THAT PATH GOD HAS WARNED HIM AGAINST, THE DAY WILL COME WHEN GOD GIVES HIM ONE FINAL CALL.

Judah, however, responded to the invitation. Under Hezekiah's reign, Judah became strong and prosperous again because they turned unto the Lord with one heart.

Our God is merciful and gracious. If you turn to Him, He will free you from the captivity of the enemy and the power of darkness that holds you within its grip.

Father, awaken us to the seriousness of the day and the age
in which we live. May we with one heart make a covenant
to serve and worship You, and to surrender ourselves
to the lordship of Jesus Christ.

AMEN.

REDIRECTED FOCUS

*"Be strong and courageous; do not be afraid nor dismayed before the king of Assyria, nor before all the multitude that is with him; for there are more with us than with him. With him is an arm of flesh; but with us is the L*ORD *our God, to help us and to fight our battles." And the people were strengthened by the words of Hezekiah king of Judah.*

— 2 CHRONICLES 32:7-8

The Assyrians went on the move to attack Jerusalem. Hezekiah wisely made preparations. He directed the people to build up the city walls, stop up the springs and wells outside the city, and stockpile spears and shields. But because of the Assyrians' brutal reputation, the people were discouraged and fearful. So Hezekiah called them together to encourage them.

He could have just told them to not be afraid, but instead, he gave them a reason not to be afraid. He redirected their focus off of the enemy and onto the Lord. He reminded them that God was on their side and willing to fight their battles.

GOD WILL FIGHT OUR BATTLES.

When impossible situations arise, we need to remember that God can do exceedingly abundantly above all that we ask or think. These battles are not against us—they are against God. And no one can move our God.

If you are worried or distressed about a problem, you haven't come to a real trust in God yet. The moment you place the whole situation in God's hands, worry will go; fear and anxiety will disappear. Rest in God. It is all in His hands.

Father, we are so thankful, Lord, that we go into the battle as victors. Help us keep our eyes upon You that we might be strong and courageous.

IN JESUS' NAME, AMEN.

NO REMEDY

And the LORD God of their fathers sent warnings to them by His messengers, rising up early and sending them, because He had compassion on His people and on His dwelling place. But they mocked the messengers of God, despised His words, and scoffed at His prophets, until the wrath of the Lord arose against His people, till there was no remedy.

— 2 CHRONICLES 36:15-16

It is an awesome thing when God declares that there is no cure, no remedy. Such was the tragic case of Judah. They worshiped other gods, refused to listen to the voice of the Lord, and turned their backs on God—until finally He turned His back on them and allowed them to be defeated by their enemies.

> IF YOU REFUSE GOD'S REMEDY, THERE IS NO OTHER CURE.

In His patience and His compassion, God had sent many prophets to warn Judah. Jeremiah was one such prophet. When he delivered the message that God had determined to turn Judah into the hands of the Babylonians, and that it would go better for them if they submitted to the Babylonians, King Zedekiah imprisoned him as a traitor. God's remedy had been refused—so God's wrath was aroused.

Whenever there is a problem, God always has a remedy. For the problem of sin, God has prescribed a remedy, a cure. It is found in the sacrifice of Jesus Christ, the Lamb of God. The Bible tells us that the blood of Christ cleanses us from all our sins. But be warned: If you refuse God's remedy, there is no other cure.

Father, we are grateful that You have been so patient with us, giving us opportunity again and again to turn from the world to live after You. Lord, help us live before You in a way that is pleasing.

IN JESUS' NAME, AMEN.

MAINTENANCE FROM THE KING

*Now because we receive support from the palace, it was not proper
for us to see the king's dishonor; therefore we have sent and
informed the king.*

— EZRA 4:14

Israel's neighbors sent this letter to Artaxerxes during the rebuilding of the temple. When their offers of help were rebuffed, they sought to hinder the work. They hired lawyers to throw a snag into the project and sent a document to the king of Persia. They said, "We believe these people will dishonor you. We couldn't just stand by and see this happen; therefore, we felt it was necessary that we inform the king."

This verse applies to us today. For we have a King as well, and we receive our maintenance from Him.

Some people say that Jesus is just a crutch for weak people. They're right. I lean upon Him all the time. If He weren't a crutch for me, I would have fallen a long time ago. He has never failed me or let me down. You don't have to worry when you are being maintained by the King.

But the world around me dishonors my King. Every time someone takes the name of my God in vain, my heart cringes.

I DON'T LIKE TO SEE MY KING DISHONORED.

Just as Israel's neighbors sent a letter telling the king what was happening, we, too, need to inform ours. We need to get on our knees before God regarding the conditions of our nation and the things that are happening—and pray that He will begin to work.

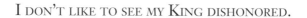

*Father, help us today to bring glory and honor to You, our King.
Give us the boldness to stand up for what is right and holy and pure.*

IN JESUS' NAME, AMEN.

AT A LOSS FOR WORDS

And now, O our God, what shall we say after this? For we have
forsaken Your commandments.

— EZRA 9:10

Just fifty-seven years after God—through Cyrus—released them from captivity so they could return to Jerusalem, rebuild the temple, and resume their worship of Him, Israel had already turned back to the very things God had previously judged them for. When Ezra heard the disturbing news, his heart sank. The people had not separated themselves from those around them, but were instead doing according to their abominations.

Ezra couldn't believe the people could so quickly forget God. Shocked, and at a loss for words, he prayed, "Lord, I don't have any excuses. What can I say?"

Though Ezra couldn't find words to speak to God, he had quite a few words for the people—words of warning and correction in which he called for a very strict and radical reform.

He called for a total separation of God's people from those things of the world that would pollute, dilute, or defile their witness. As Christians, we must do the same.

WE MUST MAKE SOME RADICAL DECISIONS CONCERNING
SEPARATION FROM THE WORLD AND ITS POLLUTION.

The enemy has declared open war against God. Are we just going to sit by and let our Lord be blasphemed? Or will we separate ourselves from the world, rise up, and take a stand for Jesus?

By our silence, Lord, we have encouraged the enemy. Help us to
stand in Your strength in this all-out war that the enemy has
declared against You. Lord, be our strength, be our fortress,
be our help.

IN JESUS' NAME, AMEN.

INSTANT PRAYER

Then the king said to me, "What do you request?" So I prayed to
the God of heaven.

— NEHEMIAH 2:4

For several months, Nehemiah had prayed for an opportunity to be used in the rebuilding of Jerusalem.

When the king noticed Nehemiah wasn't his usual happy self, he asked, "Why are you so sad?" Nehemiah described the condition of Jerusalem—the walls were in rubble, the gates had been burned, and the people were demoralized. "How can I be happy when I have heard that news?"

So the king said, "What is your request?" This was the opportunity Nehemiah had been asking for. Aware of how momentous the moment was, he offered a quick prayer to the God of heaven. The king probably didn't even notice the slight pause, but God did.

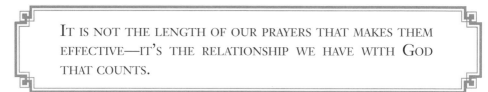

IT IS NOT THE LENGTH OF OUR PRAYERS THAT MAKES THEM EFFECTIVE—IT'S THE RELATIONSHIP WE HAVE WITH GOD THAT COUNTS.

"The effective, fervent prayer of a righteous man avails much" (James 5:16). Ezra's prayer had to be short and silent, but it was effective. God heard and responded. What a comfort to realize He hears our silent prayers.

If you don't have a relationship with God, there is only one prayer He is interested in, and that is, "God, be merciful to me, a sinner." But once you have prayed that prayer—then as a child of God, you can offer up those quick prayers any time you are in need. If you're in that right relationship, these short prayers can be dynamite.

Father, we thank You that You do answer prayer—even those
quick prayers that spontaneously arise out of weakness or turmoil.

IN JESUS' NAME, AMEN.

WHEN OPPOSITION RISES UP

But it so happened, when Sanballat heard that we were rebuilding the
wall, that he was furious and very indignant, and mocked the Jews.

— NEHEMIAH 4:1

N o sooner did Nehemiah return to Jerusalem and begin rebuilding the wall than opposition rose against him. In an attempt to stop the work, Sanballat and Tobiah ridiculed Nehemiah. But Nehemiah's response to their mockery was prayer.

Seeing that mockery didn't work, their next move was to plan secret attacks against those building the wall. So Nehemiah instructed workers to set a continuous watch against them.

The first step is always prayer—and then we act. Prayer is never a substitution for taking practical measures. You may say, "Well, I have prayed and I just have faith that the Lord will take care of things." But the Bible tells us that faith without works is dead.

IN ORDER FOR FAITH TO BE VALID, IT HAS TO LEAD TO ACTION.

Paul warned Titus that those who live godly in Christ Jesus will suffer persecution. Whenever you make a stand for God, or seek to do the work of God, opposition will rise up and seek to defeat you. When it does, we need to pray and ask God to guide us in a course of action, and then we need to take steps to rebuild our walls and set guards around them.

Now is the time to wake up and gird ourselves.

———

Father, we realize the walls have been broken down. Help us to
have the courage to stand against ridicule and mockery. And Lord,
may we determine in our heart to build those walls of defense again.

IN JESUS' NAME, AMEN.

THE NATURE OF GOD

But You are God, ready to pardon, gracious and merciful, slow to anger, abundant in kindness, and did not forsake them.

— NEHEMIAH 9:17

In this short verse, Nehemiah describes God's nature by listing a few of His attributes. The first that he mentions is God's willingness to pardon. Though His people were completely unfaithful to Him, God was completely faithful to His people. We have all fallen short of His glory, but the blood of Jesus is able to cleanse us of all unrighteousness.

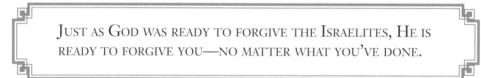

JUST AS GOD WAS READY TO FORGIVE THE ISRAELITES, HE IS READY TO FORGIVE YOU—NO MATTER WHAT YOU'VE DONE.

God is gracious. He bestows His blessings on those who do not deserve it.

God is merciful. As David—who really needed God's mercy—pointed out, God doesn't reward us according to our sins. Instead, He extends His mercy toward those who fear Him—mercy as high as the heavens are above the earth.

God is slow to anger. Sometimes I get a little upset about that. I am a lot like James and John who wanted to call down fire from heaven to consume the Samaritans who insulted Jesus. But God is slow to anger. He is patient and longsuffering.

God is kind. He was kind to Israel, He has been kind to our country, and He has certainly been kind to me.

God sees our failings, our flaws, and our weaknesses. And yet He stands ready to pardon. When we call on Him, He forgives us, washes us, and renews us. It is just His nature.

Father, we thank You for Your mercy. May we forsake our evil ways and receive Your pardon and cleansing.

AMEN.

The Haman in Our Lives

*When Haman saw that Mordecai did not bow or pay him
homage, Haman was filled with wrath. But he disdained to lay
hands on Mordecai alone, for they had told him of the people of
Mordecai. Instead, Haman sought to destroy all the Jews who
were throughout the whole kingdom of Ahasuerus—
the people of Mordecai.*

— Esther 3:5-6

Haman was an Agagite—a descendant of the Amalekites. God had ordered Saul to utterly destroy these Amalekites, but he disobeyed and allowed the king to live. As a result, the Amalekites continued to war against Israel.

In biblical typology, Haman is a type of the flesh, something God hates. Just as the Amalekites warred constantly against Israel, so too the flesh wars constantly against the Spirit. As the Amalekites attacked Israel at its weakest point, so the flesh will attack at your weakest point. Even as the Amalekites tried to keep Israel from coming into the Promised Land, so the flesh will try to hinder you from coming into victory and enjoying the promises of life in the Spirit.

God swore He would have war with Amalek from generation to generation, but He promised that one day the remembrance of Amalek would be utterly put away and Amalek would perish.

APRIL

One day the flesh will be put away forever.

We each have a Haman in our lives—that area of the flesh that has not yet been dealt with. Let us reckon it to be dead, crucified with Christ, that we might have His full victory as we walk in the Spirit.

*Father, thank You for providing victory through Jesus Christ over
the old nature. Help us press on in the Spirit, that we may know
Your power over the flesh.*

Amen.

Conquering Fear

*Go, gather all the Jews who are present in Shushan, and fast for
me; neither eat nor drink for three days, night or day. My maids
and I will fast likewise. And so I will go to the king, which is
against the law; and if I perish, I perish!*

— ESTHER 4:16

At Haman's request, the king of Persia decreed that on a certain day all of the Jews within the kingdom were to be slain. No one knows Queen Esther is a Jew. Her cousin encourages her to go to her husband and plead for her people, but doing so will put her life in jeopardy.

God's purposes will always be accomplished, regardless of what we do or don't do. Yet He allows us to be the instruments through which He accomplishes it. Esther chose to be that instrument. She recognized that God had brought her to this very special moment, and so she conquered her fear. "Even if it costs me my life," she said, "I will do it. If I perish, I perish."

Jesus told us not to worry about tomorrow, for tomorrow will take care of itself. Yet many Christians do worry. They worry because they haven't yet surrendered to the will of God.

SURRENDER BRINGS FREEDOM FROM FEAR AND ANXIETY.

The day God vacates the throne, we are all in big trouble. But as long as God is on the throne, we don't have to fear. After all, if we can trust the Lord for our eternal destiny, shouldn't we be able to trust Him with tomorrow?

*Lord, set Your people free from the concerns about the future. Help
us trust that You will work out Your eternal purpose as we commit
our ways unto You through Jesus Christ our Lord.*

AMEN.

WHY WAS I BORN?

*Why did I not die at birth? Why did I not perish
when I came from the womb?*

— JOB 3:11

In just a few moments' time, Job lost his children, his health, and all of his earthly possessions. He found himself a naked soul reduced to the bare essence of existence without any props or support.

> WHAT QUESTIONS DOES A MAN ASK WHO HAS BEEN STRIPPED OF EVERYTHING?

Job wanted to know why he was born. He didn't curse God, but he did curse the day of his birth. "Why was I ever born? What is the purpose of my life?"

If you subscribe to the evolutionary theory, the answer is obvious. There is no purpose for your life, for you exist by accident. You exist as the result of fortuitous occurrences of accidental circumstances over billions of years of time.

The Bible, however, teaches that there is life after death. This is just a place where God is preparing me in order that I might dwell with Him forever. The tests, the trials, the hardships, the disappointments are all intended to show me how temporary earthly things are, and teach me to live for the eternal and not for the present.

Why was I born? Why were you born? He created us to know and trust Him, that we might dwell with God in the glory of His kingdom forever.

*Father, teach us to trust in You, knowing that our lives are in
Your hands. We know that the enemy can do no more than what
You allow him to do. As we stumble or fail a test, it is only that we
might see how weak we are so that we will trust You more.*

IN JESUS' NAME, AMEN.

WHAT IS MAN?

What is man, that You should exalt him, that You should set Your heart on him...?

— JOB 7:17

We are each but a speck of dust on a speck of dust called Earth, which orbits around the sun in a little corner of the Milky Way galaxy. Yet, the Scriptures say that God's thoughts toward us are so great, if we could count them, they would outnumber the sands of the sea.

It is amazing that God thinks of us. Even more amazing is the fact that He magnifies us—above plants, above animals, and even above the angels. Job wanted to know why. "What is man, that You should exalt him?"

It is God's way.

> WHENEVER A LIFE IS YIELDED TO GOD, HE MAGNIFIES THAT PERSON.

God makes a person greater than they could ever be apart from His working. God does this because He loves us. He loves us so much, He gave His only begotten Son, who became what we were in order that He might make us what He is.

And thus, God develops and trains us. He allows trials and disappointments because He knows that is the only way to prepare us for eternity. Like Job, who went through a time of testing in which he lost everything he had, we sometimes go through loss or disappointment. But each loss is part of God's eternal plan as He prepares us to be with Him forever.

Father, thank You for Your faithfulness to mold us into the person You want us to be, and to take away anything which would destroy or defile us. How thankful we are that You have set Your heart on us. May we walk in that love.

AMEN.

THE CRY FOR A MEDIATOR

*For He is not a man, as I am, that I may answer Him, and that
we should go to court together. Nor is there any mediator between
us, who may lay his hand on us both.*

— JOB 9:32-33

"If you will just get right with God," Job's friends advised, "everything else will be okay." But Job didn't know how to do that. He saw the greatness of God compared with his own smallness, and realized that the gap between the infinite God and the finite creature is too great for man to ever bridge himself. Recognizing his dilemma, Job cried out for a mediator.

In the New Testament we read, "There is one God and one Mediator between God and men, the Man Christ Jesus" (1 Timothy 2:5).

JESUS IS THE BRIDGE BETWEEN GOD AND MAN.

Because Jesus and the Father are one (John 10:30), He is able to touch God. Because Jesus "became flesh and dwelt among us," (John 1:14), He also touches us. He understands our weaknesses, our fears, our temptations. And thus, Jesus is able to bring us to God.

This bridge that brought man to God was not created by man. Unlike other religions, in Christianity, man is not trying to reach God—God reaches down to man. If you want to find the eternal, true and living God, you can touch Him only by allowing Him to touch you through His Son, Jesus.

APRIL

*Father, we are so thankful You have provided that means whereby
we may be justified, not by our own works of righteousness, but by
our simple believing and trusting in our Mediator, Jesus Christ,
the One making intercession for us.*

AMEN.

NOTHING + NOTHING = NOTHING

Let him not trust in futile things, deceiving himself, for futility
will be his reward.

— JOB 15:31

In his attempt to understand why God had stripped Job of all his possessions, Eliphaz reasoned that Job had foolishly put his trust in those possessions. Though Job had not done so, Eliphaz was right in speaking against the folly of those who are lulled into a deceptive sense of security by their wealth.

The Bible warns us repeatedly about deception. Satan deceived Eve by causing her to doubt God's word and instead put her trust in Satan's empty promises. Still today, Satan tries to deceive us into thinking that God's laws aren't fair or don't apply to our lives.

> SATAN HAS DECEIVED MANY PEOPLE INTO TRUSTING IN EMPTINESS.

It's a fact: whatever we sow, we reap. Our minds are fertile fields into which we plant seeds each day. If we sow to the flesh, we can't expect to reap a spiritual harvest. Garbage in; garbage out. Mathematically speaking: nothing plus nothing equals nothing.

Some trust in wealth for security and satisfaction. Some trust in the emptiness of religious activity or ritual. Some trust in the emptiness of their own righteousness. But when you trust in emptiness; emptiness will be your only reward. Don't be deceived into thinking you can buy your way into God's grace. Put your hope in Jesus—the way, the truth, and the life.

Lord, may we begin to plant Your Word in the fertile soil of
our mind and sow to the Spirit that we might reap eternal life
through Jesus Christ.

Triumph of Faith

For I know that my Redeemer lives, and He shall stand at last on the earth; and after my skin is destroyed, this I know, that in my flesh I shall see God, whom I shall see for myself, and my eyes shall behold, and not another. How my heart yearns within me!

— Job 19:25-27

There were many things that Job did not know: he didn't know why he had lost everything, or why he was in this miserable condition, or why he had to suffer such pain. But Job knew one thing: "My Redeemer lives." And this was what he clung to.

Everyone recognizes that Job endured his afflictions with patience. The secret of his patience is faith. It is because of what Job believed that he was able to patiently endure all the sufferings that he did not understand.

Never let go of what you *do* know because of something you *don't* know.

What did Job believe that caused him to have such great patience? First, Job believed that God was in control of every circumstance that came into his life. The Lord gives, and the Lord takes away.

Secondly, he understood that God was for him. Though his wife turned against him, and his friends condemned him and accused him of heinous sins, he knew that God was on his side.

God is on your side too. When things are confusing or hard to understand, remember that.

APRIL

Father, we are thankful for the triumph of faith that brings us to glorious victory. Teach us to trust You as Job did and to patiently endure the dark night as we wait for the new day to dawn, the day of Your glorious kingdom.

In Jesus' name, amen.

THE QUEST FOR GOD

Oh, that I knew where I might find Him,
that I might come to His seat!

— JOB 23:3

E liphaz told Job that if he could just find God, things would be okay. But Job doesn't know where to find God.

Some people assert that because they cannot see God, they cannot believe in Him. But can you see the wind? Can you see electricity? You don't have to see something to feel its effects. Stick your finger in an outlet and the jolt you feel will make a believer out of you in a hurry.

Though I have never seen God, yet I have felt the presence and the influence of God within my life. I have heard His still small voice and I have seen His power at work in my life and in the lives of others around me.

Have you been searching for God? Jesus said, "I and My Father are One" (John 10:30). Are you thirsting after a meaningful relationship with God? Jesus cried out to the multitude, "If anyone thirsts, let him come to Me and drink" (John 7:37).

If your spirit is searching after God, if you find yourself thirsting after a meaningful relationship with Him, then Jesus is the end of your quest.

> WHEN YOU COME TO JESUS, YOUR SEARCH IS OVER, FOR YOU HAVE THEN DISCOVERED GOD.

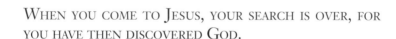

Father, thank You that we have come to know Your love. We feel
Your presence, we hear Your voice, and we see the effects of Your
hand at work in the world.

IN JESUS' NAME, AMEN.

ENCOUNTERING GOD

*I have heard of You by the hearing of the ear, but now my eye sees
You. Therefore I abhor myself, and repent in dust and ashes.*

— JOB 42:5-6

To this point in Job's story, he has defended himself to his friends. When they hinted that perhaps there was something shady in his background, Job denied it. "I have been honest and fair. I have contributed to my community and maintained my integrity." When he looked at himself in the light of others, Job came out looking pretty good.

We like comparing ourselves with others. When we make others the standard for righteousness, we often come out looking good. "I am not perfect, but I am a lot better than he is." But in the end, we won't be judged by the standards of others. The standard by which we will be judged is Jesus Christ.

When Job turned his eyes toward God, his view of himself changed. He said, "I abhor myself, and repent in dust and ashes." He who had maintained his integrity suddenly saw himself in the light of God's holiness and purity. Seeing his own filth, he repented.

> YOU MAY PRIDE YOURSELF IN YOUR ACCOMPLISHMENTS OR
> SUCCESSES. BUT MARK THIS, WHEN YOU SEE A PROUD MAN,
> YOU SEE A MAN WHO HAS NOT YET ENCOUNTERED GOD.

APRIL

Because once you truly see God, there is no place for pride—even if you are a minister, a president, or the Pope. Once a person truly sees God, the result is deep contrition and humility. The result is a repentant heart—a heart that cries out, "God, have mercy on me, a sinner."

---

*Father, our hearts long to see You that we might have a true
awareness of ourselves, and that we might be changed.
God, make us like You.*

AMEN.

THE CROSS

My God, My God, why have You forsaken Me?
— PSALM 22:1

Psalm 22 is a demonstration of God's foreknowledge of events. In this passage, God gives us advance notice of His plan for man's redemption by allowing His Son to die the ignominious death of crucifixion.

The Gospels tell us that after Jesus had been hanging on the cross for about three hours—at around noontime—the sky went dark. And out of the darkness a cry was heard from the Man on the middle cross, "My God, My God, why have You forsaken Me?" Jesus' cry brings us back to Psalm 22. But it begs the question, why would God forsake His Son at this critical hour?

GOD IS ABSOLUTE HOLINESS. THEREFORE, IT'S IMPOSSIBLE FOR HIM TO FELLOWSHIP WITH SIN.

In that moment when God laid my sin—and the sin of the whole world— upon Jesus Christ, the inevitable consequence occurred: Jesus was separated from God. He was forsaken of His Father for a time so that you would not need to be forsaken of God for eternity.

Nothing brings greater peace and confidence to your life than when you recognize the lordship of Jesus, surrender to His authority, and place your life in His hands. Not only does that decision bring you peace and confidence, it also brings you strength and endurance.

Father, we are so grateful for the cross and for the hope it brings us. We thank You that You were willing to forsake Your Son for a time in order that You need never forsake us. May we yield ourselves to be governed by Him and led by Your Holy Spirit.

AMEN.

THE LORD IS MY SHEPHERD

The LORD is my shepherd …
— PSALM 23:1

David understands the depth of these words in a way few of us do. Because he was a shepherd, he knew the relationship of the shepherd to the sheep. He knew it was the shepherd's job to protect the defenseless sheep from predators, and guide them to food and water. He knew that unless the shepherd kept the sheep from roaming, they could easily get themselves lost.

In verse 4 of this psalm, David says, "Your rod and Your staff, they comfort me." The rod was the stick the shepherd used to whack the sheep on the flank, whereas the staff was a walking stick with a hooked end, which was used to pull the sheep back.

SHEEP CAN BE VERY STUBBORN—AND SO CAN WE.

When a sheep is determined to go its own way, the shepherd will take his rod and whack it on the flanks to get it back into the flock.

Sometimes it is necessary for God to give us a whack. The Bible tells us, "Do not despise the chastening of the LORD … for whom the LORD loves He chastens" (Hebrews 12:5-6).

If you are God's child, He won't let you get away with evil. Everyone else may get away with it, but you will get caught for sure, because the Lord chastens every son whom He receives. His rod will be there to keep you in line. And His staff is there to pull you out of danger.

APRIL

Father, thank You for protecting us, guiding us, and providing for us. Thank You for loving us enough to correct us when we need it.
IN JESUS' NAME, AMEN.

THE HEAVY HAND OF THE LORD

When I kept silent, my bones grew old through my groaning all the day long. For day and night Your hand was heavy upon me; my vitality was turned into the drought of summer.

— PSALM 32:3-4

David was guilty of an adulterous relationship, which eventually led to murder. Though he tried to hide his guilt, his secret was eating him away. He couldn't clear his mind of what he had done.

When the heavy hand of God is upon your life, you will find no rest. Day and night, your conscience will plague you.

> SIN IS PLEASURABLE FOR A MOMENT, BUT IT IS A SHORT-LIVED MOMENT. ONE MOMENT'S PLEASURE CAN CAUSE A PERSON YEARS OF GRIEF, SORROW, AND HEAVINESS.

Perhaps you are experiencing the guilt David described. Your sin is plaguing you. You are seeing the consequences and it is ripping you up inside. You never intended to get this deeply involved. But you have been drawn in and you are miserable. The hand of God is heavy upon you.

I have good news for you. The moment David said, "I acknowledge my sin. I will confess" (Psalm 32:5), God forgave him. And you can be forgiven just as quickly. First John 1:9 tells us that, "If we confess our sins, He is faithful and just to forgive us our sins and to cleanse us from all unrighteousness."

Forgiveness brings release—release from guilt, from shame, and from the heavy hand of God.

———

Lord, may we experience that glorious joy of forgiveness, that we can walk free from the guilt of sin because they have been washed and cleansed by Your love, through Your Son Jesus Christ.

AMEN.

DON'T WORRY

Do not fret ...
— PSALM 37:1

In this life, we are prone to worry about many things. But David gives us the cure for worry in verses 5-7 of this psalm: "Commit your way to the LORD, trust also in Him, and He shall bring it to pass.... Rest in the LORD, and wait patiently for Him."

If we focus on a problem, it grows. It grows so big it overwhelms us, and we lose sight of the Lord. But when we focus on the Lord—on His love, grace, power, glory, and might—our problems grow so small we can hardly see them.

WE HAVE TO BE CAREFUL WHERE WE FOCUS OUR ATTENTION.

David tells us that when we commit our problems to God, two things happen: He brings it to pass, meaning He works out His will for us, and we find the rest we long for.

The psalmist declares that the person who trusts in the Lord shall not fear in the day of evil tidings. You may have heard evil tidings this week that are causing you worry. Remember: commit it to God, rest in Him, and wait patiently. Leave it in His hands. Worry will do nothing to solve your problems, but trusting brings peace and rest.

May the Lord bless you and bring you to that place of faith, trust, commitment, and rest.

APRIL

Lord, teach us to bring all things to You. When worry threatens to overwhelm, help us to commit our problems into Your hands and rest in the knowledge that You are sovereign and mighty. May we focus our hearts and our lives upon You this day.

AMEN.

The Cure for Depression

Why are you cast down, O my soul?
And why are you disquieted within me?
— Psalm 43:5

In modern terms, we could translate this verse, "Why are you so depressed? Why are you so filled with anxieties?"

Society places us under many difficult pressures. We find ourselves struggling financially, struggling with our relationships, struggling with work. The future feels uncertain. When we are unable to cope with those pressures, the result is depression or anxiety. Those feelings of dissatisfaction or hopelessness are magnified when we fail to see a way out of our circumstances—when we feel trapped in a darkened maze and can't find the way out.

David's soul was cast down. He was troubled because of the ungodly nations that surrounded and oppressed him. He was troubled because of deceitful men who had been unfair in dealing with him.

But in the midst of this depression, David reminds himself of the solution. "Hope in God" (Psalm 43:5).

> You won't find the solution to your problems by looking at other people or at yourself.

Direct your thoughts away from the problem and put them on God; away from your own weaknesses and onto His strength. You need to remember that God loves you and is in control of the circumstances that surround your life.

Father, thank You for being concerned with those things that have
brought us under such pressure, and created anxiety,
discouragement, and depression. We ask that You take these
situations and begin to accomplish Your plan.

In Jesus' name, amen.

JOY OF SALVATION

Restore to me the joy of Your salvation …
— PSALM 51:12

Joy is one of the marks of the Christian life. But joy should not be confused with happiness. Happiness is an emotion that is dependent upon the outward circumstances of my life, which means I can be very happy one moment, and very sad the next.

On the other hand, joy is an emotion evoked from internal circumstances—my relationship with God—and thus joy is a more constant experience. Because of my relationship with God, I can experience joy even in the midst of difficult or tragic circumstances.

When David sinned—and it was sin of the worst kind: adultery leading to murder—he lost the joy of his salvation, for sin breaks fellowship with God. David could no longer feel God's presence.

SIN BRINGS MISERY.

Though a person can be saved, their sin will rob them of their joy. The Holy Spirit will convict you, and this will bring heaviness until you get to the point of confession and repentance. When that happens—when we forsake our sin and return to God—He restores the joy of our salvation and brings us back into fellowship with Him.

Maybe today you are suffering guilt. Maybe like David, sin has stolen the joy of your salvation. The answer is simple: call out to God, who is merciful and ready to cleanse you from your sin and restore the joy of your salvation.

APRIL

Father, we are so grateful for Your faithfulness and willingness to forgive all who call upon Your name. How good it is to walk with You, to have that consciousness of Your nearness. We rejoice this day in the joy of our salvation.

AMEN.

Cast Your Burden on the Lord

Cast your burden on the LORD, and He shall sustain you; He shall never permit the righteous to be moved.
— Psalm 55:22

It is believed that David wrote this psalm when his son, Absalom, rebelled against him. His closest friend, Ahithophel, had also turned against him at this same time. Brokenhearted and filled with fear, David at first sought escape. But then he stopped and said, "Cast your burden on the Lord, and He shall sustain you."

> Peace comes when we turn those overwhelming issues over to God and cease trying to dictate the outcome.

David showed wisdom by turning his problem over to God. The prophet Isaiah said, "You will keep him in perfect peace, whose mind is stayed on You, because he trusts in You" (Isaiah 26:3). But if you are trying to maneuver a situation to gain the outcome you desire, you will have distress.

We find the strength to let go when we remember that God is a doting Father who loves and cares for His own. He is not going to allow anything to come into your life to destroy you. His intent is to build up your relationship so that you are able to trust Him when unexpected losses or disappointments come.

Cast your cares upon Him and leave them there. Trust in the Lord. He will take care of whatever burdens you have been carrying.

Father, we thank You that in the midst of all of our confusion—
the pressures of life, disappointments in relationships,
painful losses—You are there to help us.
Teach us to cast all our cares at Your feet.

In Jesus' name, amen.

OVERWHELMED

*From the end of the earth I will cry to You, when my heart is
overwhelmed; lead me to the rock that is higher than I.*

— PSALM 61:2

David had his share of glory, but he also had his share of problems.
When David was just a teenager, King Saul became very jealous of him
and endeavored to kill him. Still later, David struggled with problems in his
marriage and with his children. The psalms are David's prayers recorded during
the overwhelming moments in his life. And because he had so many problems,
we have so many psalms.

DAVID'S PROBLEMS ALWAYS BROUGHT HIM TO HIS KNEES.

David knew that when he reached the limit of his ability, he could cry out to
One whose power and ability is limitless. And we too can cry out to that same
Rock—to Jesus Christ, our rock of deliverance, our rock of defense, our rock of
salvation, our rock of strength.

Notice that we need to be led to the Rock. Our job is to cry out; the job of
the Holy Spirit is to lead us to Jesus.

If you are overwhelmed today, if your circumstances are more than you can
bear, let me encourage you to cry out to Jesus—to the Rock that is higher than
you, and higher than all your problems. He will deliver you. He will bring you
to a place of strength and victory.

*Father, many today are facing problems and situations that are
beyond their understanding, beyond their capacity.
I pray that Your Spirit will lead them this day to Your Son,
and that they might find in Christ their strength,
their deliverance, their health, and their peace.*

IN JESUS' NAME, AMEN.

GOD IS GOOD

Truly God is good ...
— PSALM 73:1

S ooner or later, we will each face something we cannot understand. When that happens—when the world around us seems to be falling apart and we feel confused and overwhelmed—it is important to remember this foundational truth: God is good.

Too often, in the midst of pain, we think the opposite. We look around at others who are healthy, strong, and pain-free, and we say, "I have devoted my life to God and I have tried to do the right thing. Why am I suffering? Why are the wicked *not* suffering?" Satan—who always attacks us when we are weak—is right there to join us in challenging God. He tries to shake our faith in God's goodness and His power by whispering, "If God is so mighty and so good, then why did He allow this to happen to you?"

> THE WAY TO SILENCE THE WHINING OF THE FLESH AND THE WHISPERING OF THE ENEMY IS TO REMIND YOURSELF OF GOD'S GREAT LOVE.

In reading through this psalm, it would appear that the psalmist was going through some sort of painful experience or a physical malady. Like we do at times, he felt weak. But he knew the truth about God. Toward the end of the psalm, he said, "My flesh and my heart fail, but God is the strength of my heart and my portion forever" (Psalm 73:26).

Remember that God is in control of your life. Remember that He is working all things together for your good.

Father, may we receive Your truth, and may we walk in the light of Your Word as it brings us to the knowledge of Jesus Christ our Lord. Teach us to reject Satan's lies and cling to Your truth.

AMEN.

Unite my Heart

Teach me Your way, O Lord; I will walk in Your truth; unite my heart to fear Your name.

— Psalm 86:11

hen Jesus was asked, "What is the greatest commandment of all?" He said, "You shall love the Lord your God with all your heart, with all your soul, and with all your mind" (Matthew 22:37).

What did you devote yourself to this past week? Whatever activities consumed your time, your thoughts, and your energy are the things you are truly devoted to. And if you are devoted to anything other than God, you have a divided heart.

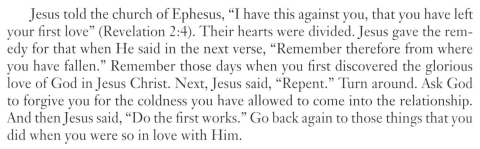

> Total devotion, total love—that's what God requires.

Jesus told the church of Ephesus, "I have this against you, that you have left your first love" (Revelation 2:4). Their hearts were divided. Jesus gave the remedy for that when He said in the next verse, "Remember therefore from where you have fallen." Remember those days when you first discovered the glorious love of God in Jesus Christ. Next, Jesus said, "Repent." Turn around. Ask God to forgive you for the coldness you have allowed to come into the relationship. And then Jesus said, "Do the first works." Go back again to those things that you did when you were so in love with Him.

Remember, repent, repeat.

Then, as you come back into fellowship with Him, follow David's example: "I will praise You, O Lord my God, with all my heart" (Psalm 86:12).

Total, absolute devotion. God deserves nothing less.

Father, search our hearts and show us those areas of attraction that may have drawn us away from that total devotion we once had for You. Renew the fire and the passion within us.

In Jesus' name, amen.

THE PATIENT GOD

He who formed the eye, shall He not see? ... shall He not correct,
He who teaches man knowledge?
— PSALM 94:9-10

Sometimes people take the attitude that God doesn't see or know when they sin. However, it isn't ineptness that keeps Him from judging. Nor is it a lack of concern. And it isn't due to weakness.

> IT IS LOVE THAT CAUSES GOD TO BE SO PATIENT AND LONG-SUFFERING WITH THE WICKED, GIVING OPPORTUNITY AFTER OPPORTUNITY FOR THEM TO TURN, TO REPENT, TO CHANGE.

But the wicked misinterpret His patience as weakness. They speak blasphemously against Him. "Does God know? Has He seen? Does He really hear?" Their assumption is that He doesn't because surely He would have done something about it if He did.

How blind we are—deliberately—to the history of mankind. God allowed those in Sodom to go a long way in their rebellion—so far that the homosexuals paraded in the streets and became physically aggressive. God allowed those in Noah's days to go so far that they threw off moral restraint and every man did what was right in his own sight. But God eventually judged that age and destroyed those people.

How long can God allow our nation to turn its back on Him? How far will God let us go? He has been far more patient than I could ever dream.

But don't mistake the patience of God as weakness, tolerance, or approval. For the day of God's righteous judgment shall come.

Father, how desperately we need You. Our world is wicked and rebellious. We need You to step in and stop men from destroying themselves. May Your kingdom come and Your will be done here on the earth, even as it is in heaven.

AMEN.

HEARKEN

Today, if you will hear His voice: "Do not harden your hearts ..."
— PSALM 95:7-8

I have stumbled many times, but each time—I must confess—God spoke to me and warned me before I fell. The problem was, I didn't heed that warning. I didn't hearken unto God's voice.

Sometimes, when God's voice breaks through and He gives us a warning about something we are about to do, we say, "Thanks, Lord, but I don't need any help there. I know what I'm doing." The truth is, we don't know what we are doing. And we *do* need His help.

As He addresses the seven churches in Revelation chapters 2 and 3, Jesus repeats the same warning to each: "He who has an ear, let him hear what the Spirit says to the churches."

THE OPPOSITE OF HEEDING IS HARDENING.

If you don't heed the voice of God, you will end up hardening yourself to hearing God.

We sometimes harden ourselves to God's voice because we don't understand the painful or difficult circumstances we find ourselves in. But there is another option. Instead of becoming bitter, instead of spending sleepless nights worrying about our problems, we can remember that God is working through the pain to purify us and mold us into the image of Jesus. We can turn those problems over to Him and trust that He will work out His perfect plan.

One choice pleases God—listening and trusting Him.

APRIL

Father, help us to keep ourselves ever attentive to Your voice.
When difficulties come, remind us that You are in control of all
things, and that You are able to work through our situation to
bring about Your will. We want to please You, Father.

IN JESUS' NAME, AMEN.

GOD'S WONDERFUL WORLD

O Lord, how manifold are Your works! In wisdom You have made them all. The earth is full of Your possessions.
— PSALM 104:24

Overwhelmed by the beauty God has created, the psalmist uses his most picturesque language to try to describe God's handiwork.

He describes the rain cycle, how God lifts the water to the tops of the mountain where it then runs down in the stream, how the springs then break forth in the valleys so that the wild animals can quench their thirst, and how, though the water flows into the sea, the sea never overflows.

In all this, the psalmist sees God's wisdom. And as he contemplates the spectacular design and beauty of the things God created, the psalmist worshiped.

There are some people today who look at nature and see the same design, the same beauty the psalmist saw—but instead of worshiping God for His creation, they worship creation itself. They worship nature. How foolish to smell a rose and touch the softness of its petals and admire the intricacies of its design and the beauty of its coloring—and then conclude, "The rose is God." That's irrational.

> THE ONLY RATIONAL THING TO DO WHEN ONE EN-
> COUNTERS THE BEAUTY OF A ROSE IS TO BREATHE IN ITS
> FRAGRANCE AND SAY, "THAT IS A CREATION OF MY GOD."

And then, like the psalmist, we ought to worship the God of all that beauty— the God of the clouds, and the mountain stream, and the sea … and the rose.

Father, we worship and praise You for the beauty of Your creation, in which we marvel at Your wisdom and Your goodness. We are amazed at the work of Your hand. May You work something beautiful within each of us.

AMEN.

Satisfaction for the Hungry Soul

Oh, that men would give thanks to the Lord for His goodness, and
for His wonderful works to the children of men! For He satisfies the
longing soul, and fills the hungry soul with goodness.
— Psalm 107:8-9

Have you ever pushed yourself away from the table at Thanksgiving and said, "I never want another bite to eat as long as I live?" At that moment, you are genuinely sincere. You really don't want another bite of food. But come evening, there you are back in the kitchen, putting whipped cream on a slice of pumpkin pie. That's because the body demands constant feeding.

THE FLESH CAN NEVER BE SATISFIED.

No matter how much you feed your flesh, it will always want more. In fact, if you give in to an area of the flesh, rather than being satisfied, it demands more and more until it eventually brings you into bondage.

Just as men have physical hunger and thirst, they also have spiritual hunger and thirst. The problem comes when you try to satisfy a spiritual need with a fleshly experience. It just doesn't work.

Are you hungry for more of God? Thirsty for peace or righteousness? In John 6:35, Jesus said, "I am the bread of life. He who comes to Me shall never hunger, and he who believes in Me shall never thirst."

Jesus is the answer to all your longings.

Father, we thank You that through Your Son, our hunger and our
thirst have been satisfied. For those still trying to fill their spiritual
need with physical experience, we ask that Your Holy Spirit
draw them back to Jesus.
In His name we pray, amen.

MAY

What Can I Give to God?

What shall I render to the Lord for all His benefits toward me?
— Psalm 116:12

Because they know Grandma loves flowers, our granddaughters will sometimes go out into our garden and pick flowers for her. They don't pick carefully. Usually, they haven't left long enough stems. And more often than not, in their quest for just the right flowers, they leave a trail of trodden down plants behind them.

The garden is not theirs. It is ours. So they are going into our garden to pick our flowers to give to Kay. But you know what? We love those gifts.

I think God receives our gifts in the same attitude. There is not a single material thing that He needs. And because "the earth is the Lord's, and all its fullness" (1 Corinthians 10:26), anything we give Him materially really belongs to Him anyway. Sometimes, when we are going through His garden looking for flowers to pick for Him, we sort of mess the place up. Yet He receives what we bring Him with loving graciousness.

When you consider all that God has done for you and all He has provided—salvation, cleansing, the hope of heaven—it makes you want to give Him something back.

> WHAT COULD WE POSSIBLY GIVE TO GOD THAT IS OF ANY VALUE TO HIM?

There's only one thing He really wants from you. Just one thing. He wants your heart.

Father, when we think of all that You've given to us—salvation, eternal life, our daily bread—we wonder what can we give to You. And so Lord, wanting to offer You a sacrifice of thanksgiving, we give You our hearts and our lives.

WANTED: DEAD AND ALIVE

Turn away my eyes from looking at worthless things,
and revive me in Your way.

— PSALM 119:37

It is interesting how charming the vain things of the world can become to us.

God placed Adam and Eve in the garden and said, "Of all of the trees that are in the garden, you may freely eat. There is only one tree that you are not to eat from, and that's the tree that is in the midst of the garden. In the day that you eat of it, you will surely die." And what tree did Eve find most attractive? Which one did she feel drawn to? The forbidden tree.

Evil is alluring, attractive—and utterly deceptive. People are drawn to the forbidden because they believe, wrongly, that it will bring satisfaction and contentment. "If I just had that, then I'd be completely happy." The reality is, however, that when we chase after what is forbidden, we're left feeling emptier than before.

> TEMPORAL EXCITEMENTS NEVER LAST LONG.

God honors our choices. If we choose to pursue fleshly experiences, hoping to find satisfaction, God will honor that decision. But when we are ready to lay aside fleshly pursuits and walk after the things of the Spirit, God will honor that choice as well.

Wise is the man who, like David, prays for God's help. "Guard my eyes, Lord. Make me dead to fleshly temptations. Make me alive to Your ways."

Father, turn us from the pursuit of empty things that offer only
false promises of satisfaction. May we be dead to the flesh and alive
to You, that we might fellowship with You
and shine like the stars forever and ever.

IN JESUS' NAME WE PRAY, AMEN.

MAY

THE BONDAGE OF INIQUITY

Direct my steps by Your word,
and let no iniquity have dominion over me.

— PSALM 119:133

A fly—unable to see the trap just ahead—gets itself caught in the spider's web. At first, it puts up a pretty good struggle. With all the energy it possesses, it thrashes about, looking for escape. But the more it thrashes, the more entangled it becomes, until eventually, it is completely bound.

Like the fly, we sometimes get ourselves caught in sin. Whether it is alcohol, drugs, gambling, pornography, fornication, or adultery, the addictive capacity of sin acts like a sticky web, drawing you in tighter and tighter until you find yourself under the bondage of corruption.

> THE MOMENT YOU GIVE YOURSELF OVER TO SIN, YOU COME UNDER SATAN'S POWER.

"All things are lawful for me, but I will not be brought under the power of any" (1 Corinthians 6:12). Jesus came into the world to destroy Satan's dominating power. He came to release you, and to "proclaim liberty to the captives" (Luke 4:18).

Wise is the man who uses his liberty to avoid the snare of evil. But if you have been captured, know that you can find freedom through Jesus. You don't have to be enslaved to the sin that threatens to destroy you. Christ can free you. Confess your sin and let Him break Satan's hold over you.

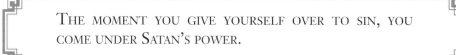

Lord, we thank You that You have power over darkness. We ask
that You strengthen us, that we would not get caught in a web of
sin, but that You would order our steps in Your Word.

IN JESUS' NAME WE PRAY, AMEN.

PLEASING GOD

For the LORD takes pleasure in His people;
He will beautify the humble with salvation.
— PSALM 149:4

When we see the pleasure that someone gets from taking a ruined object and making it like new, we are probably getting close to the heart of God. He loves to take lives that have been ruined by sin and restore them again into the image of His Son.

When God looks at you, He sees the work of His grace in you. He sees that out of the ashes of a failed life, something worthwhile and beautiful has been fashioned. God is also pleased when He sees you choosing to live after the Spirit, yielding your life to Him that He might by His Spirit conform you into the image of His Son.

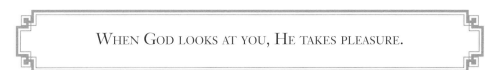

WHEN GOD LOOKS AT YOU, HE TAKES PLEASURE.

Some sights, however, do not please God. Wickedness does not please God (Psalm 5:4). Those who shrink back from their faith do not please God (Hebrews 10:38). And those who are living after the flesh do not please God (Romans 8:8). God is not pleased when you choose to live after the flesh because He knows that could destroy you.

Ask yourself honestly: Am I choosing to please myself, or God? What about the activities you have devoted yourself to—are they pleasing to God, or just to you? Remember the words of Jesus, who said, in speaking of the Father, "I always do those things that please Him" (John 8:29). When you choose to do likewise, your life will be more rewarding and more meaningful.

Live to please God.

MAY

Father, help us to live lives that bring You honor.
May we devote ourselves, Lord, to pleasing You.
IN JESUS' NAME WE PRAY, AMEN.

DISCOVERING THE WILL OF GOD

Trust in the LORD with all your heart, and lean not on your own understanding; in all your ways acknowledge Him, and He shall direct your paths.

— PROVERBS 3:5-6

We exist to glorify God and to do His will. But how do we know what He wants us to do? In this verse, Solomon gives us three steps to discovering God's will for our lives.

First, "Trust in the Lord with all your heart." You will not always understand what God is doing—or why. You have to put your full and complete trust in Him.

Second, "Lean not on your own understanding." I am amazed at all of the strategy sessions that are called by church councils to try to organize outreach programs in the most logical, appealing way. The will of God is not discovered in planning sessions but in prayer meetings.

Third, "In all your ways acknowledge Him." Don't make a decision until you have first inquired of the Lord.

GOD LEADS IN VERY SIMPLE, NATURAL WAYS.

Though we would prefer to hear God's will first—so we can decide whether or not we like it—that's not how God leads. You don't usually hear an angel singing and gesturing you to follow in a certain direction. Just live your life committed to Him; trust Him, and acknowledge Him when you have an impulse to move in one direction or another. When you do this, then "He shall direct your path."

Lord, we offer our bodies and our lives as instruments through which You can work to accomplish Your will on the earth.

IN JESUS' NAME WE PRAY, AMEN.

THE WAY OF THE RIGHTEOUS

In the way of righteousness is life, and in its pathway there is no death.
— PROVERBS 12:28

In order that we might know what it is to be righteous, God gave Moses the Ten Commandments. The first four commandments declared what it took to be right with God. The next six commandments listed what was necessary to be right with man.

If we just left the story there, we would be in a lot of trouble, because none of us could ever be righteous. But because He knew man could not live up to that standard of righteousness, God established another criteria. If we just put our trust in God, He would account that faith as righteousness.

What are you trusting? You are trusting that the eternal God, the Creator of this universe, so loved the world, (and that includes you), that He sent His only begotten Son to die for your sins and to take your guilt.

> JESUS PROMISED THAT THOSE WHO BELIEVED IN HIM WOULD NEVER DIE.

Jesus doesn't promise that we will live forever in these bodies, but that we will live forever in God's presence—never to experience separation from Him.

Writing to the Ephesians, Paul said, "And you He made alive, who were dead in trespasses and sins" (Ephesians 2:1). By putting your trust in Jesus Christ, you can be made spiritually alive today. You can become conscious of God, of His love, and of His purpose and plan for your life.

MAY

Father, we thank You for Your provisions whereby we have been accounted righteous. Help us, Lord, to live in that righteousness, in the path of which there is no death.

IN JESUS' NAME, AMEN.

The Wrong Way

There is a way that seems right to a man,
but its end is the way of death.

— Proverbs 14:12

Ultimately, there are only two destinations in life. You are either on the path that leads you to heaven or you are on the path that leads you to hell.

In speaking of those two paths, Jesus said, "Enter by the narrow gate; for wide is the gate and broad is the way that leads to destruction, and there are many who go in by it" (Matthew 7:13).

THE WISE WALK PURPOSEFULLY.

The wise look ahead and set goals for their lives—things they hope to achieve by the time they reach the end of their life's path. They think ahead to the moment they will stand before Jesus. They walk to win the words, "Well done, good and faithful servant" (Matthew 25:21).

The foolish, however, walk aimlessly. Believing Satan's lie that "all roads ultimately lead to God," they ignore the warnings along the path. All roads do not lead to the true and living God. Some roads lead to death—and eternal separation from the one true God.

Take a look at your life. Examine the path below your feet. Have you chosen the path that leads to Jesus? And what are you trusting to determine this—the word of man, or the Word of God?

Father, we ask that Your Holy Spirit would guide us in the path
of life that leads to Your abode. We're so thankful, Lord, that Your
Son cleared a way for us—a road that leads straight to You. May
we walk in His way, in His truth, and in His light.

IN JESUS' NAME WE PRAY, AMEN.

Our Strong Tower

The name of the Lord is a strong tower:
the righteous run to it and are safe.

— Proverbs 18:10

In ancient times, people built high towers along the walls that surrounded their cities. From these towers, a person could see for a long distance and could easily spot approaching enemies. When warfare broke out, towers offered a height advantage. Spears could not reach you, but your spears could easily be thrown down upon your attackers. For these reasons, people ran to the towers when danger approached.

We, too, have a strong tower—a place of refuge to which we can run when life's battles loom.

Our refuge is the name of the Lord.

Countless times, when I have needed Him most, I have run to the name of Jesus and found safety. In times of distress, times of fear, times of uncertainty, times of feeling hopeless and helpless and weak, I have run to that place where I know I will find comfort and safety. I have run to Jesus.

He is Jehovah-jireh; He has provided for my need of salvation. He is Jehovah-nissi, my banner. His banner over me is love. He is Jehovah-shalom, my peace. He is Jehovah-tsidkenu, my righteousness. He is Jehovah-shammah— wherever I am, He is there.

Jesus is our Savior, our Rock, our Refuge. He is our Strong Tower.

Are you overwhelmed today? Feeling insecure or uncertain? Run to Jesus.

Father, we thank You for that help, that strength, that confidence
that we receive in and through the name of Jesus,
the name above all names.

In His name we pray, amen.

MAY

THE PERFECT FRIEND

A man who has friends must himself be friendly, but there is a friend who sticks closer than a brother.

— PROVERBS 18:24

We are not always lovable. That is because we are prone to mood cycles. I might be lovable one moment, and quite the opposite the next.

A GOOD FRIEND LOVES YOU NO MATTER YOUR MOOD.

It can be hard to find a friend like that. But I do have one Friend who loves me regardless of my mood. He knows every part of my character—all the good, and all the bad. In fact, there are no secrets between us. He knows all my flaws, all my weaknesses. Yet He still loves me.

He is the one who initiated our friendship. And He is the one who sustains it. He sticks with me through thick and thin, and when others have deserted me, He remains. He has promised that He will never leave me, never forsake me (Hebrews 13:5).

I have failed my Friend countless times, but He has never failed me. He forgives each of my offenses. He counsels me when I need advice, and I have never yet found Him to be wrong. His thoughts are always of me. He never seems to think of His own welfare, but He is always concerned with mine. In fact, He loves me so much that He laid down His life for me.

He did it for you, too.

Father, we thank You for Your only begotten Son, who laid down His life that we might be Your friends. Lord, we pray that even as Abraham was called Your friend, so too we may be called the friend of God. We want to know You intimately.

IN JESUS' NAME WE PRAY, AMEN.

THE FEAR OF THE LORD

Do not let your heart envy sinners,
but be zealous for the fear of the LORD all the day ...
— PROVERBS 23:17

Satan always paints the life of sin as exciting and enjoyable. If you take that picture at face value, it is easy to envy those engaged in the pleasures of sin. But you have to look further.

> YOU HAVE TO COMPARE THE END RESULT OF A LIFE OF WICKEDNESS WITH THE END RESULT OF A LIFE OF RIGHTEOUSNESS.

Life can end with death and eternal separation from God; or it can be rewarded with eternal life with God in heaven. Instead of envying sinners, we're told in this proverb that we're to walk in the fear of the Lord all day long. Some have a wrong idea about the fear of the Lord. They think it's the same fear that grips your heart when you suddenly spot a red-and-blue flashing light in your rearview mirror. But that is the wrong kind of fear.

The right kind of fear is what you would feel if you were about to give a speech before the President of the United States. You would wonder, "Is my suit pressed? Is my speech appropriate?"

If we would be awed to appear in front of the President, how much more so should we feel awed in the presence of the God who created the universe? Wise is the man or woman who fears the Lord—and uses that fear to live a life pleasing to Him.

MAY

Father, help us to have enough wisdom to look down the road to
see where the path is leading us. Give us the wisdom to turn from
our sin and commit our lives to following Jesus.

IN HIS NAME WE PRAY, AMEN.

TOMORROW'S UNCERTAINTY

*Do not boast about tomorrow, for you do not know what a day
may bring forth.*

— PROVERBS 27:1

We don't know a lot about the future, but we do know one thing: it is uncertain.

The Christian, however, actually knows something else. The Christian knows that no matter what tomorrow brings, God will be there. Jesus promised, "I will never leave you nor forsake you" (Hebrews 13:5). That means that if pain or sorrow or tragedy comes tomorrow, you'll be able to see it through because the Lord will be with you.

> GOD'S WILL IS TOMORROW'S UNKNOWN FACTOR.

James tells us that it is not wrong to make plans, but when we make them, we need to make them with a contingency factor. "Come now, you who say, 'Today or tomorrow we will go to such and such a city, spend a year there, buy and sell, and make a profit;' whereas you do not know what will happen tomorrow. For what is your life? It is even a vapor that appears for a little time and then vanishes away. Instead you ought to say, 'If the Lord wills, we shall live and do this or that'" (James 4:13-15).

"If the Lord wills." The way to take the uncertainty out of tomorrow and bring in certainty is to trust it to Him. Believe that God loves you and has a plan for your life. Trust that He is with you regardless of what comes—and leave yourself open to be directed and guided by Him.

*Father, we thank You that Your hand is upon the circumstances
surrounding our lives. Help us, Lord, to take You
into consideration in all of the plans that we make.*

IN JESUS' NAME WE PRAY, AMEN.

LIFE IN THE SON

I have seen all the works that are done under the sun;
and indeed, all is vanity and grasping for the wind.

— ECCLESIASTES 1:14

Solomon lived for knowledge, pleasure, wealth, power, and fame—but at the end of his life, all that remained was frustration, emptiness, and an unsatisfied heart.

Life under the sun (apart from God) is empty. Life *in* the Son, however, is rich and fulfilling, because the labor you do for the Lord is never done in vain. How opposite that is from the things done for self—selfish ambitions, goals and aspirations. Not long after you have left this earth, those achievements done selfishly will be gone and forgotten.

> ONLY THE LIFE LIVED IN JESUS HAS ETERNAL, LASTING BENEFIT.

At the end of his life, the apostle Paul wrote, "I have fought the good fight, I have finished the race, I have kept the faith. Finally, there is laid up for me the crown of righteousness, which the Lord, the righteous Judge, will give to me on that Day" (2 Timothy 4:7-8).

"And this is the testimony: that God has given us eternal life, and this life is in His Son. He who has the Son has life" (1 John 5:11-12).

How glorious to come to the end of your days and look forward to an incorruptible, undefiled inheritance—an inheritance waiting in God's kingdom. For the one who has lived his life in the Son, the end of the road is not emptiness, sorrow or regret. It is just the beginning.

MAY

Father, our cup runs over and we can't contain our feelings of
joy and blessing that we have experienced in our life in the Son.
Thank You for Your grace towards us.

IN JESUS' NAME WE PRAY, AMEN.

WHO KNOWS?

For who knows what is good for man in life,
all the days of his vain life which he passes like a shadow?
— ECCLESIASTES 6:12

Life is short, life is uncertain, and a life lived after the flesh is unfulfilling. This much we know. But after that, we don't know much.

If we could choose between wealth and poverty, we would overwhelmingly choose wealth. Yet, which is best? The Bible contains many warnings for the rich. We don't know what wealth might do to our attitude toward life and toward God.

> WHO KNOWS WHAT IS BEST FOR US? WE DON'T KNOW.
> ONLY GOD KNOWS.

Given the choice, we would choose health over sickness. Yet, which is best? Would sickness draw me closer to God and bring me into a richer relationship with Him? Or would it cause me to become angry with God?

What is best, success or failure? Again, given the choice, success would win hands down. Yet how many people have come to Christ because of some failure in their lives? At the point of despair and personal failure, many are driven to the cross.

Since we can't know what the future holds, isn't it wise to place tomorrow in the hands of the One who does know? Since we don't know what is best for us, isn't it folly to contend with God over the things He allows to enter our lives?

The wise man submits himself to God and trusts that He will do what is best.

Father, trusting Your infinite wisdom, we place our future in Your
hands, knowing that You alone know what tomorrow holds.
IN JESUS' NAME WE PRAY, AMEN.

Sow

He who observes the wind will not sow,
and he who regards the clouds will not reap.

— Ecclesiastes 11:4

Everything we do in life involves risks and difficulties. For the most part, we don't let potential risks stop us from achieving our goals. We see those risks as challenges—and we forge ahead. If we don't, we limit what we are able to accomplish in our lifetime.

Solomon speaks about those who let the presence of wind keep them from sowing, and the possibility of rain keep them from reaping. If fearful hesitation can keep you from reaping a material harvest, how much more so is it true of spiritual things?

When sown, God's Word falls on different kinds of soil. Not all are receptive. We sometimes look at certain people and conclude that they're so far gone, there's no point in sharing the gospel with them. But that's wrong. To *not* sow God's Word because of real or imagined difficulties is to disobey the plain command of Jesus to carry His gospel into all the world.

Benjamin Franklin said, "A man who is good at making excuses is seldom good for anything else." There is no excuse for disobedience.

> We are called to sow seed in unlikely places—and leave the results to God. We're not called to judge the condition of the soil.

The psalmist said, "He who continually goes forth weeping, bearing seed for sowing, shall doubtless come again with rejoicing, bringing his sheaves with him" (Psalm 126:6). A harvest awaits. Ignore the wind and the rain, and the logic that would sideline you. Sow the seeds entrusted to your care.

MAY

———⟫●⟪———

Father, help us to be faithful in planting Your Word and Your love
into the lives of all those around us.

In Jesus' name, amen.

HIS BANNER OF LOVE

He brought me to the banqueting house,
and his banner over me was love.

— SONG OF SOLOMON 2:4

During a courtship, we usually try hard to hide the truth about ourselves, for we are afraid if the other person knew the truth, they wouldn't love us anymore. We want them to think we are always sweet and we never get angry. Then we get married—and the truth is quite a shock.

That's one of the wonderful things about Jesus. He knows everything there is to know about you—even things you don't know about yourself. He sees your weaknesses and flaws, knows you backward and forward, inside out and upside down, and still He loves you. He has invited you into His banqueting house, and His banner over you is love.

What is the banner? It is God declaring to the world, "This is the one I love."

Many times God's love comes to me just when I have been my worst. When I have been miserable, unworthy and completely undeserving, that is when God seeks to show me just how great and how unconditional His love is for me. He does this so that I can rest in the knowledge that His love doesn't alter from day to day.

> IN ALL YOUR LIFE, YOU'VE NEVER EXPERIENCED A LOVE LIKE THE LOVE GOD HAS FOR YOU.

God's love seeks only your best. His love is pure enough to overcome your failures and strong enough to endure your weaknesses. God's love is everlasting.

Father, we thank You for Your unconditional love which we have
come to experience and to trust. We pray for those who have not
yet given themselves to You. May they come this day to know Your
love, which passes human knowledge.

IN JESUS' NAME, AMEN.

An Invitation

Come, my beloved … let us get up early to the vineyards; let us see
if the vine has budded, whether the grape blossoms are open, and
the pomegranates are in bloom. There I will give you my love.

— Song of Solomon 7:11-12

Desiring intimacy with him, Solomon's bride issues an invitation to her beloved. She asks him to come with her to examine the fruit in the vineyard.

Have you ever invited the Lord to inspect your life in this way? If He were to look over your life, would He see that you are bearing the fruit of the Spirit? If present in your life, the fruit of the Spirit will demonstrate itself as patience, gentleness, goodness, longsuffering, and meekness.

Invite the Lord to inspect your life.

Sometimes, when we invite the Lord to inspect the garden of our lives, we realize we have been neglectful. We have let the busyness and cares of life keep us from tending the garden as we should. Thorns have grown up and choked out some of the sweetness and beauty that should be there. Fruit isn't developing.

It is then that we realize how much we need the Lord. We need Him to search us, to know our hearts, to try our thoughts.

Call upon the Lord to examine your life. Sit at His feet and pour your heart out to Him. Receive the love He gives you in return. Don't neglect the One who loves you. The time you spend with God is more important than any work you could ever do for Him.

MAY

Lord, come into Your garden and examine the fruit of our lives. May
You be pleased with what You see there. Lord, we want to spend more
time with You sharing love together in sweet communion.

In Jesus' name we pray, amen.

THY KINGDOM COME

*For unto us a Child is born, unto us a Son is given; and the
government will be upon His shoulder. And His name will be
called Wonderful, Counselor, Mighty God, Everlasting Father,
Prince of Peace. Of the increase of His government and peace
there will be no end, upon the throne of David and over His
kingdom, to order it and establish it with judgment and justice …*

— Isaiah 9:6-7

I s it any wonder we are anxious for the kingdom of God to come?

The kingdom of man is full of war, pain, suffering, and heartache—all the result of man's rejection of God's love.

WHEN JESUS REIGNS, THE WORLD WILL BE GLORIOUS.

Today, the world is governed by Satan and those he inspires in rebellion against God, but someday, when the world is governed by the One called "Wonderful, Counselor, Mighty God, Everlasting Father, Prince of Peace," we will experience something entirely different. There will be such peace and joy on the earth (Isaiah 2:4) that even the animal kingdom will no longer be savage (Isaiah 11:6-9). Death will cease (Isaiah 25:8) and there will be no more physical infirmities (Isaiah 29:18).

All that awaits the coming of God's kingdom. But in actuality, the kingdom of God exists now wherever God reigns. If God rules in my life, I am in the kingdom of God. Though still living in this world, I have already begun to experience God's kingdom. I am comforted by His peace, assured by His love, and overwhelmed by the joy of His salvation.

May He come soon—and may we do His will while we wait.

*Father, we long for that day when Jesus reigns on the earth. We
thank You for the hope we have while we wait.*

AMEN.

UNGODLY AMBITIONS

How you are fallen from heaven, O Lucifer, son of the morning!…
For you have said in your heart: "I will ascend into heaven, I will
exalt my throne above the stars of God … I will be like the Most
High." Yet you shall be brought down to Sheol …

— ISAIAH 14:12-15

All of us belong in one of two categories. You are either trying to be *like* God in order to bring glory to Him, or you are trying to *be* God in order to bring glory to yourself. Satan wanted worship and adoration—and his ambition brought him down. Any who seek to take God's glory will, like Satan, be humbled.

I HAVE NO DESIRE TO BE GOD, BUT I DO WANT TO BE LIKE GOD.

I want my life to be a reflection of God. I long to be conformed into His image by His Spirit—not that I would receive glory for myself, but that as others see the love He manifests through me, they would glorify Him. My desire is to live the life Jesus described in Matthew 5:16: "Let your light so shine before men, that they may see your good works and glorify your Father in heaven."

There is only one God. Worship belongs to Him alone. And only a foolish creature would seek to dethrone God or steal His glory. As for me, it is enough to love and serve the true and living God, the Creator of the heaven and the earth.

Father, we thank You that You have called us and chosen us.
As Your children, our desire is to be like You in our attitudes,
our responses, our actions, in our thoughts and deeds.
May Your Holy Spirit continue to mold us.

IN JESUS' NAME, AMEN.

God Smites to Heal

And the LORD will strike Egypt, He will strike and heal it;
they will return to the Lord, and He will be entreated
by them and heal them.
— ISAIAH 19:22

Some of you are experiencing turmoil right now. Like Egypt, your problems seem to compound one on top of the other, and you are in fear of what can happen next.

Some of you are going through a civil war—the war between the spirit and the flesh. And the flesh is winning. You find yourself doing things that you hate yourself for, but you don't have the power to resist. You feel hopeless. You feel you have been smitten by God.

GOD'S SMITING IS ALWAYS INTENDED TO HEAL—NEVER TO DESTROY.

God sees you doing those things that are harmful and damaging to you. And like a good, loving Father, He chastises you. He does this because you are His own, and He loves you, and He wants you to be healed. He wants to free you from those things that are destroying you. If you don't respond to the chastisement He has already brought, then He will chastise you again—and perhaps more painfully.

If your life is just one grand mess today and you feel you have been under the chastisement of God, you can begin the healing process right now by repenting and returning. Call on His name and He will begin to heal you of the calamity you have brought upon yourself.

Father, we thank You that when we go astray or become involved in
destructive things, You don't leave us in the place of misery.
In love, You chastise us in order to heal us.
Help those who are struggling today.
IN JESUS' NAME, AMEN.

WHERE TO TURN WHEN TROUBLED

And so it was, when King Hezekiah heard it,
that he tore his clothes, covered himself with sackcloth,
and went into the house of the LORD.

— ISAIAH 37:1

When the powerful Assyrian army threatened to besiege Jerusalem until its inhabitants starved to death, Hezekiah responded to the crisis by going straight into the house of God.

> WHEN YOU NEED TO GET YOUR LIFE IN PERSPECTIVE, THERE'S NO BETTER PLACE TO GO THAN INTO THE HOUSE OF GOD.

Asaph, the psalmist, said, "My feet had almost stumbled; my steps had nearly slipped. For I was envious of the boastful, when I saw the prosperity of the wicked.... When I thought how to understand this, it was too painful for me—until I went into the sanctuary of God; then I understood their end" (Psalm 73). Being in God's presence, in God's house, gave Asaph an eternal perspective.

An amazing transformation happens when we view our problems from God's perspective. Troubles that look huge and hopeless when seen from our human perspective will suddenly seem like nothing—because we know that the God who rules the universe can handle them.

The Lord has promised to help those who call on His name. "Call upon Me in the day of trouble; I will deliver you" (Psalm 50:15).

MAY

———⊰•⊱———

Correct our vision, Lord. Give us an eternal perspective,
that we might bring our life into balance.

IN JESUS' NAME, AMEN.

Peace Like a River

Oh, that you had heeded My commandments! Then your peace
would have been like a river, and your righteousness
like the waves of the sea.

— Isaiah 48:18

Israel had stopped heeding God. They had turned their backs on His commandments and wouldn't listen to His voice; yet they still claimed to be His people, and they still swore by His name.

God knew they had chosen a path that was going to bring them pain. He warned them and pleaded with them through His prophets. However, they continued to ignore Him and disregard His commandments. As a result, their lives were filled with misery, pain, and calamity. God saw their suffering and said, "If you had only listened, you could have had peace like a river." But instead of peace, they had only turmoil, devastation, and constant upheaval.

> God wants your life to overflow with joy—and peace.

Out of their great love for their children, parents will try to keep them from making mistakes. We want our children to have good lives, lives filled with joy. We want them to have peaceful lives.

God is our parent. He has those same desires for us—for you. Because He loves you, He wants you to have a good life, a life of blessing and contentment.

And so God reminds you today: "Heed My commandments; listen to My voice."

Father, how thankful we are that You love us with a stubborn love
that refuses to let go. Teach us, Lord, to listen to Your voice and to
hearken to Your commandments, that we might walk in the path of
peace and righteousness until there be peace like a river.

In Jesus' name, amen.

WHEN GOD SAYS "NO"

"For My thoughts are not your thoughts, nor are your ways My ways," says the LORD. "For as the heavens are higher than the earth, so are My ways higher than your ways, and My thoughts than your thoughts."

— ISAIAH 55:8-9

Is it loving to give your children everything they want? "Daddy, I want a whole box of lollipops. If you really love me, you would give it to me." But because you do love them and you don't want them to rot their little teeth out, you limit the lollipops. Children don't understand rotten teeth and nutrition, so they may feel that you don't love them or that you are mean. But it is your love that causes you to say "no" even though it may be disappointing to them. Now magnify that many, many times over and you have the conditions that exist between man and God.

GOD HAS THE ADVANTAGE OF FOREKNOWLEDGE.

A "no" from God does not indicate a lack of concern or of love. Sometimes He says "no" because He is protecting us. Sometimes He says "no" or takes something away in order to teach us to trust and rely completely in Him.

God knows the future and knows the consequence of every action. What may look to me like a tremendous blessing may, in reality, be a curse in the long run. And what looks to me like a curse might turn out to be a tremendous blessing.

We are concerned with present comfort, but God is concerned with our eternal welfare. Remember that the next time He says "no."

Father, forgive us for the times we have challenged You and questioned Your love. Help us, Lord, to trust You with the circumstances of our lives.

IN JESUS' NAME, AMEN.

MAY

BE NOT AFRAID

*"I create the fruit of the lips: Peace, peace to him who is far off
and to him who is near," says the LORD, "and I will heal him."
But the wicked are like the troubled sea, when it cannot rest,
whose waters cast up mire and dirt.*

— ISAIAH 57:19-20

an you imagine God pacing the floor, worried and stressed over some situation? It doesn't happen.

He inspired the prophet Isaiah to write, "You will keep him in perfect peace, whose mind is stayed on You, because he trusts in You" (Isaiah 26:3).

> HE IS A GOD OF PERFECT PEACE; AND HE DESIRES THAT SAME PEACE FOR HIS CHILDREN.

And near the end of His earthly ministry, Jesus promised, "Peace I leave with you, My peace I give to you … Let not your heart be troubled, neither let it be afraid" (John 14:27).

Paul said the peace of God is a peace that passes human understanding (Philippians 4:7). In a world filled with tremendous pressure and turmoil, how wonderful it is to experience such comfort.

Satan often tries to take me away from the peace of God by whispering, "But what if…?" If you listen to Satan's challenges, you will begin to lose God's peace. You begin to wonder, "How will I work my problem out?"

"Don't be afraid," Jesus said. "Keep your mind stayed on God," Isaiah said. Remember the wisdom in those words. And remember that when we have no answers, God knows all. Trust Him—and take the peace He offers.

---

*Father, we thank You for the gift of peace, and we offer our lives
that You would rule and reign in our hearts. Teach us to keep our
hearts and our minds steadfast in Jesus Christ.*

IN JESUS' PRECIOUS NAME, AMEN.

GOD HAS ORDAINED YOU

*Then the word of the LORD came to me, saying: "Before I formed
you in the womb I knew you; before you were born I sanctified you;
I ordained you a prophet to the nations."*

— JEREMIAH 1:4-5

Jeremiah's life and ministry began in the mind of God before Jeremiah was ever born. The same is true of each of us. Before we were conceived, God knew us and prepared a perfect plan for each of us—a purpose we are to fulfill for His glory.

As we age, we can look back and see how God prepared us for the work that He would have us do. However, we still have our free will, which God will not violate. So not all of us are actually fulfilling God's purpose for our lives. Many have rejected God's will for their lives in order to follow their own desires.

> GOD HAS A WORK FOR EACH OF YOU TO ACCOMPLISH FOR HIS GLORY.

The Scriptures tell us that, "The Lord … is not willing that any should perish but that all should come to repentance" (2 Peter 3:9), yet not all come to repentance. That's God's will, but many do perish because they fight against it. So although God has ordained and separated a person, that person must surrender himself to do that will of God to fulfill His plan.

The Lord has a calling for each of us to accomplish for Him. God's strength is sufficient for you to fulfill that plan, so why not surrender to His will?

*Father, help us to be faithful to the call You have placed upon our
lives. Help us give ourselves to You to be used as You desire.
May we bring Your will to pass on this earth
and bring Your love and truth to a needy world.*

IN JESUS' NAME, AMEN.

MAY

No Pretense

*"And yet for all of this her treacherous sister Judah has not turned
to Me with her whole heart, but in pretense," says the Lord.*

— Jeremiah 3:10

Judah witnessed the destruction of the northern kingdom of Israel as they turned away from God into idolatry. Though King Josiah initiated spiritual reform, it wasn't a complete reformation. Though they had become outwardly religious, inwardly their hearts were unaffected.

Today, many people might go to church, but only on special occasions or when it is convenient for them. Others attend church faithfully—out of habit. But even as they sit in the service, their mind is out on the golf course or where they want to go for lunch. Though their body is in church, their heart is someplace else.

> Many people today settle for a halfhearted relationship with God.

Jesus told the church of Ephesus that they had lost their first love. He told the church in Laodicea, "Because you are lukewarm, and neither cold nor hot, I will vomit you out of My mouth" (Revelation 3:16). Rate your relationship with God. Is it hot, cold, or lukewarm? Do you have the same fervency you once had for God, or is the emotion gone, and you are operating now out of mere duty or habit? Is your worship genuine, heartfelt adoration, or is it merely a pretense?

If the Holy Spirit has shown you an area of pretense, an area where you have allowed your heart to be divided, repent and renew your commitment. God deserves true worship from you. He deserves your whole heart.

---

*Father, give us a pure heart—one that is wholly devoted to You.
Bring us back into a place of blessing,
and a place where we can be a blessing to You.*

In Jesus' name, amen.

The Old Path

Thus says the LORD: "Stand in the ways and see, and ask for the old paths, where the good way is, and walk in it; then you will find rest for your souls. But they said, 'We will not walk in it.'"

— JEREMIAH 6:16

Israel was a mess. Their prophets spoke lies, telling the people, "Peace, peace," when in actuality, war and destruction were coming. Israel refused to recognize God any longer. Instead, they worshiped gods of materialism, pleasures, and education. Covetousness reigned. Even the priests were corrupt. The foundations of their society had eroded away.

Seeing their future, God warned them. "You are plunging towards destruction. Stop for a moment and look where this path is leading you."

And then the Lord advised that they "ask for the old paths." What were those old paths? Belief in God and belief in the infallibility of God's Word.

THE OLD PATH IS ONE OF TOTAL RELIANCE UPON GOD.

God's path is the only path that offers true rest. When you completely trust God, placing all things in His hands, you find the rest your soul yearns for.

Perhaps you have been caught up in the restlessness of this world and you find yourself on a treadmill—always walking and never getting anywhere. The pressures of life have you full of worries and anxieties. Look at the path beneath your feet. Move yourself back to the old path. It is as easy as getting on your knees before God. Ask Him to forgive you for straying and to bring you back to a place of dependence and trust.

Father, forgive us for wandering. We ask that You bring us to that place of complete trust in You. Bring us back to the old path of faith.

AMEN.

MAY

THE SKILLFUL POTTER

I went down to the potter's house, and there he was, making
something at the wheel. And the vessel that he made of clay was
marred in the hand of the potter; so he made it again into another
vessel.... Then the word of the LORD came to me, saying: "O house
of Israel, can I not do with you as this potter?"

— JEREMIAH 18:3-6

C lay is one of the most common materials on earth. In its raw form, it has very little value. Its potential lies in the hands of the potter. If skillful, he can take that lump of clay and shape it into a beautiful, expensive vessel worth thousands of dollars. All the clay has to do to obtain its full potential is just yield itself completely to the potter's touch.

> IF YOU SUBMIT TO HIM, YOU WILL GRADUALLY BEGIN TO
> SEE THE SHAPE GOD IS FORMING IN YOU.

As the potter begins, he kneads the clay to remove any lumps and to create elasticity so that the clay will conform to his touch. Sometimes as God begins His work in our lives, we get impatient. We want to see immediate change. But unless time is taken to prepare the clay properly, it can never be made into a valuable vessel.

God already has in His mind what He wants to do with the lump of clay that is you. Stay on the wheel. Yield to His touch. And watch the beauty He creates in you.

Father, we want to become vessels of glory that please You. Forgive
us for our stubbornness and for our resistance to Your touch.
May we surrender ourselves fully unto You.
IN JESUS' NAME WE PRAY, AMEN.

What God Thinks of You

For I know the thoughts that I think toward you, says the Lord,
thoughts of peace and not of evil, to give you a future and a hope.
— Jeremiah 29:11

Sometimes, when we have failed in our Christian walk by disobeying God or yielding to fleshly impulses, we become disgusted with ourselves. We often then take those same feelings and project them onto God. "He must be angry and disgusted, too. In fact," we reason, "He probably doesn't even love me anymore."

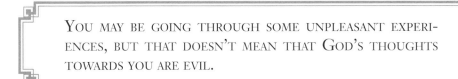

You may be going through some unpleasant experiences, but that doesn't mean that God's thoughts towards you are evil.

The people Jeremiah was writing to had real cause to believe that perhaps God was angry with them. They were living in captivity in Babylon as a result of their own sin. They had turned away from God and trusted in lies. Because they had chosen a path that would have ultimately led to their destruction, they were now going through a necessary time of chastisement. So you can imagine what they believed God was thinking about them.

But the prophet Jeremiah was assuring them that the thoughts of God toward His children are always thoughts of peace and not of evil.

This is true of you too. God loves you. God's thoughts towards you are of peace, and He's using those circumstances to work out His eternal plan in you.

Have you failed Him today? He hasn't failed you. His love is as sure as it was yesterday, as sure as it will be tomorrow. That's a love you can count on.

Thank You, Father, that Your thoughts concerning us are those of
peace and love. Help us to keep our eyes on eternity
and not our circumstances.

In Jesus' name, amen.

MAY

LOVING DISRUPTION

Moab has been at ease from his youth; he has settled on his dregs,
and has not been emptied from vessel to vessel, nor has he gone
into captivity. Therefore his taste remained in him,
and his scent has not changed.

— JEREMIAH 48:11

Moab—situated as they were in wine country—would have understood this analogy very well. When making wine, they put the juice of the grapes into large jugs. As the juice fermented, the dregs, or lees, would settle at the bottom. They then poured the wine from jug to jug, always leaving as much of the sediment as possible in the bottom of the previous jug. In this way, they produced pure wine. However, if they waited too long and the wine settled in its dregs, it began to rot. That rotten taste and smell would permeate the flavor of the whole jug.

Moab had settled in his dregs and become rotten. A life of ease, with no conflicts or disturbances, had spoiled and weakened him.

When God sees that we have begun to settle in our lees, tolerating evil and compromise, He often begins to pour us from vessel to vessel. He brings disruption to unsettle us so that our lives won't take on the taste of the world.

We don't like being poured from jug to jug.

DISRUPTION IS UNSETTLING AND UNCOMFORTABLE. BUT IT
SERVES AN IMPORTANT PURPOSE.

Disruption not only purifies us, it also brings us back to our knees, where we gain a closer relationship with our Father.

We are so grateful, Father, that You love us. Continue pouring
us from vessel to vessel, as through the process of disturbances You
make us what You would have us to be—pure for Your glory.

IN JESUS' NAME, AMEN.

THE CALL TO MOTHERS

Let tears run down like a river day and night; give yourself no relief; give your eyes no rest. Arise, cry out in the night, at the beginning of the watches; pour out your heart like water before the face of the Lord. Lift your hands toward Him for the life of your young children …

— LAMENTATIONS 2:18-19

Believing themselves to be both sophisticated and strong, Israel tried to eliminate God from their national life. They considered Him to be no longer necessary. As a result, Babylon devastated Jerusalem.

Israel is mourning its ravaged city. Jeremiah, seeing that desperate times call for desperate measures, issues a call to all the mothers of its nation.

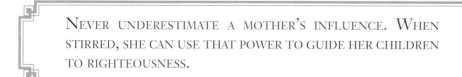

NEVER UNDERESTIMATE A MOTHER'S INFLUENCE. WHEN STIRRED, SHE CAN USE THAT POWER TO GUIDE HER CHILDREN TO RIGHTEOUSNESS.

Our country is in dire need of that kind of influence. Consider the atmosphere of our public school system. In 1963, the U.S. Supreme Court deemed it unlawful to pray or read the Bible in our schools. Since that decision, what has happened? On a national average, SAT scores have consistently dropped, violence and crime have become more prevalent, and drug abuse has skyrocketed.

The only real answer to ungodliness is a return to godly principles—those principles upon which our nation was founded. Not just mothers, but fathers too must teach our children what is right and wrong—from God's perspective. We need to teach the next generation to seek God through prayer.

Here is a radical suggestion: this week, let's turn our televisions off and turn our faces toward God. Let's pray for our nation—and for our children.

Stir us, Father, to call upon Your name. Cause us to pray for our children, for our schools, and for our nation.

AMEN.

From Depression to Hope

*This I recall to my mind, therefore I have hope. Through the
Lord's mercies we are not consumed, because His compassions fail
not. They are new every morning; great is Your faithfulness. "The
Lord is my portion," says my soul, "therefore I hope in Him!"
The Lord is good to those who wait for Him, to the soul who seeks
Him. It is good that one should hope and wait quietly
for the salvation of the LORD.*

— LAMENTATIONS 3:21-26

s is usually the case, it was thinking about himself that caused Jeremiah's depression. But when he changed his way of thinking—from himself to God—the depression left. When he remembered God and meditated on His character, peace and hope filled his mind.

WHEN HOPELESSNESS VANISHES, HOPE TAKES ITS PLACE.

Instead of thinking about himself, Jeremiah thought about God's nature. He thought about the Lord's mercy, through which we are not consumed. He thought about God's faithfulness. God always does exactly what He says He will do, and He is able to bring forth good out of the deepest mess. He thought about the fact that the Lord is our portion. What more could we want or need? He thought about the goodness of God, who works all things together for our benefit.

Then Jeremiah concluded that it is good to "hope and wait quietly for the salvation of the LORD."

Are you worried today? Change your thoughts. Don't meditate on your pain—meditate on your Savior. Set your eyes on Jesus and remember His character. His love has never failed you. His mercies are new every morning.

*Father, help us set our eyes on You instead of ourselves.
Fill our hearts with Your hope and love today.*

AMEN.

The Call of God

*And go, get to the captives, to the children of your people, and
speak to them and tell them, "Thus says the Lord GOD,"
whether they hear, or whether they refuse.*

— EZEKIEL 3:11

God has called us each to a ministry within the body of Christ. Not all are apostles, not all are prophets, not all are evangelists, not all are pastors or teachers, but we all have a place of service. God has a task and a purpose for you. And if He calls you to a ministry, you can be sure that He will equip you for it.

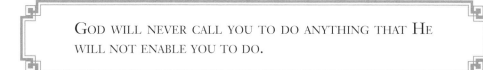

GOD WILL NEVER CALL YOU TO DO ANYTHING THAT HE WILL NOT ENABLE YOU TO DO.

Ezekiel was commanded to speak to the people, "Whether they listen, or not." The ministry is not easy. Often it can be very discouraging. The people won't always respond to the things that you tell them. Sometimes people get angry with you because you dare to speak to them the things of the Lord.

But when your life is over, there is only one thing that will count—and that is your obedience to the will of God. Everything you may have done for yourself, all of the wealth that you may have amassed, all of the accomplishments that will be written in the obituary will be meaningless.

Give your life to that which really counts—that which is eternal. Live your life for Him.

---

*Father, thank You for the power of the Holy Spirit that enables us
to fulfill our calling. May we always minister from a position of
compassion, understanding, and love. And yet, Lord, may we not
be guilty of failing to warn the people of all that You have said.*

IN JESUS' NAME, AMEN.

FALSE HOPE

So I will break down the wall you have plastered with untempered
mortar, and bring it down to the ground, so that its foundation
will be uncovered; it will fall, and you shall be consumed in the
midst of it. Then you shall know that I am the LORD.

— EZEKIEL 13:14

The prophets were lying to the people. Wanting to give a popular message, they spoke words of peace, when the truth was that Israel was on the brink of destruction. These prophets "built a wall" in the minds of the people, behind which they wrongly believed they would find comfort and safety against the enemy. But the security they found in the prophets' words was a false security. When tested by storms, the wall wouldn't stand.

> A TRUE SERVANT OF GOD DARE NOT PREACH A COMFORT-
> ING MESSAGE TO THOSE LIVING IN SIN.

People want to hear a comforting message that says it really doesn't matter to God what you do as long as you have a good attitude, or as long as it feels right. Yet those who comfort you in your sin are false prophets. They build untempered walls behind which you find nothing but false security.

I have been called to faithfully and truthfully warn those who have chosen a path of sin. But I am also to speak good tidings for those who surrender their lives to Jesus Christ. He is the wall built with tempered mortar. Put your trust in Him, so that when storms come, you'll find true safety.

Lord, we know that our hope is not in vain. Jesus Christ will see
us through the greatest storms of life, and will one day present us
faultless before Your presence with exceeding joy.

IN JESUS' PRECIOUS NAME, AMEN.

MISPLACING BLAME

*"Therefore I will judge you, O house of Israel, every one according
to his ways," says the Lord GOD. "Repent, and turn from all your
transgressions, so that iniquity will not be your ruin."*

— EZEKIEL 18:30

The Israelites blamed their suffering in captivity on the sins of their fathers. But God challenged that mind-set. He called them to take responsibility for their own sins.

Like it or not, you are responsible for the person you are and the things you do. Every man is judged for his own ways. When you stand before God you will answer for only one person—and that is you.

STOP BLAMING OTHERS FOR YOUR SINS.

You may have had a terrible past. You may have had neglectful or unfit parents and a miserable childhood. You may have suffered unimaginable abuse. In Jesus, there is healing for all those hurts. Your past can be erased and you can be all God intends for you to be. But as long as you look for someone else to blame, you will never see a need to repent for your own actions.

If you continue in unrighteousness and continue placing blame for your sin on someone else, your sin will ultimately ruin you. But God wants more for you. He wants to bless you. Jesus said, "I have come that they may have life, and that they may have it more abundantly" (John 10:10).

Stop blaming others for your sins. Repent, turn to Jesus, and receive the new life He wants to give you.

*Father, we thank You that we can have that new life and new heart
You have offered to us. May we accept the responsibility for our own
sin and turn from it to find a new and blessed life in Jesus Christ.*

AMEN.

YOU SHALL KNOW

I, the Lord, have spoken it; it shall come to pass, and I will do it; I
will not hold back, nor will I spare, nor will I relent ...
and they shall know that I am the LORD.

— EZEKIEL 24:14, 27

God told Ezekiel of the complete destruction about to come upon Jerusalem. He said, "I have spoken it; it shall come to pass." On the very same day Ezekiel marked that calendar, which was to be the beginning of the end, the Babylonians began the siege against Jerusalem. God fulfilled His Word.

> WHEN GOD FULFILLS HIS WORD CONCERNING THE END TIMES AND BEGINS TO POUR OUT HIS JUDGMENT UPON THE EARTH, PEOPLE WILL KNOW THAT HE IS GOD.

Many people today challenge the Word of God. They scoff at the promises of Jesus, thereby fulfilling the prophecy given by Peter, when he said, "Scoffers will come in the last days, walking according to their own lusts, and saying, 'Where is the promise of His coming?'" (2 Peter 3:3-4). These mockers view the Bible as a collection of fanciful stories created by men who needed to believe in something. But they have no explanation for why Bible prophecies have come to pass so accurately.

How important it is for us to acknowledge God and surrender our lives to Him now. His judgment is coming, and only those who are His will escape the coming of His wrath.

Father, speak to our hearts through Your Word, that we might
realize the certainty of those things You have declared. May we
walk after You and commit ourselves fully and completely to You.

IN THE NAME OF JESUS WE ASK, AMEN.

PRIDE

Because … its heart was lifted up in its height, therefore I will deliver it into the hand of the mighty one of the nations, and he shall surely deal with it; I have driven it out for its wickedness.

— EZEKIEL 31:10-11

It was God who planted Assyria by the water so that their roots could get plenty of nourishment. It was God who had made them great and beautiful, but they began to take credit for their power, boasting in what they had done.

TAKING CREDIT FOR WHAT GOD HAS DONE IS ALWAYS A DANGEROUS THING.

Too often, men who have been used by God or who have been specially gifted by God begin to look at their accomplishments as though they were somehow responsible for their success. They begin to take glory that really belongs to the Lord. But God said that He will allow no flesh to glory in His sight. The one who exalts himself will be brought low.

A greatly successful ministry can pose a danger, because people suddenly want to learn your secrets. The temptation is to point to the things God has done as though we ourselves had devised them.

Anything we have that is good or valuable has been given by God. It is God who has given us strength, talents, and understanding. We must give credit to God for those things that He has done.

To God be the glory; great things He has done!

———

Father, may we acknowledge You as the giver of life and of strength. May we continually give You the glory You so richly deserve.

IN JESUS' NAME, AMEN.

JUSTICE

Yet the children of your people say, "The way of the Lord is not
fair." But it is their way which is not fair!

— Ezekiel 33:17

It's interesting that the people in this passage are angry with God for His grace. God had declared that if a man was destined to die because of his wickedness, that man could be forgiven if he would turn from his sins and begin to walk in God's statutes. God also promised that if a man repented, none of his past sins would ever be mentioned to him again.

Now, that upset a lot of the people. They didn't like God so easily forgiving sin. Where is the justice in that? Surely man must do something to earn God's forgiveness.

There is much that we don't know about God and about His justice. What will His final disposition be to that person who has lived in some remote place and has never heard of God's provision for salvation through Jesus Christ? No one knows. But when he stands before the Lord and we hear the sentence he has been given, we will most certainly say, "True and righteous are Your judgments" (Revelation 16:7).

> RATHER THAN CRITICIZE GOD, WE NEED TO LEARN FROM HIM. WE NEED TO HAVE THE SAME LOVE, COMPASSION, AND READINESS TO FORGIVE AS GOD DOES.

How beautiful that a life of wickedness can be blotted out in a moment! Man may shake his head and say, "That's not fair," but God would answer, "My ways are higher than yours."

Father, how thankful we are for the grace and mercy You've
extended to us. Forgive us our transgressions,
even as we forgive those who transgress against us.

In Jesus' name, amen.

Inspiration, not Perspiration

They shall have linen turbans on their heads and linen trousers on their bodies; they shall not clothe themselves with anything that causes sweat.

— Ezekiel 44:18

When we think of sweat, we think of fleshly activity. And there might be cases where in serving the Lord we do perspire—like during building projects and things of that nature. But when it came to the worship of God, expressing praise, adoration, and thanksgiving, God said He didn't want anything that caused sweat.

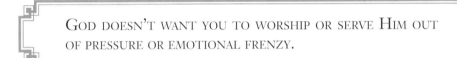

God doesn't want you to worship or serve Him out of pressure or emotional frenzy.

The Lord doesn't want you to feel that He has put such an intolerably heavy burden upon you that you have to strain in order to accomplish His will. Some speak of the great sacrifices that they have made to serve the Lord. But God never requires you to give up one worthwhile thing to follow Jesus—only the junk that has been cluttering your life.

God desires that you worship from a heart overflowing with love, simply because you're reacting to the love He manifests toward you. No sweat, no false stimulation, just a pure, natural expression of gratitude.

May our worship be inspired by a pure heart—with thanksgiving for those things God has done in our lives, and awe for His glory, His majesty, and His beauty.

Father, we desire to serve from a place of gladness and gratitude.

In Jesus' name, amen.

HE IS THERE

... the name of the city from that day shall be:
THE LORD IS THERE.
— Ezekiel 48:35

In his attempt to describe the future glory of the nation of Israel, Ezekiel said, "It will be called Jehovah-shammah—the Lord is there." He cannot think of anything more glorious than the fact that the Lord is there.

Some people think they would like to escape the presence of God. They work hard to eliminate God from our national life—no mention of God in public schools, no reminder of God in public places. They think they would enjoy being where God isn't, because then they'd have no restrictions. They could do whatever they like. But you have to remember that in a world without limitations, everyone else has the same liberties you do. And you wouldn't last long under those conditions.

THANK GOD WE CAN'T ESCAPE HIS PRESENCE.

Because God is there, we have hope, strength, and purity. Without Him, we have only darkness.

Though God is always there, we sometimes forget. That is when we have a tendency toward sinning. It is also when we begin to despair over our circumstances. But that is the point at which we need a consciousness of God's presence the most.

The awareness of the presence of God will keep us from sin. It will chase our despair. It will enable us to rejoice in the darkest hour of our lives. Cultivate that awareness. Remember the One who has promised to be with us on the mountaintop, in the valley, and everywhere in between.

Father, we thank You for the gift of Your presence.
Help us to remember You are there, that our hearts
might be lifted from despair to thanksgiving.

AMEN.

With You in the Fire

"Look!" he answered, "I see four men loose, walking in the midst of the fire; and they are not hurt, and the form of the fourth is like the Son of God."

— Daniel 3:25

When Daniel's friends, Shadrach, Meshach, and Abed-Nego, refused to bow to the image Nebuchadnezzar had set up, the king became furious, and ordered the three to be thrown into the burning furnace. But God always has the last word. Within the furnace, the men were untouched by the flames. When the king opened the furnace, he was startled to see not just three men inside, but four. And that fourth was "like the Son of God."

Within this story we see a demonstration of the abiding presence of Jesus Christ, who preserves His people through the darkest hours and the fiercest trials. We would like it if God would just keep us from the fire altogether. That would be our preference. But many times He chooses not to do that.

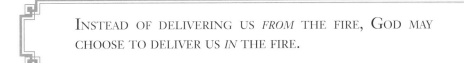

Instead of delivering us *from* the fire, God may choose to deliver us *in* the fire.

Fire refines. God desires purity in His people, so He often lets us spend some time in the furnace so that the impurities within us may be burned away.

You may be going through a fiery trial today, but know this—you are not in that fire alone. The Lord is there with you, and when the trial has served its purpose, He will deliver you.

Father, we thank You that we are never alone—even in the deepest pain or the darkest hour. How grateful we are for Your presence in the midst of difficulties. How blessed we are that You choose to go through our trials with us.

In Jesus' name, amen.

THE EASY WAY OR THE HARD WAY

Now I, Nebuchadnezzar, praise and extol and honor the King of heaven, all of whose works are truth, and His ways justice. And those who walk in pride He is able to put down.

— DANIEL 4:37

ebuchadnezzar was an extremely gifted man—perhaps *too* gifted. He began to be lifted up with pride. He began to feel that his accomplishments were all the result of his own brilliance.

The Bible tells us that, "Pride goes before destruction" (Proverbs 16:18). God warned Nebuchadnezzar of the dangerous path he was walking. But Nebuchadnezzar chose to ignore that warning.

> GOD IS SO FAITHFUL. HE ALWAYS WARNS US WHEN WE HEAD TOWARD DANGEROUS GROUND.

When God issues a warning, you can learn the lessons He wants you to learn in one of two ways: the easy way or the hard way. The easy way is to heed His warning. The hard way is to continue walking toward trouble.

Nebuchadnezzar chose the hard way. He again became prideful, and in that same hour, he went insane. It took seven years for him to recognize God's sovereignty.

The Lord loves us too much to let us get by with those things that will destroy us. Because we belong to Him, He will always bring the warnings and the lessons we need to keep us from trouble. Whether we learn them the easy way or the hard way is entirely up to us.

Father, we thank You that You love us enough to keep us from folly. Give us a hunger for Your Word, in which we will find all the wisdom we need for life and godliness.

IN JESUS' NAME, AMEN.

DOING THE KING'S BUSINESS

And I, Daniel, fainted and was sick for days;
afterward I arose and went about the king's business.
— DANIEL 8:27

From this passage, we can conclude that Daniel was a representative of the Babylonian government for King Belshazzar. He had been entrusted with the king's business and he faithfully set about to fulfill that responsibility.

We, too, have been entrusted with the King's business and called to represent Him wherever we go. But the kingdom of our Lord, unlike all earthly kingdoms, will last forever. For ours is an eternal kingdom.

> YOUR KING HAS BUSINESS FOR YOU TO DO THIS DAY.

"Our citizenship," Paul wrote, "is in heaven, from which we also eagerly wait for the Savior, the Lord Jesus Christ" (Philippians 3:20). What a privilege it is to represent Jesus on the earth. He has given us the authority to speak for Him and to speak in His name. But while it is a privilege, it is also a tremendous responsibility, for wherever we go, people will judge Him according to what they see in us.

The King we serve does not like to be misrepresented. We are to love as He loves, give as He gave, forgive even as He has forgiven us. The King that we represent is kind, compassionate, merciful, and gracious, and He has asked that we represent Him in the same way.

Your King has business for you to do this day. May you serve Him with gladness and with faithfulness.

Father, we thank You for the honor and privilege of representing
You. Help us, Lord, that by our actions and through our words, we
might be fit ambassadors for our wonderful King.
WE PRAY THIS IN THE NAME OF JESUS, AMEN.

THE WEAPON OF PRAYER

*Do not fear, Daniel, for from the first day that you set your heart
to understand, and to humble yourself before your God, your
words were heard; and I have come because of your words.*

— DANIEL 10:12

Daniel sought understanding from God, and to that end, he prayed for twenty-one days. Finally, a heavenly visitor informed Daniel that God had heard his prayers and had sent the messenger to bring the answers he had asked for.

However, as the messenger was coming to Daniel, he was caught up in a battle with the powers of darkness that controlled the nation of Persia. He fought for twenty-one days before Michael, one of the chief princes, came to his aid and freed him. Only then could he complete his mission.

A SPIRITUAL CONFLICT RAGES IN THE UNIVERSE AROUND US.

Whether you know it or not, or whether you like it or not, you are in a battle right now. Strong forces are fighting for control of your mind. Only the power of the Holy Spirit can help you stand against the spiritual forces that seek your destruction.

Ephesians 6:12 explains the nature of the battle this way: "We do not wrestle against flesh and blood, but against principalities, against powers, against the rulers of the darkness of this age, against spiritual hosts of wickedness in the heavenly places."

Ephesians 6 also describes the spiritual armor God has provided for your protection. Your job is to put that armor on, and then to pray. The real fighting takes place on your knees—and that is also where the victory will be found.

---

*Help us, Lord, to set aside every weight and sin that threatens to
entangle us, that we might run this race for Your glory.*

AMEN.

SOWING AND REAPING

They sow the wind, and reap the whirlwind. The stalk has no bud;
it shall never produce meal. If it should produce,
aliens would swallow it up.

— HOSEA 8:7

God gave birth to Israel, but they forsook Him, and began sowing to the wind. As a result, He removed His protection and left them to their own devices. And now, He is warning, the wind that they sowed was about to reap a whirlwind from the north—Assyria, who would sweep down and scatter the nation of Israel.

SOW CAREFULLY.

"Whatever a man sows, that he will also reap," Galatians 6:7 tells us. And nature proves that principle to be true. We reap in kind. If you sow corn, you get corn. You don't get beans. If you sow mercy, mercy will be extended to you. If you sow forgiveness, you will receive forgiveness. If you sow wild oats … then you had best be prepared to reap the consequences for that.

The problem is that we tend to not be selective enough. Too often, we sow mixed seed. We come to church and sow God's Word into our minds, but then we go home, flip on the television and start sowing to the flesh. A mixed crop comes up, and with it comes a lot of confusion.

If you sow to your flesh, all you can ever hope to reap is corruption. But if you sow to the Spirit you will reap the fruit of the Spirit and life everlasting.

Father, keep us from being deceived into thinking we can sow
whatever we want and not have to suffer the consequences for
those choices. May we sow in righteousness.

IN JESUS' NAME, AMEN.

A HEART CONDITION

*Their heart is divided; now they are held guilty. He will break
down their altars; He will ruin their sacred pillars.*

— HOSEA 10:2

Israel gave God a place in their heart—but only a small place. They couldn't offer Him their whole heart, because they had also chosen to worship other gods.

Jesus told us that it isn't possible to serve two masters (Matthew 6:24). Yet that is exactly what many people try to do. Instead of giving God total devotion, they settle for giving Him just a nod now and then.

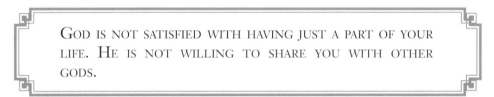

GOD IS NOT SATISFIED WITH HAVING JUST A PART OF YOUR LIFE. HE IS NOT WILLING TO SHARE YOU WITH OTHER GODS.

God desires—God deserves—to have your whole heart, your whole soul, your whole mind.

How is your heart today? Is it given wholly to God, or is it divided? It can be difficult to accurately assess your own heart because, as Jeremiah points out, "The heart is deceitful above all things, and desperately wicked; who can know it?" (Jeremiah 17:9). The only way to know the true condition of your heart is to ask the Lord to search your heart for you.

What can you do if God reveals to you that your heart is divided? Follow the example of David, who asked God to unite his heart. Or accept the challenge of Joshua, who urged, "Choose for yourselves this day whom you will serve … as for me and my house, we will serve the LORD" (Joshua 24:15).

---

*Father, help us to live a life that is truly devoted to You. Remove
anything that is causing us to offer You a divided heart.*

IN JESUS' NAME, AMEN.

WRESTLING WITH GOD

*He took his brother by the heel in the womb, and in his strength
he struggled with God. Yes, he struggled with the Angel and prevailed; he wept, and sought favor from Him.*

— HOSEA 12:3-4

How could a man ever wrestle with God—or an angel of God—and prevail?
It doesn't seem possible. Yet Hosea tells us it happened, and the explanation
is found at the end of the sentence: "He (Jacob) wept, and sought favor with
Him." In other words, Jacob said, "Please don't go without blessing me!"

Jacob's wrestling match occurred the night before he was to meet up with
his brother, Esau, who was on the march with 400 men. No amount of conniv-
ing or scheming could save him this time. Jacob knew there was no escape. And
so he wrestled with the Angel, clung to Him, and begged for a blessing.

IT'S TIME TO SURRENDER AND WEEP BEFORE THE LORD.

Sometimes I see men wrestling with God and I wonder, *What is it going to
take to bring them to their knees?* In Jacob's case, it took a crippling. When he
couldn't run anymore, couldn't scheme anymore, couldn't trick his way out of
his circumstances anymore, he finally surrendered himself to God.

Maybe you are in the place of Jacob where you just don't know what you are
going to do. When you finally come to the end of your own strength and you
surrender yourself to the Lord, that is the point at which you begin to discover
the power of God at work in your life.

*Father, we can see that victory comes when we surrender to You.
Cripple us, Lord, if that is what it takes to bring us
to a place of complete surrender.*

IN JESUS' NAME, AMEN.

FASTING

*"Now, therefore," says the LORD, "turn to Me with all your heart,
with fasting, with weeping, and with mourning."*
— JOEL 2:12

Our nature has two sides: the flesh side, and the spirit side. We feed the flesh side pretty consistently—usually a minimum of three times a day, with liberal snacks in between. But we are not usually as consistent about feeding our spirit.

Fasting is a way to deny the flesh and strengthen the spirit. If you fed your spirit as consistently as you feed your flesh, you would be spiritually fat. Fasting reverses the usual process—it starves the flesh and feeds the spirit.

FASTING WAS NOT JUST AN OLD TESTAMENT DISCIPLINE.

Isaiah told the people they weren't fasting the way God wanted them to. "In the day of your fast you find pleasure" (Isaiah 58:3). In other words, they sought pleasure when they should have been focused on God. It would be like taking a day to fast but spending the entire day watching TV. Our flesh craves entertainment, but the purpose of a fast is to put the flesh in its place and seek God.

When you fast, and spend time in prayer and reading God's Word, your spirit becomes stronger and stronger, and the hold of the flesh is weakened. We then find ourselves having victories in our spiritual battles.

Fasting was not just an Old Testament discipline. God is calling His people to fast today. Our world is in desperate trouble. We who love God need to deny our flesh, seek His face, and strengthen our spirits for battle.

---

*Father, we desire to turn from our sin that You would manifest
Your grace and mercy toward us. Help us to seek You with all of
our hearts—fasting and mourning before You for our
nation and for our families.*

AMEN.

THE CHOSEN

*"You only have I known of all the families of the earth; therefore
I will punish you for all your iniquities." Can two walk together,
unless they are agreed?*

— AMOS 3:2-3

G od chose Israel—not because they were good, or powerful. He chose them simply because He loves them. And it is through the nation of Israel that God chose to bring the Savior into the world.

Like Israel, we too have been chosen not because of our own goodness or because we have something God needs. God chose us because He loves us and wants fellowship with us.

FELLOWSHIP IMPLIES UNITY.

In order to have fellowship with God, you must be in agreement with God. That means you must follow the rules He has established. We are in no position to strike deals with the Lord: "You do this for me and I will do this for You." We are helpless sinners who stand bankrupt before God. And He looks on us with compassion and says, "I choose you."

Being the chosen people of God creates a great responsibility. We know His ways. We know His requirements. We walk in the light and have understanding of His Word; therefore, we will be judged by a higher standard. If we choose to sin, God will chastise us because we are His.

What a blessing it is to be loved by God, chosen by God, and forgiven by God. Let's walk together in unity with Him and display His majesty to a world that does not know Him yet.

*Father, how thankful we are to be Yours. May we never veer from
the truth, but may we walk with You in obedience.*

IN JESUS' NAME, AMEN.

PREPARE TO MEET GOD

Therefore thus will I do to you, O Israel; because I will do this to you, prepare to meet your God, O Israel!
— AMOS 4:12

God warned Israel repeatedly. He brought calamities upon them. He tried to turn them back from their chosen path of destruction. But for all that, they would not return to Him. Now the time of judgment was at hand. The prophet Amos issues a warning to the people: "Prepare to meet your God!"

This time, however, the meeting would not be for purposes of love and fellowship and unity. This meeting would be adversarial.

IT IS SHEER FOLLY TO MEET GOD AS AN ADVERSARY.

The Scripture declares, "Woe to him who strives with his Maker!" (Isaiah 45:9). How could you ever hope to win in a battle with God? Yet some of you are striving with God. God has been speaking to you about those things in your life that are dishonest, corrupt, or displeasing to Him. The Holy Spirit has convicted you, but you have ignored His voice and set yourself against Him.

Someday you are going to meet God and you need to be prepared. Nothing is hidden from His eye. He knows every thought, every motive of the heart. We are guilty. But we are also blessed—for we have an Advocate who represents us before the Father. "Who is he who condemns? It is Christ who died, and furthermore is also risen, who is even at the right hand of God, who also makes intercession for us" (Romans 8:34).

Praise God for His Son!

*Lord, may we experience the joy of meeting You each day—
the joy of Your presence, the power of Your Spirit,
and the glory of walking with You.*
IN JESUS' NAME, AMEN.

POSSESS YOUR POSSESSIONS

But on Mount Zion there shall be deliverance, and there shall be
holiness; the house of Jacob shall possess their possessions.
— OBADIAH 1:17

God had promised to give Israel the whole land, all the way to the Mediterranean Sea. It was theirs already—all they had to do was to put their foot down and claim it. Sadly, they failed to do that. They limited what God would have given them.

Paul described God as, "Him who is able to do exceedingly abundantly above all that we ask or think" (Ephesians 3:20). There is no limit to what God can do.

WE ARE THE ONES WHO LIMIT OUR BLESSINGS.

Do you have that rest, joy, and peace that God has promised? If not, then you are not possessing your possessions. You have failed to take all of the territory that belongs to you. Too many Christians are discouraged, worried, and defeated instead of experiencing that fullness of joy that God wants His children to experience. If you don't have that indescribable joy, then you haven't possessed all of your possessions. It's there; it's available for you—you just haven't taken it yet.

The Lord speaks of the coming day when Jacob will possess his possessions. We can possess our possessions today. Don't settle for a mediocre life below the level that God wants you to live. Let's pursue the things of God, let's pursue the power of God; let's pursue an anointing of the Spirit of God.

Believe … and take what is yours.

———————

Lord, we thank You for Your precious promises.
Help us to rely upon Your strength and to claim
those places of victory You have for us.
AMEN.

JUNE

LYING VANITIES

They that observe lying vanities forsake their own mercy.
— JONAH 2:8 (KJV)

After three miserable days and nights—days and nights he brought upon himself—Jonah hit dry ground and sought the Lord. And then he declared what he had learned in the belly of the whale: "They that observe lying vanities forsake their own mercy."

What were the lying vanities Jonah had observed? First, he believed that he could run from the call of God; second, he believed he could find a place where God wasn't and actually hide from God's presence; and lastly, he believed that his way was better than God's way.

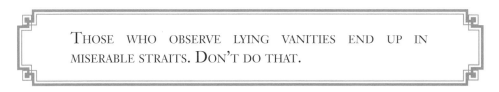

> THOSE WHO OBSERVE LYING VANITIES END UP IN MISERABLE STRAITS. DON'T DO THAT.

God is extremely merciful and extremely wise. His ways are always best, and He desires nothing but good for your life. "I know the thoughts that I think toward you … thoughts of peace and not of evil, to give you a future and a hope" (Jeremiah 29:11). There is nothing better for you than to find the will of God and to do it. You can't improve on that; that's life at its highest. It's the place of satisfaction and contentment, and you'll never be fully content or satisfied with anything less.

Don't create problems for yourself. Instead, submit to the One who loves you. You can arrive voluntarily, or you can arrive smelling like a fish—but you're going to go where God wants you to go.

Father, we thank You for contentment that comes from yielding ourselves to Your will for our lives, and thus finding that joy, peace, and satisfaction of knowing You're in control.
IN JESUS' NAME, AMEN.

No Restrictions

*Is the Spirit of the LORD restricted? Are these His doings? Do not
My words do good to him who walks uprightly?*
— MICAH 2:7

I s the Spirit of God restricted? Is He limited to whom He can speak through,
or what He can say? Is the Spirit to be blamed for what is happening to the
nation, or for the seeming weakness of the church today? The answer is no.

GOD HAS NO RESTRICTIONS, NO LIMITATIONS.

The Spirit of God is not restricted in any way. Though we are weak and inef-
fectual, He is not. The Holy Spirit speaks to our hearts and declares, "Not by might
nor by power, but by My Spirit" (Zechariah 4:6). And though I am baffled by the
conditions of the world, He is not. He still has a heart for the world and still desires
to draw the lost to Jesus Christ.

You can be an instrument in His hand regardless of your own abilities. God
can use you without a seminary degree, and without a Ph.D. If you yield to Him,
He can and will use you to share the truth of Jesus Christ with a dying world. We
can be the light of the world and the salt of the earth if we will yield ourselves to
God's Spirit and let Him work out His plan through our lives.

May God work through us to bring this world to its knees.

*Father, we thank You for the power of the Holy Spirit to effect
changes in lives and in societies. God, we pray for a spiritual
awakening in our nation, through the anointing
and the empowering of Your Spirit.*
IN THE NAME OF JESUS, AMEN.

WHO IS A GOD LIKE OUR GOD?

Who is a God like You, pardoning iniquity and passing over the transgression of the remnant of His heritage? He does not retain His anger forever, because He delights in mercy.

— MICAH 7:18

The psalmist describes God as "merciful and gracious, slow to anger, and abounding in mercy;" a God who "has not dealt with us according to our sins, nor punished us according to our iniquities" (Psalm 103:8,10). So great is His compassion that He told Ezekiel to pass on a message to the people. "Say to them: 'As I live,' says the Lord GOD, 'I have no pleasure in the death of the wicked, but that the wicked turn from his way and live. Turn, turn from your evil ways! For why should you die, O house of Israel?'" (Ezekiel 33:11).

THERE IS NO GOD LIKE OUR GOD.

Who is a god like our God, who is so merciful, so ready and willing to forgive our transgressions? Who is a god like our God, who guides us to the path of righteousness and throws our sins into the depths of the sea?

There is no god like our God. He is a Father to the fatherless. He is the Conqueror of sin and death. He is the Rock to which we can run for shelter. He is the Pardoner of all our offenses.

How blessed we are to serve the God of mercy!

Father, we thank You for Your character—for Your love, Your compassion, Your mercy, Your forgiveness, Your righteousness, and Your power. Oh Lord, we love You. Draw us and guide us.

IN JESUS' NAME, AMEN.

TRUST IN THE LORD

The LORD is good, a stronghold in the day of trouble; and He knows those who trust in Him.

— NAHUM 1:7

God never promised that once you committed your life to Jesus, He would keep you immune from pain and problems. He only promised that when you went through trials—notice that is "when," not "if"—He would go through the pain with you, and would see you through to the other side.

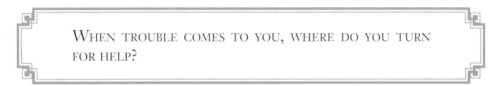

WHEN TROUBLE COMES TO YOU, WHERE DO YOU TURN FOR HELP?

Do you turn within, hoping to find power within yourself? Do you look to other people to help? Or do you try to get by with the help of some motto: "What you can't cure, you must endure," or, "Just grin and bear it," or, "I think I can, I think I can, I think I can," like the little red engine?

Everyone has trouble. That is an inescapable part of life. We live in a world in rebellion against God, and as a result we live in a world filled with chaos. In the day of trouble, there's only one stronghold to whom you can turn and find safety, and that is the Lord Jesus Christ.

Don't turn to others. Don't turn within. Don't think some optimistic little saying will get you through your troubles. Instead, put your trust in the Lord. He will walk through the trouble with you, and when you have emerged on the other side, you will see the wisdom of His plan.

*Father, when the storm rages all around us, draw us to Yourself.
We know that You are good and loving. Teach us to trust You
in the midst of our confusion.*

IN JESUS' NAME, AMEN.

WHEN GOD IS SILENT

*O LORD, how long shall I cry, and You will not hear? Even cry out
to You, "Violence!" and You will not save.*

— HABAKKUK 1:2

It is difficult to endure the silence of God—those times when we pray but it
seems He doesn't hear because nothing changes.

That was Habakkuk's frustration. Israel had turned its back on God. The
nation was in moral chaos. Alarmed, Habakkuk cried out, "God, You are doing
nothing!" The Lord answered, "Look among the nations and watch—be utterly
astounded! For I will work a work in your days which you would not believe,
though it were told you" (Habakkuk 1:5).

GOD'S WAYS ARE NOT OUR WAYS.

Sometimes we misinterpret God's silence for indifference, but the truth is,
God is always at work.

God then gave Habakkuk a prophecy concerning the perilous days ahead.
He described the judgment that would come through the hand of the Chaldeans, whom He was raising up for that purpose. And then, urging Habakkuk to
hold on and keep trusting in Him, God encouraged the prophet with words that
have continued to encourage believers throughout the centuries: "The just shall
live by his faith" (Habakkuk 2:4).

You may be feeling today that God doesn't hear you, or worse—that He doesn't
care. But I can assure you from the Word of God that He does hear, He does care,
and He is at work on your behalf—even when He seems silent. Look away from
your problems. Ignore the circumstances. Instead, cast your cares on the One who
loves you and who has promised to meet all your needs.

*Father, bring us to this level of faith; that when we don't under-
stand what You are doing, we can say, "Lord, just keep doing it."*

AMEN.

GOD REJOICES OVER YOU

The LORD your God in your midst, the Mighty One, will save;
He will rejoice over you with gladness, He will quiet you with His
love, He will rejoice over you with singing.

— ZEPHANIAH 3:17

We who are parents know what it is to rejoice over our children. And God feels the same way. He rejoices with joy over those who have become His children through faith in Jesus Christ. Zephaniah tells us that God "rejoices over you with gladness."

He then tells us that God "will quiet you with His love." What a wonderful picture that is! The Bible tells us that God loved us so much that He laid His life down for us. The love of Jesus for us is everlasting, eternal, unchanging. Despite tribulations, trials, or hardships, His love is unmoved. Let the implications of that sink down in your heart. We need to meditate on the depth of God's passion for us.

WHEN WE UNDERSTAND OUR FATHER'S GREAT LOVE FOR US,
OUR HEARTS ARE QUIETED AND WE REST IN THAT TRUTH.

Zephaniah then says that God will "rejoice over you with singing." Can you imagine the Lord singing a love song to you, accompanied by a heavenly orchestra?

Life is uncertain. There is much we do not know. But because of the Word of God, we know the only thing that matters—the Lord loves us. Let the storms rage, let the arrows fly. Come what may, we are loved.

Father, we are amazed by Your love. How we long for that day
when You shall dwell in the midst of us,
our mighty God, our King of kings.
IN JESUS' NAME, AMEN.

DESIRE OF NATIONS

For thus says the LORD of hosts: "… I will shake heaven and earth,
the sea and dry land; and I will shake all nations, and they shall come
to the Desire of All Nations, and I will fill this temple with glory."
— HAGGAI 2:6-7

Those who returned from Babylonian captivity had become discouraged in the building of the temple, so they began fixing up their own houses instead. Haggai rebuked them and told them that this was why they were not prospering. But the people complained that the new temple, in comparison to the splendor of Solomon's temple, seemed insignificant and pitiful. So Haggai is encouraging them that one day, the glory of the Lord would fill the temple once again.

GOD WILL NOT STAND BY FOREVER AND LET WICKEDNESS REIGN.

Scripture describes the day of God's judgment—the great tribulation—when the heavens, the earth, and the seas will be shaken. After that, the "Desire of All Nations" shall come.

Jesus said to the Jews, "You shall see Me no more till you say, 'Blessed is He who comes in the name of the Lord!'" (Matthew 23:39). Though Scripture taught that the "Desire of All Nations" would establish a kingdom of righteousness, peace, and joy, the Jews rejected Him the first time He came. They had no desire for Him.

What about you? Is Jesus the desire of your heart today? Do you long for the establishment of His kingdom?

Father, we thank You for the promise of Your coming kingdom.
In the midst of a world filled with sin and chaos, we cling to Your
Word and we wait for Jesus Christ, the Desire of All Nations,
to come and establish Your righteous kingdom.

AMEN.

SING AND REJOICE

*"Sing and rejoice, O daughter of Zion! For behold, I am coming
and I will dwell in your midst," says the LORD. "Many nations
shall be joined to the Lord in that day,
and they shall become My people."*

— ZECHARIAH 2:10-11

When the people returned to the city from their Babylonian captivity, Jerusalem was wasted and desolate. But Zechariah encouraged them that someday, God will choose Jerusalem again. The Lord of hosts will take His portion again in Judah and will dwell in the midst of His people.

> THE ONLY THING THAT PROVOKES SINGING AND REJOIC-
> ING IN MY HEART IS THE PROMISE OF THE COMING OF JESUS
> CHRIST.

The prospect of the coming of the Lord should inspire singing and rejoicing in our hearts. As I look at the world today, I don't see much to rejoice in or to sing over. My heart weeps for the abounding evil we see around us. Nothing in this world inspires the kind of rejoicing the prophet refers to in this passage.

Every day that passes brings us one day closer to that glorious day—that day of singing and rejoicing, when the Lord shall come and dwell in the midst of the people.

We live in momentous times, when events are coming together to usher in the return of Jesus. As long as God gives us breath, we need to warn others of the evil days to come, but we also need to proclaim the glorious day that is coming—the day of the Lord's return.

*Lord, may Your kingdom come and Your will be done on earth,
even as it is in heaven. Our hearts long for that day when You
will dwell in peace and righteousness in the midst of Your people!*

AMEN.

JUNE

Moving Mountains

"Not by might nor by power, but by My Spirit," says the Lord of hosts. "Who are you, O great mountain? Before Zerubbabel you shall become a plain!"

— Zechariah 4:6-7

The people weren't prepared for what they found when they came back from captivity. The devastation was overwhelming. Where the temple of God once stood there was now just a huge mountain of rubble.

Such a mountain! Discouragement fell on the people as they had tried to remove the rubble. But the word of the Lord came through Zechariah to Zerubbabel, the man leading in the re-building of the temple. "Who are you, O great mountain? You shall become a plain!"

Often when we look at a task the Lord has given us it seems overwhelming. We wonder, "How in the world can this ever be accomplished?" But God's answer to us is the same as it was to Zerubbabel. "This mountain cannot be moved on your own strength. Only My Spirit can accomplish this work."

You may be facing a mountain today—a financial mountain, a health mountain, or maybe a relationship mountain. You have tried your hardest to remove the rubble, but you are tired, and weary, and ready to give up.

> It is good to come to the end of yourself. That is when you finally reach for God.

Ask the Holy Spirit for help. Let God show Himself strong on your behalf. Drop your shovel, stand back, and watch Him move that mountain.

Lord, we come to You today weary of the task and drained of our strength. We need Your help. We need the power of Your Holy Spirit to tackle this task. Fill us, Lord. Be our strength today.

In Jesus' name, amen.

Prisoners of Hope

Return to the stronghold, you prisoners of hope. Even today
I declare that I will restore double to you.
— Zechariah 9:12

In the previous verse, Zechariah addressed those who were imprisoned in a pit with no water. But now he addresses those who are imprisoned by hope.

For the believer, we are clutched, or "imprisoned," by the hope of the coming of the Messiah. We can't escape it. We don't want to escape it. It is what we long for, what we wait for. We know that when Jesus comes again, humanity's sufferings will finally end. Wars will end. Heartache will cease. He will rule and reign in peace and righteousness. And He will free us from that pit in which we may find ourselves today.

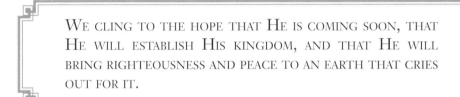

WE CLING TO THE HOPE THAT HE IS COMING SOON, THAT HE WILL ESTABLISH HIS KINGDOM, AND THAT HE WILL BRING RIGHTEOUSNESS AND PEACE TO AN EARTH THAT CRIES OUT FOR IT.

Oh, how necessary hope is! How we need it to sustain us. In a world that is falling apart, a world in which men's hearts fail them for fear, how wonderful it is to have that hope in Jesus Christ.

The Lord promises those who are the prisoners of hope that He will restore double to them. He tells in the latter portion of the chapter how He will subdue their enemies, how He will glorify His people, and how He will make them like gemstones in a crown, "lifted like a banner over His land" (Zechariah 9:16).

Come quickly, Lord Jesus!

Father, our eyes and our hope are set on You. We long for Your
return; we wait with anticipation for the day when You
come to establish Your kingdom.
IN JESUS' NAME WE PRAY, AMEN.

A Covenant Before God

*Yet you say, "For what reason?" Because the L*ORD *has been wit-*
ness between you and the wife of your youth, with whom you have
dealt treacherously; yet she is your companion and your wife by
covenant.

— MALACHI 2:14

The Israelites tried. They covered their offerings with tears, but the Lord refused to accept them. When they asked, "For what reason?" God told them it was because of the way they treated their wives.

They had made divorce too easy. If a man became enamored with a young, pretty girl, he could discard his wife by simply declaring, "I divorce you" three times. And then the companion of his youth, the woman who stood by him through all the lean years and made sacrifices to help him get started in life, the woman who had borne his children and kept his home, had no choice but to leave.

GOD HATES DIVORCE.

God hated divorce then, and He hates it now. And I have learned that if God hates something, I had better take care that I hate it also.

The Scripture tells men that we are to love our wives even more than we love ourselves. We are to love her "as Christ also loved the church and gave Himself for her" (Ephesians 5:25).

There is great pressure against marriage today. May we who are married remember that we have made a covenant with each other before God, "For better or for worse, for richer or for poorer, in sickness and in health, to love and to cherish until death do us part."

⟞⟩⬦⟨⟝

Father, help us to love each other as You have loved us, and to
treat one another with compassion and kindness.

IN JESUS' NAME, AMEN.

THE BOOK OF REMEMBRANCE

Then those who feared the LORD spoke to one another, and the Lord listened and heard them; so a book of remembrance was written before Him for those who fear the Lord and who meditate on His name.

— MALACHI 3:16

ave you ever noticed how keyed in you are on your own name? Say two people are in conversation behind you, and one of them mentions your name. Don't you automatically perk up? You wonder, "What are they saying about me?"

The Lord is just as keyed in on His name. Whenever our conversation turns toward Him, He hearkens. "What's that? What are they saying about Me?"

Unfortunately, sometimes what God hears isn't so pleasant. Israel had a habit of murmuring against the Lord, and against those things He allowed in order to bring them to a place of blessing. Rather than encouraging one another with God's promises, they murmured against the discomfort of the experience. And many times we are guilty of the same thing.

GOD, IT WOULD SEEM, IS QUITE A BOOKKEEPER.

God records those who fear Him and who talk about Him to one another. It is an awesome thought to realize that my name is written in God's book of remembrance!

I pray that you will find yourself speaking often of God's love and of His goodness; that you will share with others about what the Lord means to you. Let's keep that recording angel busy as he writes in the book of remembrance. Let's give him a lot to write about as we share with one another the goodness and the blessings of our Lord.

Lord, may we indeed speak often, one with another, of Your glories. Thank You for redeeming us and for treasuring us.

IN JESUS' NAME, AMEN.

REPENT

*In those days John the Baptist came preaching in the wilderness of
Judea, and saying, "Repent ..."*
— MATTHEW 3:1-2

What does it mean to repent? It is more than just saying you are sorry. Real repentance is being so sorry, so contrite, that you do not repeat the offense again. If a person declares that they have repented of a certain action or sin and they continue in that same action, there is good reason to doubt the genuineness of the repentance.

For God to work in a life, the first step is a true turning away from sin. And this happens when we encounter the kindness, or goodness, of God. As Paul wrote, "The goodness of God leads you to repentance" (Romans 2:4). When we realize that God is merciful, gracious, loving, and willing to forgive our transgressions, that is when our hearts are softened toward repentance.

> WITHOUT TRUE REPENTANCE, THERE ISN'T REAL FORGIVENESS.

If you have harbored a secret sin in your life and you have not genuinely turned away from it—maybe you've just become better at hiding the sin, and more careful about covering your bases—don't deceive yourself. God knows your heart. He knows your sin. And He will not be mocked.

Meditate on the goodness of God. Think about His love for you, His abounding mercy, and His willingness to not only forgive you but to change your life and help you conquer those destructive desires. Forsake the sin, turn from it with finality. And receive the forgiveness that cleanses.

———

*Father, may Your Holy Spirit speak to us concerning the necessity
of true repentance. May we bear fruit that will demonstrate a true
repentance, a true turning from evil, a true forsaking
of those things that destroy our lives.*
IN JESUS' NAME, AMEN.

TEMPTATION

*Then Jesus was led up by the Spirit into the wilderness
to be tempted by the devil.*

— MATTHEW 4:1

The Bible teaches us that temptation usually falls in one of three realms: the lust of the flesh, the lust of the eye, or the pride of life. Jesus was tempted in all of these areas. After forty days of fasting, He was hungry. Hunger itself is not a sin. But Satan turned it into a temptation. "Since You are the Son of God, why don't You turn these stones into bread?" In other words, Satan was suggesting that Jesus let His bodily appetites rule over His spirit.

> THIS IS ALWAYS THE HEART OF TEMPTATION: TO LET THE FLESH RULE OVER THE SPIRIT.

And thus, in every situation I must determine whether I will yield to the desires of my flesh or to the desires of the spirit.

Jesus used the Word of God to answer every temptation Satan brought. That is why it is so important for us to have the Word of God stored away in our hearts. The abiding Word of God in you will be the secret of your strength in overcoming whatever temptation Satan brings your way.

Prepare yourself now, for temptation will surely come. Plan your steps before you face the choice. When God's Word says one thing and Satan says another, what will you do? Will you yield yourself to God and follow after His Word, or will you let your flesh rule over your spirit?

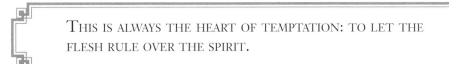

*Father, we confess that so often we have failed the test; that we've
allowed the flesh to rule over the spirit. Forgive us, Lord,
and cleanse us. Let us be governed by Your Holy Spirit
and by Your eternal Word of truth.*

IN JESUS' NAME, AMEN.

No Worries

Therefore I say to you, do not worry about your life, what you will
eat or what you will drink; nor about your body, what you will put
on. Is not life more than food and the body more than clothing?
— MATTHEW 6:25

Faith and worry are mutually exclusive. If you have real faith in the providence and care of God, you will not worry over your circumstances. Any worry you have demonstrates a lack of faith.

Because of your faith in Jesus Christ, you are now a child of God. Knowing that He is your heavenly Father should dispel any concern over the issues of life. Your Father knows that you need food and clothes, so you don't have to worry about it. Jesus taught us that our Father loves us so much, He even watches over the trivial details of our lives, and knows our needs before we are aware of them.

It is a matter of priority. What are you putting first—food and clothing? If so, you are no better off than the heathen. But if you seek first the kingdom of God and His righteousness, then God will take care of the other things.

> DON'T PUT THE WRONG THINGS AT THE TOP OF YOUR PRIORITY LIST.

Those who waste their lives pursuing non-productive, temporal things have nothing eternally to show for their lives when they get to the end of the road. Therefore, let a man examine himself. Look at your own heart—and determine to put God first.

Father, help us to give You the place of highest priority in our
lives. Forgive us, Lord, for the time we spend thinking
about physical things that will pass away.
IN JESUS' NAME, AMEN.

LOSE YOURSELF

He who finds his life will lose it,
and he who loses his life for My sake will find it.
— MATTHEW 10:39

I hear a lot of people talking today about the need to "find themselves." But according to Jesus, the best thing you can do is to lose yourself.

Speaking to His followers one day, Jesus explained the first requirement for discipleship. "If anyone desires to come after Me," He said, "let him deny himself, and take up his cross daily, and follow Me" (Luke 9:23). To seek Jesus, you must deny self. You must give up the habit of self-centeredness.

The greatest example of selflessness the world has ever seen happened on the cross. Though His preference would have been to let that cup (the cross) pass from Him (Matthew 26:39), Jesus laid aside His own will to obey His Father's will.

LOSE YOURSELF IN JESUS CHRIST.

The one who lives only for himself and thinks only of himself will lose everything in the end. That's because you can't keep any of those things that you do for yourself. All the successes, all the accomplishments, all the trophies will ultimately burn in the fires that will test our works. The only things you can take with you—the only things that will last forever—are those things you do for Jesus Christ.

Want to find yourself? Want to find the deepest possible meaning in life? Then deny yourself. Lose yourself in Jesus Christ and in so doing, you will find joy and peace that will last for eternity.

Father, help us to live by these spiritual principles You have
elucidated for us. Help us come to that place
where it is none of self and all of Thee.
AMEN.

THE LIGHTER YOKE

Come to Me, all you who labor and are heavy laden, and I will
give you rest. Take My yoke upon you and learn from Me, for I
am gentle and lowly in heart, and you will find rest for your souls.
For My yoke is easy and My burden is light.

— MATTHEW 11:28-30

Life is full of burdens. We are burdened with responsibilities, with expectations, with our own desires, with the drive to accumulate possessions or seek pleasure. But Jesus has extended a twofold invitation to those who labor under those heavy loads: "Take My yoke upon you and learn from Me."

The yoke was a farming implement—a wooden harness oxen wore so they could pull the plow. In using this term, Jesus is saying, "I have a work for you to do. And I want to take the reins of your life and begin to direct you."

> IT'S EASIER TO LIVE FOR GOD THAN TO LIVE FOR YOURSELF.

Jesus then said, "Learn of Me." In that phrase, He invites a scrutiny. The more you study Him, then the more you will love Him as you learn of His great love for you.

And what was Jesus' burden? His first recorded words were, "I must be about My Father's business" (Luke 2:49). Jesus lived to do His Father's will. In saying, "My burden is light," He is declaring that it is far easier to please God than it is to please yourself. Find the man who has peace and satisfaction, and you will find a man committed to Jesus Christ.

Lord, so many are troubled over the pressures of this life. But we
thank You that even while living in this fast-paced world,
we can still have rest in our souls by committing ourselves to You.

IN JESUS' NAME, AMEN.

UNFORGIVABLE

*Therefore I say to you, every sin and blasphemy will be
forgiven men, but the blasphemy against the Spirit
will not be forgiven men.*

— MATTHEW 12:31

If you are worried that you may have committed the unforgivable sin, I can assure you that you haven't. Once a person has committed the unforgivable sin, they are not worried about it at all.

THE UNFORGIVABLE SIN IS THE CONTINUED REJECTION OF THE HOLY SPIRIT.

When you sin, God's Spirit strives with you, convicting you of that sin. We often call it the voice of conscience. When we heed Him, confess our sins, and turn from them, "He is faithful and just to forgive us our sins and to cleanse us from all unrighteousness" (1 John 1:9). But God said His Spirit would not always strive with men. There can come a time in a person's life when they no longer hear the convicting voice of the Holy Spirit.

The rejection of the Spirit's witness to your heart—that Jesus is the Messiah, that He died for your sin, and that He rose again—is the beginning of the path that leads to the unpardonable sin. The continued rejection of Jesus Christ as your Savior will ultimately bring you to the place where He will cease to strive with you and you cannot believe. And if you die rejecting Jesus Christ as your Savior, there is no forgiveness, neither in this world nor in the world to come.

⸺⊰●⊱⸺

*Father, there are people in our lives who have been saying "no"
over and over—those whose love for darkness exceeds their love for
the light. But You love them in spite of their rebellion. May they
hear and respond to Your Spirit before they go too far.*

AMEN.

KEEP YOUR EYES ON JESUS

*And when Peter had come down out of the boat, he walked on the
water to go to Jesus. But when he saw that the wind was
boisterous, he was afraid; and beginning to sink
he cried out, saying, "Lord, save me!"*

— MATTHEW 14:29-30

After rowing all night, the disciples had only reached the middle of the sea. And now great waves had formed and heavy rains began to beat upon them. Suddenly, in the midst of the storm, they see a figure walking towards them on the water. Terrified, they cry out—but a calming voice answers them. "Don't be afraid," Jesus says. "It's only Me."

FEAR AND FAITH ARE MUTUALLY EXCLUSIVE.

Peter, ever the bold one, says, "If it is really You, Lord, then bid me to come to You." When Jesus tells him to come, Peter gets out of the ship and begins to walk across the water. But it is a short walk. Just a few steps into his journey, Peter takes his eyes off Jesus and puts them on the boisterous waves at his feet—and begins to sink.

Overwhelming situations can cause us to take our eyes off of Jesus. When we do that, we often sink in despair. But if we are wise, like Peter, we remember to cry out to the only One with the power to help us, "Lord, save me!"

Fear and faith are mutually exclusive. Faith cancels fear, and fear cancels faith. If you keep your eyes on Jesus, your faith will help you walk on water and overcome any difficulty life brings.

*Lord, teach us this day to keep our eyes on You. For those feeling
overwhelmed, who fear they might be sinking, remind them of
Your nearness, Your love, and Your willingness to save.*

IN JESUS' NAME, AMEN.

Not a Word

*And behold, a woman of Canaan came from that region and cried
out to Him, saying, "Have mercy on me, O Lord, Son of David!
My daughter is severely demon-possessed."
But He answered her not a word.*
— MATTHEW 15:22-23

The woman's plea was passionate, but Jesus answered her not a word. When He finally did speak, it was to the disciples. He declared to them that the woman was outside of the covenant God had made with Israel. But the woman wasn't discouraged. In fact, she agreed with Jesus. "That is true, Lord. I don't deserve it. But I'm not asking for bread—only for the crumbs that fall from the table."

> GOD'S SILENCE DOESN'T ALWAYS MEAN "NO."

Jesus knew from the beginning that He would heal her daughter. Yet He wanted to draw the woman's faith out to its fullest expression. Each time He took one step back, she came two steps closer. Refusing to become discouraged, she held on until she heard the words she wanted to hear, "O woman, great is your faith! Let it be to you as you desire" (Matthew 15:28).

Sometimes, God is simply waiting. He might be working in your heart, or tarrying in order to strengthen your faith. Don't get discouraged when the answer is not immediately forthcoming. Hold on. Keep asking. Demonstrate your faith, and wait for the words you long to hear, "Let it be as you desire."

*Father, draw us ever closer to You, into a more intimate, complete
relationship. Teach us patience as we wait for Your response to our
requests. Strengthen our faith, and give us opportunities
to prove that faith to You. May we rest in Your love.*

IN JESUS' NAME, AMEN.

TRUE FORGIVENESS

Then Peter came to him and said, "Lord, how often shall my
brother sin against me, and I forgive him? Up to seven times?"
Jesus said to him, "... up to seventy times seven."
— MATTHEW 18:21-22

I have a suspicion that Peter was hoping to impress the Lord with this question. In his own mind, seven times probably seemed like quite a stretch. So when Jesus corrected him, saying "seventy times seven," Peter probably thought, "Yikes!"

Forgiveness is a prerequisite if we want our own sins to be forgiven. Jesus emphasized that truth in His teaching on the Lord's Prayer. "Forgive us our debts, as we forgive our debtors" (Matthew 6:12). A few verses later, He added, "But if you do not forgive men their trespasses, neither will your Father forgive your trespasses" (6:15).

FORGIVENESS IS NOT A MATTER OF MATHEMATICS. IT IS A MATTER OF SPIRIT.

When God forgives, He forgets. He never brings it up again. We would do well to imitate Him. He has forgiven us such a great debt, yet it is amazing what little things will rankle us and cause us to be angry and resentful toward others. Too often, our attitude is, "I will forgive—but I won't forget." Jesus would answer, "That is not forgiveness."

For the believer, forgiveness isn't an option—it is a requirement. But God will enable you to do whatever He requires. If you lack the strength to forgive, all you have to do is ask the Holy Spirit to work that forgiveness through you. What a glorious thing it is when God's love flows through us to heal another.

———⟫●⟪———

Lord, search us and know our hearts. If we need to forgive,
help us to do so by Your Holy Spirit.

IN JESUS' NAME, AMEN.

Love Grown Cold

And because lawlessness will abound, the love of many will grow cold.

— Matthew 24:12

There are some who once burned with holy zeal for the Lord. They had a deep devotional life, full of time spent in the Word and in prayer. But their fire went out. Satan crept in gradually, destroying both their witness and their relationship with the Lord. Though they'd once rejoiced to have been delivered from the mire and muck of the world, they have returned, like pigs, to that same mire and muck. As Jesus foretold in Matthew 24, their love has waxed cold.

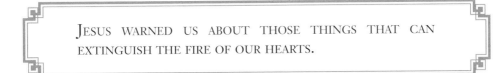

Jesus warned us about those things that can extinguish the fire of our hearts.

"Take heed to yourselves, lest your hearts be weighed down with carousing, drunkenness, and cares of this life, and that Day come on you unexpectedly" (Luke 21:34). Carousing means giving yourself over to the appetites of the flesh. Drunkenness—whether by alcohol, drugs, or yes, even excessive TV watching—is the numbing or clouding of your brain to the point where you can no longer think clearly. The cares of this life are those things that keep you so busy that you no longer have time for the things of the Spirit.

What is the condition of your heart today? Does your love for Jesus burn brightly there, or has your love for Him waxed cold?

Father, we don't want our love for You to wax cold.
Keep love's fire burning in our hearts, that our zeal
for You would be a bright witness to the world.

In Jesus' name, amen.

THE DAYS OF NOAH

But as the days of Noah were,
so also will the coming of the Son of Man be.
— MATTHEW 24:37

In the days of Noah, God saw that the wickedness of man was great on the earth, and that every imagination of the thoughts of man's heart was evil continually. It is not hard to make a comparison to today. Our world is full of violence and corruption. Television and movie industries pollute the minds of people until the thoughts and the imagination of man's heart is only evil continually. And just as in the days of Noah, people eat and drink, marry, and carry on their business without thought to the soon coming of the Lord.

> THE WORLD CAN'T CONTINUE ON MUCH LONGER THE WAY THINGS ARE, SPIRALING EVER DOWNWARD.

A day of reckoning approaches, and nothing in the world's arsenal can save us. Education won't save us. Neither will science. The government won't. The United Nations won't. Not even Green Peace can save our planet. The only sure hope for the future is the return of Jesus Christ. He alone has the power to save and deliver.

As we see the deteriorating conditions of the world around us, we shouldn't get discouraged. Instead, we should be motivated. We need to rise to the challenge and live lives that are godly, righteous, and holy, as we wait for the return of our Lord.

Father, as we look at the world today, we see the same conditions
that existed in the days of Noah, and we realize that judgment is
not far off. May we humble ourselves, pray, and seek Your face,
and may we turn away from all wickedness.

IN JESUS' NAME, AMEN.

The Faithful Servant

*"Well done, good and faithful servant; you were faithful over a
few things, I will make you ruler over many things.
Enter into the joy of your lord."*

— MATTHEW 25:21

All of us need to take a personal inventory and ask ourselves, what is it that
God has entrusted to me? When we appear before the judgment seat of
Christ, every one of us will give an account for what we did with our lives, our
talents, and our resources.

> WHAT HAS GOD PUT IN MY KEEPING THAT HE WILL SOME
> DAY REQUIRE AN ACCOUNTING FOR?

In this parable, Jesus tells us of one to whom five talents were entrusted.
When his master returned, the servant had much to show him. "Lord," he said,
"you gave me five talents, and I have earned you five more." To which his master
replied, "Well done, good and faithful servant." He then promised to entrust
even more responsibility to his servant, and invited him to enter into "the joy
of your lord."

All that I have done and am doing in my life is for the purpose of one day
hearing those words, "Well done." That is the motivation behind all I do. It is
what I am looking toward and working for. If Jesus came today, would you be
pleased to show Him what you've been doing with the things He has entrusted
to you?

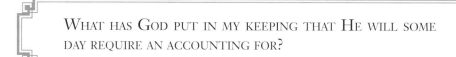

*Father, we thank You for that which You have entrusted into our
keeping and into our care. Help us not to be lazy about the service
we do for You, but may we be diligent in using those things that
You have given to us—using them, Lord, for Your purpose.*

IN JESUS' NAME WE PRAY, AMEN.

The Road to Denial

A servant girl came to him, saying, "You also were with Jesus of Galilee." But he denied it before them all, saying, "I do not know what you are saying."
— MATTHEW 26:69-70

How is it that a man who walked in such close fellowship with Jesus could deny his Lord? Just a handful of mistakes led Peter from fellowship to denial.

Peter's first mistake was arguing with Jesus (Matthew 26:31-35). If you ever find yourself in an argument with the Lord, know this for sure: you are wrong.

> JUST A HANDFUL OF MISTAKES WILL TAKE YOU FROM FELLOWSHIP AND LEAD YOU TO DENIAL.

Secondly, Peter boasted of his commitment. "Even if all are made to stumble because of You, I will never be made to stumble" (Matthew 26:33). Beware of overconfidence in your flesh.

Then, Peter chose sleep over prayer (Matthew 26:40, 43). We often treat prayer as an afterthought, or as being optional. I am certain that if we would pray more, we would sin less.

And then, Peter put distance between himself and Jesus. "But Peter followed Him at a distance" (Matthew 26:58). The secret of the Christian life is to stick as closely to Jesus as you possibly can.

Finally, we find Peter warming himself by the soldiers' fire (Mark 14:54). It is always dangerous to seek warmth from the enemy.

Peter denied the Lord, but his faith did not fail. If, like Peter, you have failed, Jesus wants to help you start over—this time holding tightly to His hand, sticking closely by His side, and avoiding the enemy's fire.

Father, we thank You for Your mercy, Your grace, and Your forgiveness of our sins. We are so grateful that despite our failures, You are able and willing to restore us to a place of usefulness and service.

IN JESUS' NAME, AMEN.

SUFFICIENT POWER

And Jesus came and spoke to them, saying, "All authority has been given to Me in heaven and on earth."

— MATTHEW 28:18

The same Jesus who had the power to bring the universe into existence, and the power to forgive sins, and the power to cast out demons, and the power to uphold all things by His Word (Hebrews 1:3), is the same Jesus who told His disciples—and us—to, "Go therefore and make disciples of all nations, baptizing them in the name of the Father and of the Son and of the Holy Spirit" (Matthew 28:19).

It would seem that since we are weak, and since Jesus has all that power, perhaps He should be the one to go. But He also said, "Lo, I am with you always" (Matthew 28:20). So when He sends us off to carry out the Great Commission, He is really saying, "You go, and I will be with you."

OH, THAT YOU ONLY KNEW THE EXCEEDING GREATNESS OF THE POWER THAT GOD HAS MADE AVAILABLE TO YOU!

You don't have to be bound by the desires of your flesh. You don't have to live in defeat. You don't have to live in bondage. All the power in the universe is available for you through Jesus Christ—sufficient power for any and every emergency. Whatever power you need to fulfill His calling, to be perfected in His image, to be all God wants you to be, is yours today through Jesus.

Father, may we know the exceeding greatness of Your power to us who have come to believe in Jesus Christ. May we go forth in Your name, empowered by Your Holy Spirit to carry the gospel into the needy world around us.

AMEN.

HIS TOUCH

Now a leper came to Him, imploring Him, kneeling down to Him
and saying to Him, "If You are willing, You can make me clean."
Then Jesus, moved with compassion, stretched out His hand and
touched him, and said to him, "I am willing; be cleansed."

— MARK 1:40-41

No one knew how leprosy was transmitted from one person to another; all that was known was that the disease—which progressively rotted the flesh—was incurable and fatal. Leprosy parallels sin, which also progressively rots its victims and leads to their death. Thus, in Scripture, leprosy is a type of sin.

Society ostracized the leper and required that he warn those who approached him of his condition by crying out, "Unclean, unclean." Yet we find this man kneeling at the feet of Jesus, expressing faith in the ability and the power of Jesus to cleanse him of his leprosy. To him, his healing was simply a matter of willingness on the part of Jesus.

NO ONE IS BEYOND THE TOUCH OF JESUS.

Compassion caused Jesus to reach out and touch the man. In doing so, He made Himself ceremonially unclean. But He also extended a loving touch to someone who probably had not felt human touch for years.

Then Jesus said those glorious words, "I am willing; be cleansed."

What happens when a sinner comes to Jesus? Moved with compassion, Jesus reaches out and touches that life. No matter how far gone their disease, no matter how much sin has eaten away, no matter that no one else wants to touch that life, Jesus will. No one is beyond His touch.

Lord, thank You that when we were rotting away with the
ravages of sin, You reached out to us, touched us, forgave us,
and cleansed us. We love You, Lord.

AMEN.

THE PLOT AGAINST JESUS

Then the Pharisees went out and immediately plotted with the
Herodians against Him, how they might destroy Him.
— MARK 3:6

Logic tells you it would be lawful to do good, no matter what day it was. But because Jesus dared to heal a man on the Sabbath—and then defend His actions against their tradition—the Jews sought to kill Him.

Even today, some feel they must destroy Jesus. The movie industry frequently casts Christians in a negative light, seeking to destroy the influence of Jesus in our society. Organizations have long since fought to remove Jesus from the public sector of our nation, and unfortunately, the Supreme Court has helped them.

> DON'T SIT ON THE FENCE AND LOOK THE OTHER WAY.

Why is this happening? It is because, as Jesus said, men love darkness rather than light. Jesus spoke out against adultery, hatred, lying, and cheating, and instead taught forgiveness. He taught that we must love God and love one another. But those who are filled with hatred toward God and their fellowman feel they must destroy the message of Jesus. If they can do that, then perhaps they can live their sinful lives without guilt.

I believe in the coming days we will see more of our religious liberties taken and even more oppression of Christianity by the government. Those bent on destroying Jesus won't stop until they can see His influence removed from our society.

Don't sit on the fence. Don't look the other way. Make an active stand for the Lord wherever He is attacked.

Father, we get so upset at those who go against You, but we know
that Your kingdom is coming. Hasten the day, Lord. Bring to pass
Your kingdom of righteousness, joy, and peace.
IN THE NAME OF JESUS, AMEN.

TWO QUESTIONS

But He said to them, "Why are you so fearful?
How is it that you have no faith?"
— MARK 4:40

The disciples had good reasons to be fearful: a fierce storm had come upon them, waves sloshed over the bow, and the boat was beginning to sink. And yet, the Lord slept through the storm.

When trouble comes upon us, overwhelming us with its intensity, threatening to sink us, it can sometimes seem that the Lord isn't concerned with our predicament. Our calls go unanswered and we wonder why the Lord isn't helping, why our situation isn't changing.

We never face a storm alone. The Lord is with us—always. And when Jesus is on board, there's no need to fear.

Jesus had two questions. After asking, "Why are you so fearful?" He then asked, "How is it that you have no faith?" When our problems seem big, our faith can get small. It was fear that caused the disciples to lose their faith.

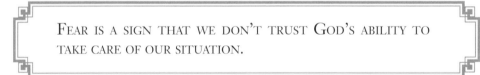

FEAR IS A SIGN THAT WE DON'T TRUST GOD'S ABILITY TO TAKE CARE OF OUR SITUATION.

It is glorious to know that our heavenly Father is watching over us, that He loves us, that He cares for us, and that He is in control. When we don't understand what is happening around us, we can still trust Jesus. We don't need to fear. Jesus is on board, He is able to calm the storm, and He will bring us safely into that eternal harbor.

Father, we thank You for the peace of Christ that passes human
understanding, that in the midst of the storm our hearts
can be at rest because our trust is in You.

IN JESUS' PRECIOUS NAME, AMEN.

Touching Jesus

*When she heard about Jesus, she came behind Him in the crowd
and touched His garment. For she said, "If only I may touch His
clothes, I shall be made well."*

— MARK 5:27-28

This woman believed that Jesus had power. She was convinced that if she could touch even the hem of His garment, she would be healed of her plague. However, obstacles blocked her way. The crowd thronged Him, pushing, shoving, moving Jesus along. But her own desperation and determination pushed the woman through that crowd until she finally got close enough. Reaching out, she grabbed the one thing within her reach—the hem of His garment.

Suddenly Jesus stopped and asked, "Who touched My clothes?"

MANY IN THE CROWD HAD PRESSED AGAINST JESUS, BUT ONLY ONE MADE CONTACT WITH HIM.

Maybe you are part of the crowd. You're pressing in on Jesus, but not really touching Him. That is not sufficient. It is not enough.

When Jesus touches you, He brings love, healing, deliverance, power, and life. He wants to give you all those things. He wants to bring what you need and what you long for. He wants to heal your wounds, fill you with His love, deliver you from the power of darkness, and enable you to live the life you were created to live.

Oh, how we need the touch of Jesus in our lives! I encourage you to push through the crowd and get in touch with Jesus today. Reach out in faith and touch Him now. Let Him touch you in return. In the moment you make contact with Him, you will find the healing, deliverance and help you need.

---

*Jesus, may we reach out to You today and be delivered
from the things that plague us. Touch us, Lord.*

AMEN.

UNBELIEF

Now He could do no mighty work there, except that He laid
his hands on a few sick people and healed them.
And He marveled because of their unbelief.

— MARK 6:5-6

Throughout the area of Galilee, Jesus met with throngs of people. Everywhere He went, He brought blessing. He comforted the brokenhearted. He healed the blind and the lame. He preached the good news to the poor. By the time He returned to Nazareth, a multitude of believers followed in tow.

But Nazareth didn't receive Jesus the way others had. No sick were brought to Him. No hurting came for comfort. Instead, the unbelieving people stood by watching and scoffing and questioning. Where did this hometown boy get this wisdom? Where did He get this power?

> OUR LIMITATIONS COME WHEN WE REFUSE TO RECEIVE GOD'S POWER.

Jesus loved the people in His hometown just as He loved the people everywhere He went. There was much He wanted to do for them, but their unbelief kept them from receiving. His power wasn't limited; God's power is limited by nothing. The limitation came in their refusal to receive His power. Because of their unbelief, they didn't bring the lame, the blind, or the sick. They didn't give Jesus an opportunity to minister.

Jesus wants to bless you today. He wants to heal, soothe and teach you, but when you forget He is there and He is able, when you keep Him at arm's length because of your unbelief, you rob yourself of blessing.

Be aware of the danger of unbelief. Guard your heart. Nurture your faith in Jesus, that you would never limit His work in your life.

———

Father, we pray that we would not be guilty of unbelief.
Help us to trust You to do that work in our lives.

IN JESUS' NAME, AMEN.

FORGIVE

And whenever you stand praying, if you have anything against
anyone, forgive him, that your Father in heaven
may also forgive you your trespasses.
— MARK 11:25

Our bodies are amazing. Within the chemical laboratory that is you, different emotions cause different chemical reactions. As Proverbs tells us, "A merry heart does good, like medicine" (17:22). Laughter and happiness have healing value. But the opposite is also true. Bitterness and anger create destructive chemicals that begin to destroy our health and our well-being.

RESENTMENT IS DESTRUCTIVE.

When we carry hurts and offenses with us, our bodies suffer. It doesn't matter if you are justified for being angry. It doesn't matter that the other person deserves your resentment. The fact remains that you will hurt yourself when you hold on to resentful feelings. The offense may seem unforgivable, but you still need to forgive.

Some wounds run so deep that it seems impossible for us to forgive, but it's not. Your Father can help you. Just hold the offense before Him and ask the Lord to free you from the anger you're feeling, and the desire for revenge. Ask the Lord to help you to forgive the offender—just as He forgave you when you were undeserving or unworthy of His forgiveness. Remember: Jesus did more than just teach forgiveness; He practiced it. As He was being nailed to the cross, He prayed, "Father, forgive them, for they do not know what they do" (Luke 23:34).

Don't let bitterness destroy your life. If you want to bless Jesus, others, and yourself—forgive.

Father, although we have sinned against You again and again,
You have forgiven us—again and again. Help us to be like You.
Help us to forgive as we have been forgiven.

BEARING FRUIT

*Now at vintage-time he sent a servant to the vinedressers, that he
might receive some of the fruit of the vineyard ...*
— MARK 12:2

God loves to walk in His vineyard. Why? He is looking for fruit.

In John 15:8, Jesus says, "By this My Father is glorified, that you bear
much fruit." Paul goes on, in Galatians 5:22-23, to explain the fruit of the Spirit
as being "love, joy, peace, longsuffering, kindness, goodness, faithfulness, gentleness, and self-control." This is the fruit God sought from the nation of Israel,
and this is what the Lord is seeking from us.

WHAT FRUIT IS COMING FORTH FROM YOUR LIFE?

In contrast to fruit is work. Fruit develops naturally as a result of relationship, whereas works are those things that are produced by effort, by organiza-
tion and by coordination.

The Lord is not interested in coming to a factory and hearing the noisy roar
of the motors and the clanging of the steel, and seeing the grime that is usually
found in such busy places. The Lord wants to come to His garden, that He
might partake of and enjoy the fruit He finds there.

What fruit is coming forth from your life? Is it the works of the flesh, or the
fruit of the Spirit? If you want to bear fruit for God—easily and naturally—then
you need to attend to your relationship with Him. You need to seek Him, think
about Him, and study His character.

Fruit will never come by will or determination. It comes by simply walking
with the Gardener, and abiding in His love.

*Father, let us know and experience Your love on a daily basis and
share it with those with whom we come into contact. May they see
that love and realize that we are Your disciples.*

AMEN.

Return of the King

Then they will see the Son of Man coming
in the clouds with great power and glory.
— Mark 13:26

When Jesus came the first time, it was as a servant. "For I have come down from heaven, not to do My own will, but the will of Him who sent Me" (John 6:38). His first coming was full of sorrow, rejection, and pain. His next coming will be far different. He will return in power and glory—the King of kings, here to establish God's reign over the earth.

The Jews were confused by Jesus, because they focused on only one half of the Old Testament prophecies concerning the coming Messiah. They were watching for the coming of a glorious kingdom; a utopia on earth, with no more heartache or sickness. Other verses spoke of the Messiah being despised, rejected, pierced, and beaten. They prophesied that He would come in lowliness, riding on a donkey. But because the Jews couldn't reconcile the two portraits of the Messiah, they rejected Him when He appeared. They didn't understand that both descriptions were true, and that they'd find their fulfillment in two separate comings: one to make a sacrifice for man's sins; one to reign in glory, majesty, and power.

JESUS SUMS UP THIS PORTION OF SCRIPTURE WITH A SINGLE WORD: "WATCH!"

We should be watching for our Lord's return. We should be waiting in expectancy, right up to the minute of His return—that should He come today, we would have no business yet undone.

Father, thank You for the glorious hope we have of the soon return
of Jesus Christ. We wait for that day with longing and anticipation,
wanting to see Your kingdom established in righteousness and peace.

IN JESUS' NAME, AMEN.

Strength in the Spirit

Watch and pray, lest you enter into temptation.
The spirit indeed is willing, but the flesh is weak.

— Mark 14:38

We often forget the humanity of Jesus. We are so focused on His divinity we forget that He was both God and man. But He did have a human side, and we see evidence of that in the garden of Gethsemane—where He faced the greatest challenge of His life. And we need to praise Him for what He endured. Jesus took on a body of flesh to gain sympathetic understanding of our weaknesses. Because He struggled with His humanity there in the garden, He understands the struggles we face today.

Our hearts want to do the right thing. Our hearts want to please God, but the flesh is so weak. Are we always doomed to fail? Thank God He has made provision for the weakness of our flesh. Jesus said, "You shall receive power when the Holy Spirit has come upon you" (Acts 1:8). God's provision for our weak flesh is the empowering of His Holy Spirit.

THE EMPOWERING OF THE HOLY SPIRIT CAN OVERCOME THE FLESH.

When you rely on the Holy Spirit, those areas of your greatest weakness can become the areas of your greatest strength. When you rely on your own strength, however, thinking you are fully capable of handling things by yourself, that is when you are in danger.

The flesh is not reliable. God's Spirit, however, can fill your gaps, strengthen your weaknesses, equip you for work, guide you through difficulties, and change you into the image of Christ. Which would you rather rely on?

—⬦—

Father, we thank You for the help that is ours through the power
of the Holy Spirit. Lord, help us to rely upon You
instead of ourselves.

In Jesus' name, amen.

The Tragedy of Unbelief

And when they heard that He was alive and had been seen by her,
they did not believe.

— MARK 16:11

The tomb was empty. The stone was rolled away. And Jesus—who had triumphed over hell and the grave—had risen to life again.

They should have anticipated His resurrection. Hadn't He told them over and over again that He would be crucified, but that He would rise again on the third day? You would think on that third day they would have been exhilarated and waiting with anticipation. But when Mary comes to them with the life-changing news, they don't believe her. Doubt keeps them in tears. And they continue mourning for One who was no longer in the grave.

UNBELIEF BRINGS TRAGEDY.

Adam did not believe God's statement, so he ate the fruit and brought sin and death into the world. The people in Noah's day did not believe his warnings, so the flood came and they were destroyed. Because the children of Israel did not believe that God would drive out the inhabitants of the land, they perished in the wilderness.

What is unbelief costing you today—peace of mind? A joyful heart? Are you fretting over circumstances or because you feel your life is out of control, even though Scripture tells you not to worry? Are you disbelieving God's promises, God's power, and God's love for you?

May God give us faith to trust and believe—regardless of the circumstances, regardless of our feelings.

———

Father, give us the faith to rely on Your promises and Your charac-
ter, knowing that You are sovereign, mighty, powerful, and
loving. Remind us daily that You are still on the throne.

AMEN.

THE GREATNESS OF JESUS

*And behold, you will conceive in your womb and bring forth a
Son, and shall call His name JESUS. He will be great, and will
be called the Son of the Highest; and the Lord God will give Him
the throne of His father David.*

— LUKE 1:31-32

How great is the Son? He is so great that John wrote, "In the beginning was the Word, and the Word was with God, and the Word was God. All things were made through Him, and without Him nothing was made that was made" (John 1:1,3). He's so great that Paul elaborated on that by writing, "For by Him all things were created that are in heaven and that are on earth, visible and invisible, whether thrones or dominions or principalities or powers. All things were created through Him and for Him" (Colossians 1:16). He is not only the Creator, He is the central object of creation. You were created for Him, and for His good pleasure.

We are told that He, "being in the form of God, did not consider it robbery to be equal with God, but made Himself of no reputation … He humbled Himself and became obedient to the point of death, even the death of the cross. Therefore, God also has highly exalted Him and given Him the name which is above every name, that at the name of Jesus every knee should bow … and that every tongue should confess that Jesus Christ is Lord" (Philippians 2:6-11).

> HOW BLESSED WE ARE TO LOVE AND BE LOVED BY SUCH A
> GREAT GOD!

*Father, we are awed by Your nature—Your majesty, power, glory,
wisdom, patience—and awed by Your beauty.
May You come quickly for us, Lord Jesus.*

IN JESUS' PRECIOUS NAME, AMEN.

Prepare Ye the Way of the Lord

Prepare the way of the LORD; make His paths straight. Every valley shall be filled and every mountain and hill brought low; the crooked places shall be made straight and the rough ways smooth; and all flesh shall see the salvation of God.

— LUKE 3:4-6

The King was coming. And John the Baptist had been called to be His forerunner—to announce that His kingdom was at hand and to urge the people to prepare themselves through repentance. In essence, John was called to smooth the way for the Lord's arrival.

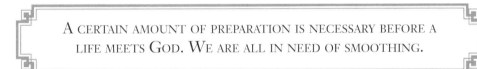

A CERTAIN AMOUNT OF PREPARATION IS NECESSARY BEFORE A LIFE MEETS GOD. WE ARE ALL IN NEED OF SMOOTHING.

Jesus—the holy, righteous King—was coming at a time of great spiritual, moral decay. The atmosphere was hostile to righteousness and to the things of the Lord. So John went about urging the people to repent. "Even now the ax is laid to the root of the trees," John warned them. "Therefore every tree which does not bear good fruit is cut down and thrown into the fire" (Luke 3:9). When the people asked, "What shall we do then?" John answered, "He who has two tunics, let him give to him who has none; and he who has food, let him do likewise" (3:11). In other words, stop thinking about yourselves. Consider others. Straighten out those crooked ways in your life. Get ready for the King.

Our King is coming! With David, let's pray, "Search me, O God, and know my heart; try me, and know my anxieties; and see if there is any wicked way in me" (Psalm 139:23-24).

---

*Lord, we invite You to smooth out the rough spots within us.
Have Your way with our hearts, Father.*

AMEN.

LED

Then Jesus, being filled with the Holy Spirit, returned from the
Jordan and was led by the Spirit into the wilderness …
— LUKE 4:1

In speaking of Jesus, John said, "He who says he abides in Him ought himself also to walk just as He walked" (1 John 2:6). The question is, how did Jesus walk? The answer is that He walked in the Spirit.

When your life is led by the Spirit, that means God will sometimes interrupt your plans. When that happens—when your day gets taken in another direction, or unexpected company drops by—you ought to stop and say, "Lord, what do You have in mind here?"

GOD'S HAND IS IN EVERY DISRUPTION AND EVERY DETOUR.

Notice that Jesus was led by the Spirit into the wilderness to be tempted by Satan. We sometimes have the mistaken notion that a life led by the Spirit is a life full of roses and no problems. But that is not true. A life led by the Spirit may go in directions you didn't plan. Will you trust Him even when you don't understand?

God's Spirit is with you. He will work all things out for you. As Jesus was filled with the Spirit, led by the Spirit, and empowered by the Spirit, so too we need to be filled, led and empowered. Trust Him with your life—no matter how often He interrupts you, no matter where He chooses to take you.

Father, we offer You our time and our plans. Insert Yourself in our
day, Father. Bring those conversations, those situations where You
want to bring Your light. May we live each minute to Your glory.
IN JESUS' NAME, AMEN.

POWER OVER TEMPTATION

*Then Jesus ... was led by the Spirit into the wilderness, being tempted
for forty days by the devil. And in those days He ate nothing, and
afterward, when they had ended, He was hungry.*

— LUKE 4:1-2

Satan loves to attack or tempt us when we are in a weakened physical condition. Such was the case with Jesus. Knowing that after forty days without food Jesus was weak and hungry, Satan suggested He use His divine powers to meet the needs of His flesh. In other words, "Let the spiritual be subservient to the physical."

None of us have divine power, but we still face that same temptation. Satan constantly is trying to get us to put the physical level of life above the spiritual level; to allow ourselves to be ruled by the flesh and not the Spirit.

Jesus responded to Satan's temptation with the Word. That is always the best way to handle Satan. "It is written," Jesus said, "'Man shall not live by bread alone, but by every word of God'" (Luke 4:4). Jesus confirmed that the spiritual life is always superior to the physical life.

> JESUS TRIUMPHED OVER TEMPTATION AND CAN HELP YOU TO HAVE VICTORY ALSO.

Jesus knows we are tempted to think more of bread than of the Word. He was tempted in that same way so that He could understand us and help us in our struggles.

When Satan is trying to lure you away, Jesus can come alongside and say, "I know what you are thinking. I know that you are tempted. I understand." But because He triumphed over temptation, He can also help you to have victory.

*Father, how thankful we are that because You overcame
temptation, You're able to help us overcome.
Lord, we are powerless without You. Be our strength.*

IN JESUS' NAME WE PRAY, AMEN.

BLIND TRUST

*But Simon answered and said to Him, "Master, we have toiled
all night and caught nothing; nevertheless
at Your word I will let down the net."*

— LUKE 5:5

"Launch out into the deep and let down your nets for a catch," Jesus told Simon Peter (Luke 5:4).

But they had already been fishing all night. And those seasoned fishermen had caught nothing. You can almost hear the polite yet condescending tone in Peter's voice. He may as well have said, "You are a good teacher, but I am the fisherman. You may know things about God, but I know fish."

FAITH OBEYS, REGARDLESS OF PERSONAL UNDERSTANDING.

But Peter didn't say any of that. Instead, he said, "Nevertheless, at Your word I will let down the net." And because he obeyed blindly—not because the request was logical but because it came from Jesus—they pulled up a net so loaded with fish, it nearly broke.

Our best efforts can lead to empty nets. But obedience can bring success beyond our wildest dreams. There were many years in my own ministry where I threw out nets and brought back nothing. But when the Lord purposed to fill the nets, they were suddenly filled to overflowing. It had nothing to do with my own abilities or my own power. It happened simply because God purposed it. And all the glory goes to Him.

God's command may seem contrary to your logic. But if you listen for direction and act in obedience, you will find the difference between failure and success. "Nevertheless, at Your word I will do it." Let those be words we live by.

―――

*Father, make us such obedient children that at the slightest whisper
from You, we act. Teach us to trust Your voice over our own.*

AMEN.

THE BALANCED LIFE

And Jesus answered and said to her, "Martha, Martha, you are
worried and troubled about many things. But one thing is needed,
and Mary has chosen that good part,
which will not be taken away from her."

— LUKE 10:41-42

Concerned over all the little details of dinner, Martha spent her night resenting her work and missing out on the most important task—sitting at the feet of Jesus. She was so busy serving Jesus, she had no time to spend with Jesus.

Serving the Lord is a wonderful and necessary thing. However, that service should come from a place of joy and excitement. We should never find ourselves complaining to Jesus about the things we do for Him.

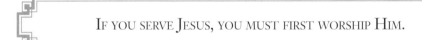

IF YOU SERVE JESUS, YOU MUST FIRST WORSHIP HIM.

In contrast to Martha, Mary "chose that good part." The good part was intimacy with Jesus. While Martha ran around the kitchen, Mary sat at His feet taking in every word.

Since both service and worship are necessary ingredients in the life of a believer, we are basically talking about the need for balance. The well-balanced life is one that manifests love for the Lord through service for the Lord, but which also includes time for fellowship and worship. Both are needed. Is your life balanced? Are you serving out of love, or obligation?

If you would serve Him, you must first worship Him. It is when we sit at His feet that we gain the strength we need for life. When we sit in worship before Him, He then guides us in our activities.

Father, thank You that whenever we drop to Your feet, You are
there waiting for us. Teach us, Lord. Tell us how we can serve
You—because we want to bless You.

IN JESUS' NAME, AMEN.

The Abundance of Things

*Take heed and beware of covetousness, for one's life does not consist
in the abundance of the things he possesses.*

— Luke 12:15

Two brothers had been fighting over their inheritance. One thought the other was trying to cheat him, so he asked Jesus to intervene. But Jesus refused to become involved in an argument over things. Instead, He warned them against covetousness. After sharing a parable and pointing out the care God gives the ravens and the lilies, He then concluded by saying, "Seek the kingdom of God, and all these things shall be added to you" (Luke 12:31).

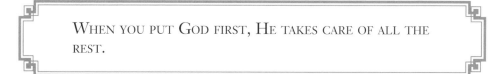

WHEN YOU PUT GOD FIRST, HE TAKES CARE OF ALL THE REST.

It is amazing how distorted and out of balance a person's life can get when they live only for material things. But when a person begins to follow after the things of the Spirit, their life comes into balance. Not only that, they gain peace, contentment, and joy they didn't have before.

Jesus said, "It is your Father's good pleasure to give you the kingdom" (Luke 12:32). But is that what you value? Is your interest in eternal things, or only in temporal, material things—things that are passing away?

You might be very successful. But no matter how much you may amass, your life does not consist in chasing after bodily appetites. It doesn't consist in the abundance of your possessions but in a real relationship with God, as your spirit is alive unto Him through your faith in Jesus.

———

*Father, help us not to learn the hard way the truths we need
to know. Help us live life with an open hand, not grasping this
world, but reaching toward Your kingdom.*

AMEN.

THE WAY UP

For whoever exalts himself will be humbled, and he who humbles himself will be exalted.

— LUKE 14:11

At the home of the Pharisee—where He had been invited for dinner—Jesus watched people maneuvering to get the places of importance around the table. Finally, He told them why that wasn't wise. "What if someone more honorable than you comes along and the host has to say to you, 'Sorry, fellow, you are in the wrong seat. Why don't you move down to a lower seat?'" Jesus then added, "Don't embarrass yourself. It is better that you take a lower seat, and let the host come to you and say, 'Why are you sitting down here? I'd like you to move to a better seat.'" Jesus concluded by saying, "Whoever exalts himself will be humbled, and he who humbles himself will be exalted" (Luke 14:11).

> SPIRITUALLY SPEAKING, THE WAY UP IS DOWN, AND THE WAY DOWN IS UP.

If you will humble yourself, you will be brought up. Take the lowest place and you will be invited to come higher. But if you take the highest place, you are apt to be asked to step down.

May God help us to live our lives as servants—conscious of the needs of others and willing to reach out and minister however we can. May we follow the example of our Lord, who took no thought to Himself, but lived a humble life of service to all.

Lord, we see how You laid aside Your glory to come to earth, live in lowliness, and die for us. We see that You have been exalted now to the highest place; that You are King of kings and Lord of lords. Teach us to follow Your example.

IN JESUS' NAME, AMEN.

THE RICHEST MAN

*Therefore if you have not been faithful in the unrighteous
mammon, who will commit to your trust the true riches?*

— LUKE 16:11

Jesus told of a servant who had begun squandering his master's goods upon himself. When the master heard rumors of this, he called the servant to account. The servant—surmising he would soon be out of a job—quickly used his master's resources to set himself up for the future he knew was coming.

Let's say you have fifty years left in which to enjoy the blessings God has given you. But if you use those things only for yourself, and don't consider the kingdom of God and the eternal future, you are going to be sorry. Though you may be well off now, you will spend eternity destitute.

Let me assure you that the poorest man in heaven is far better off than the richest man in hell. But God will one day call on each of us to account for how we used the things He placed at our disposal. If you are wise, you'll use these things for the kingdom of God.

Both heaven and earth have riches. Earth's riches are measured in bank accounts, portfolios, and in the heaps of possessions men spend their lives accumulating. Those riches will burn if moth and rust and thieves don't get to them first. Heaven's riches, though, are eternal. No fire can touch them. No moth or rust can damage them. No thief can steal them away. Whatever you deposit in heaven will be waiting, right there, for the day you enter those gates.

DEPOSIT YOUR RICHES CAREFULLY.

*Father, make us good stewards of what You have entrusted to us.
Give us Your perspective on what are true riches.*

IN JESUS' NAME, AMEN.

The Nine

*And one of them, when he saw that he was healed, returned,
and with a loud voice glorified God, and fell down on his face at
His feet, giving Him thanks. And he was a Samaritan. So Jesus
answered and said, "Were there not ten cleansed?
But where are the nine?"*

— Luke 17:15-17

If you were dying and without hope, and someone came along and healed you, don't you think the least you would want to do is say thank you? Jesus healed ten lepers. But only one returned to express his gratitude.

It is easy to look at this story and shake our heads at the ungrateful nine. But are we sometimes part of the nine? How often has God blessed us and we have grabbed the blessing and run, not looking back or looking up? How often has He kept us from close calls, and we have continued on our way without thanking Him?

MANY ARE QUICK TO BLAME GOD FOR EVERYTHING—
INSTEAD OF THANKING HIM.

"Oh, that men would give thanks to the LORD for His goodness, and for His wonderful works to the children of men!" (Psalm 107:8). God is so good to us, so worthy of our praise.

The nine are quick to blame God for the things that go wrong in their lives, but not quick enough to thank Him for the things that go right.

The nine are like the boy sliding down the side of the roof crying, "Oh Lord, help me!" When his pants get caught on a nail, he comes to a ripping stop. Looking up, he says, "Never mind, Lord, the nail caught me."

Are you with the one—or with the nine?

---

*Father, we come in Jesus' name to give thanks to You today for
Your goodness and for Your wonderful works to us.*

WATCH AND PRAY

Watch therefore, and pray always that you may be counted worthy
to escape all these things that will come to pass,
and to stand before the Son of Man.

— LUKE 21:36

God has been patient and long-suffering. He has put up with an awful lot of abuse, but the day is coming when the Lord will take His vengeance.

Jesus had just described for His disciples the great tribulation period, that time when God will unleash the forces of nature. Cataclysmic signs in the heavens will cause famine, pestilence, and tremendous earthquakes. But immediately after those events, Jesus said, "They will see the Son of Man coming in a cloud with power and great glory" (Luke 21:27).

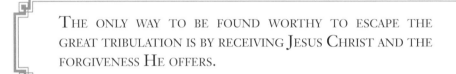

THE ONLY WAY TO BE FOUND WORTHY TO ESCAPE THE GREAT TRIBULATION IS BY RECEIVING JESUS CHRIST AND THE FORGIVENESS HE OFFERS.

As He was describing these events, Jesus instructed us to pray for two things. First, that we will be accounted worthy to escape the coming calamity, and secondly, that we might stand before the Son of Man.

The children of God have not been appointed to wrath but will stand in that glorious company in heaven singing the worthiness of the Lamb to take the scroll and to break the seals.

Jesus did warn in verse 34, "Take heed to yourselves, lest your hearts be weighed down with carousing, drunkenness, and cares of this life, and that Day come on you unexpectedly." Don't let life steal your attention. Don't be unprepared for His coming.

Be watching and praying—always.

———

Lord, our hope is built on nothing less than the blood of Jesus and
His righteousness. Deliver us from the wrath to come, we pray.

IN JESUS' NAME, AMEN.

Unfailing Faith

*And the Lord said, "Simon, Simon! Indeed, Satan has asked for
you, that he may sift you as wheat. But I have prayed for you, that
your faith should not fail; and when you have returned to Me,
strengthen your brethren."*

— Luke 22:31-32

Jesus chose Peter to be a leader in the church, and thus, Satan desired to destroy him. Satan always targets the leadership within the church, because he knows if he can destroy a leader, he destroys many.

But Jesus didn't pray that Satan had to leave Peter alone. Instead, He prayed that Peter's faith would not fail. We probably would have prayed, "Lord, keep Peter out of the sifter. Don't let him have any problems." But that would have kept Peter from the growth that comes through experiencing difficulty.

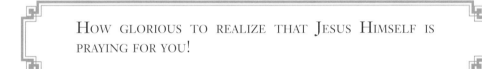

How glorious to realize that Jesus Himself is praying for you!

In John 17:20, Jesus includes you in His prayer. He said, "I do not pray for these alone, but also for those who will believe in Me through their word." If you have come to believe in Jesus as the Son of God, then that prayer was for you.

We, like Peter, may be defeated in a few of the battles along the way, but the ultimate victory belongs to Jesus who is praying for us that our faith will not fail. And when we come through in His strength, we can then turn and share understanding and compassion with those going through the same issues.

*Lord, we thank You that when we stumble, You lift us into Your
arms of love, dust us off, wash us, cleanse us,
and put us back on the path.*

In Jesus' name, amen.

DESTROY THIS TEMPLE

Jesus answered and said to them, "Destroy this temple, and in three days I will raise it up."
— JOHN 2:19

When Jesus walked into the temple and saw the disgraceful merchandising going on, He was so upset that He made a whip and began to drive out the moneychangers, overthrowing their tables and rebuking them. Of course, this upset the religious leaders who owned the concessions, and they demanded that Jesus show them some sign of His authority to do these things. He replied, "Destroy this temple, and in three days I will raise it up."

They thought He was referring to Herod's temple, but Jesus was talking about His own body. Jesus would later say of His life, "No one takes it from Me, but I lay it down of Myself. I have power to lay it down, and I have power to take it again" (John 10:18). That is quite a boast—a boast upon which the authenticity of the gospel rests.

> IF THE CRUCIFIED BODY OF JESUS HAD STAYED IN THE TOMB, THERE WOULD BE NO CHRISTIAN FAITH, NO CHURCH.

The gospel is predicated upon the resurrection of Jesus Christ from the dead. He did exactly what He said He would do. He rose from the dead, ministered to His disciples for forty days, then ascended into heaven where today He is at the right hand of the Father, making intercession for us. And one day soon He is coming to take us to be with Him.

Father, we thank You for the resurrection. It is the sign that authenticates all that Jesus said—that You are loving, forgiving, gracious, and merciful. Thank You for giving us that full, rich life as we walk with You.

IN JESUS' NAME, AMEN.

LIVING WATERS

*Jesus answered and said to her, "Whoever drinks of this water
will thirst again, but whoever drinks of the water
that I shall give him will never thirst."*

— JOHN 4:13-14

Deep within every man there is an intense thirst for God. As David said,
"My soul thirsts for You; my flesh longs for You in a dry and thirsty land
where there is no water" (Psalm 63:1).

Man tries to satisfy that thirst in different ways and through different experiences—drugs, alcohol, or, like the Samaritan woman, relationships. But those
things can't quench the thirst for God.

THE THIRST IN MAN IS A THIRST FOR GOD.

If you drink of the water from the wells of life, you will thirst again. It would
be wise to write that over each of your ambitions. "Go ahead, drink of that
water. But you will thirst again." Write that over every material thing you hope
to possess—the new car, new home, boat, or whatever. Write that over every
goal of your life. Achieve it, but you will surely thirst again.

When Jesus talked to the Samaritan woman about the living water, He was
talking about the only thing that can possibly satisfy the deep thirst of the soul—
a relationship with God.

Are you thirsty today? Forget the world's water. Drink deeply of the living
water—and find the satisfaction you long for.

*Lord, we thank You that You made a way for us to satisfy the deep
thirst of our soul. May we come, may we drink,
and find that satisfaction that our soul is seeking.*

IN JESUS' NAME, AMEN.

THE JESUS OF THE SCRIPTURES

You search the Scriptures, for in them you think you have eternal life; and these are they which testify of Me.

— JOHN 5:39

The Bible is all about Jesus. In fact, Jesus is the central, overriding, pivotal focus of Scripture. You can find Him in every page. "Behold, I have come—in the volume of the book it is written of Me—to do Your will, O God" (Hebrews 10:7).

God gave many scriptures in the Old Testament to describe the nature, the character, and the circumstances of the coming Messiah, so that when He came, there would be no question that He was the true Messiah. To help them recognize the Savior, God gave over 300 predictions and identification markers about His birth, birthplace, childhood, ministry, rejection, death and resurrection.

> LIVING FOR JESUS IS NOT A ONCE-A-WEEK KIND OF AN EXPERIENCE.

The Jews knew the Scriptures backwards and forwards. They had studied them diligently, faithfully. But Jesus said of them, "You search the Scriptures but you won't come to Me that you might have life." Knowing the Scriptures is not sufficient to receive the gift of eternal life. A lot of people have a false sense of security regarding their salvation, simply because they say that they believe God, but eternal life does not come from knowing the Bible—it comes by receiving the Jesus of the Scriptures.

Living for Jesus is a daily, hourly, minute-by-minute experience. It is yielding your life to Him and walking in fellowship with Him. It is falling in love with Him to the point where He becomes the very center and focus of your life.

Lord, we want to give You more than just a passing glance. We want to make You the very center and substance of our lives.

AMEN.

THIRSTY?

*If anyone thirsts, let him come to Me and drink. He who believes
in Me, as the Scripture has said, out of his heart
will flow rivers of living water.*

— JOHN 7:37-38

When Jesus said this, I believe that the disciples didn't really understand what He meant. But when John wrote this gospel years later, he had the advantage of hindsight. So in verse 39 he added his own commentary: "But this He spoke concerning the Spirit, whom those believing in Him would receive; for the Holy Spirit was not yet given."

> GOD DESIRES THAT OUR LIVES BE A VESSEL TO CON-
> TAIN THE SPIRIT OF GOD, AND THAT WE WOULD THEN
> CHANNEL GOD'S SPIRIT TO A THIRSTY WORLD AROUND
> US.

So often we act as sponges, soaking up all we can get, but without having any overflow. There is nothing left for those around us. God is not just interested in what He can do *in* you, but what He can do *through* you.

Paul wrote to the Galatians, "The fruit (or the issue) of the Spirit is love" (Galatians 5:22). The world hungers after true, divine, agape love. That is what the world needs to see in us. When your life overflows with the Spirit of God, then that is what issues forth from you. It issues forth like a torrent of living water, blessing all of those that are around you because of what God has done in you and is now doing through you.

———⊱⋅⊰———

*Lord, may we receive the fullness of Your Holy Spirit in our
lives until He flows forth from us like a torrent of living water,
bringing Your love and Your light to those around us.*

IN JESUS' NAME, AMEN.

Free Indeed

If you abide in My word, you are My disciples indeed. And you
shall know the truth, and the truth shall make you free.

— JOHN 8:31-32

People like to talk about freedom. But true freedom is not the freedom to do what you wish—it is the freedom *not* to do what is wrong. When Jesus sets you free, the freedom He gives is true freedom. It is the freedom not to do those things that were destructive to you and to those around you.

Some who are enslaved to sin wrongly believe they are free. But Jesus said, "Whoever commits sin is a slave to sin" (John 8:34). Whether it is an obvious sin, like drug and alcohol abuse, or a secret sin that no one knows about but you, sin has the power to grab a hold of you and keep you in its grip, helpless to extricate yourself.

GOD HAS GIVEN US A FREE WILL.

Paul said, "All things are lawful for me" (1 Corinthians 6:12). That is broad. But then he went on to say, "I will not be brought under the power of any." Oh yes, I have the freedom to do something, but if in the exercise of that freedom I am brought into bondage, then I am no longer free. I have exercised my freedom in such a way as to bring myself into slavery.

Maybe you find yourself bound by something today. You feel you can't get free. But when you come to know the truth—Jesus Christ—then the truth will make you free.

Father, thank You for that wonderful freedom that we have in
Christ Jesus. We are free to live as You would have us to live, free
to walk in fellowship with You in the power of the Spirit.

AMEN.

FAULT FINDERS VS. HEALERS

And His disciples asked Him, saying, "Rabbi, who sinned,
this man or his parents, that he was born blind?"

— JOHN 9:2

When an accident occurs, two types of emergency vehicles arrive on the scene. The first to arrive are usually the police. They try to determine who is at fault and, if necessary, give a citation to the guilty party. The paramedics arrive next. They really have no concern as to who is at fault—they just want to alleviate the pain and suffering.

The disciples passed by a man born blind. Like policemen, they wanted to immediately assess blame for the casualty. Jesus declared that neither the parents nor this man was at fault, but that the works of God might be made manifest in him when Jesus healed him.

> GOD HAS CALLED US TO BE PARAMEDICS RATHER THAN POLICEMEN.

How do you look at human tragedy? Do you come like a policeman, or like a paramedic? Jesus said that God did not send Him into the world to condemn the world, but that the world through Him might be saved.

Often a person's life is shattered because they are reaping the consequences of their own rebellion against God. Do you shake your finger in their face and say, "If you had not done this or that, you wouldn't be in this situation"? Do you have your codebook out, citing them for their violation of the law? Or do you come as a paramedic seeking to bind up their wounds?

Ours is not the responsibility of finding the reason for the suffering, but to seek to heal the damage that has been done, even as Jesus did.

Father, may we be Your witnesses,
doing Your work in this hurting world.

IN JESUS' NAME, AMEN.

PRAY, REASON, COMMIT

Now My soul is troubled, and what shall I say? "Father, save Me from this hour"? But for this purpose I came to this hour. Father, glorify Your name.
— JOHN 12:27-28

esus knew the cross was God's will. Yet as He faced the horrendous ordeal before Him, His heart was troubled. As He waited there in the garden, Jesus did three things that enabled Him to obey.

First, He prayed. What a wonderful example to us, for we too will face times of uncertainty or even fear, times when we need to cry out to the One who cares about all the details of our lives.

> WHEN YOU ARE TROUBLED BY CIRCUMSTANCES THAT YOU DON'T UNDERSTAND, FOLLOW JESUS' EXAMPLE.

Secondly, He reasoned. He talked it through and reasoned that the painful experience ahead of Him would work out God's eternal purposes. "For this purpose I came to this hour."

And then thirdly, He committed Himself to obedience. "Father, glorify Your name." In other words, "I am committed to bringing You glory, Father, regardless of what it costs Me."

Follow Jesus' example. Pray first. Prayer changes things. Sometimes, the thing that needs changing the most is our attitude. Prayer also gives us the strength to endure a trial and the capacity to accept it. Next—reason. Realize that God loves you supremely and is working out His eternal plan in your life. His plan may bring temporary discomfort, but it will also bring eternal good. And then thirdly, commit. "Have Your way, Lord. Use my life to bring glory to Your name."

Father, teach us to follow the example of Jesus when we face uncertain or frightening situations. Remind us to pray, to reason through the problem, and to commit ourselves to bringing You glory.

IN JESUS' NAME, AMEN.

PROMISES, PROMISES

Peter said to Him, "Lord, why can I not follow You now? I will lay down my life for Your sake."

— JOHN 13:37

Even while Peter was making this beautiful, heartfelt declaration of his devotion, Jesus knew that before the sun rose the following morning, Peter would deny Him three times.

It is so very easy to make a verbal commitment. But when it comes right down to where the rubber meets the road, we are not always faithful to those promises.

WORDS ARE CHEAP.

We make vows to God when we are trying to make a deal with Him, to get Him to acquiesce to our desires. "Lord, if You will do this for me, then I will do this for You." Or we make vows right after a failure. As we are getting up again, we say, "Lord, I will never do that again." Our words prove we are putting confidence right back in the flesh, but as long as we are still trusting ourselves, we are setting ourselves up for failure.

Only God knows whether or not we will keep our promises. As the psalmist said, "O LORD, You have searched me and known me. You know my sitting down and my rising up; You understand my thought afar off. You comprehend my path and my lying down, and are acquainted with all my ways" (Psalm 139:1-3).

Don't promise anything to God on the basis of your flesh, for your flesh will fail you. Promise only to do those things Jesus prompts you to do, and rely on Him for the strength to obey.

Father, let our every prayer reflect our complete dependence on You and our unfailing trust in Your sovereignty and wisdom.

IN JESUS' NAME, AMEN.

NATURAL FRUIT

I am the vine, you are the branches. He who abides in Me, and I
in him, bears much fruit; for without Me you can do nothing.
— JOHN 15:5

People would like to produce fruit apart from the vine. They think they might squeeze out a fruit or two by living good lives or by becoming better people. But the fact is, apart from Jesus, we can do nothing. It is only as we abide in Him that the Holy Spirit begins to form fruit in us—naturally.

What fruit does the Spirit produce? The fruit of the Spirit is agape love—deep, fervent love—love that suffers long and is kind; love that does not envy, does not exalt itself, does not behave in an unseemly manner, love that does not get cliquish, love that does not seeks its own. This is an amazing love. It's love that is not easily provoked, love that doesn't think evil of others, love that bears all burdens, love that believes all things, love that never fails.

> IT IS IMPOSSIBLE FOR YOU TO PRODUCE, MIMIC, OR CONJURE UP THE LOVE OF THE HOLY SPIRIT.

If God's Spirit dwells in you, then the natural result will be the fruit of agape love. We are impatient for that fruit. We would like to plant an apple tree today and eat the apples tomorrow. But fruit does not grow overnight. Do not be impatient with God and with the Holy Spirit as He develops fruit in your life. It will develop in His time—and what a beautiful day that will be when you bring forth fruit.

Thank You, Father, for the indwelling of Your Holy Spirit.
Lord, teach us to be patient as the fruit of Your Spirit
begins to develop in our lives.
AMEN.

SET APART

Sanctify them by Your truth. Your word is truth.
— JOHN 17:17

The word "sanctify" means to be set apart. In the temple, vessels were set apart to be used exclusively in the worship of God. They were to be used for no other purpose. And that is what sanctification means for us—that we might be set apart from the world and freed from the world's influences, that we might be committed and dedicated unto Him, that we might be God's own property.

OUR LIVES ARE BOMBARDED BY SIN ON A DAILY BASIS.

Every time you turn on the television or the radio, every time you step into a mall or a grocery store, seductions and enticements try to draw you after the things God has declared to be impure. We need to partake of the Word daily in order to counteract these influences of the world. At the end of each day, let the Word of God cleanse you from all of the junk you have been exposed to.

As Jesus said in John 15:3, "You are already clean because of the word which I have spoken to you." It is His Word that cleanses away the filth we have been exposed to each day.

Because we love God, we should want to fulfill His desires. If He desires that we be kept from the world, set apart, then we should want that too. We should be diligent to make our stand against evil. And if God says that the Word is what cleanses us, then we should go to the Word daily.

Father, we thank You that You have loved us and have taken us out of the world and given us heavenly citizenship. Set us apart, Lord, through Your Word.

IN JESUS' NAME, AMEN.

It is Finished

So when Jesus had received the sour wine, He said, "It is finished!"
And bowing His head, He gave up His spirit.
— John 19:30

When Jesus cried, "It is finished," it was not a cry of defeat but of glorious victory. Through the cross, Jesus defeated Satan's power to enslave man, to destroy man, and to separate man from God. Through the cross, Jesus made a way for man to approach God and to live in fellowship with God once again.

We have been given the power to live the life God wants us to live. We have been given the power to be like Him—to be restored to the image of God. That is God's desire and purpose for your life.

> THE POWERFUL GRIP THAT SIN ONCE HELD OVER YOU,
> OVER ME, HAS BEEN BROKEN.

God wants to restore that which was lost in the garden of Eden. To that end, God's Spirit works in our lives day by day, conforming us, molding us, shaping us back into God's ultimate intention for man, that we might live in fellowship with God and reflect His love and grace and kindness and mercy to this dark world in which we live. The barriers that once held us away from God have been removed. Now that the work of redemption is a finished work, we are able to live in fellowship with the Lord.

The work is over. It is finished. Jesus conquered sin, death, hell, and the grave. He conquered Satan. And as the result, we can now experience the great blessedness of living with and for our God.

———⟶⟐⟵———

Father, may we take full advantage of the time You have given us
in this life to know You, to serve You, and to love You.
In Jesus' name, amen.

THE RESURRECTION

But Mary stood outside by the tomb weeping, and as she wept she stooped down and looked into the tomb.

— JOHN 20:11

Scripture captures the very moment when heartache turned to hope. Mary—seeing the stone rolled away from the front of the tomb—stoops down and looks inside. Her weeping will turn to temporary confusion, no doubt, but what she doesn't yet realize is this is the day when God would give "beauty for ashes, the oil of joy for mourning, the garment of praise for the spirit of heaviness" (Isaiah 61:3).

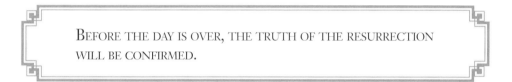

BEFORE THE DAY IS OVER, THE TRUTH OF THE RESURRECTION WILL BE CONFIRMED.

Jesus will appear to Mary and the disciples, and they will discover that all His words were true—that He is indeed the Son of God, that He is the Lamb of God who gave Himself as a ransom for sin, that He is all that He claimed to be, that He is the resurrection and the life, the way and the truth.

On this new day, this first day of the week, something new was born. The bridge between man and God was gapped, and a new relationship was made possible. Because He lives, we can live. Because He conquered the grave, we need no longer fear death. Because He defeated sin, we can be free from sin's clutches.

There in front of that empty tomb, Mary experienced the truth of the psalmist's words: "Weeping may endure for a night, but joy comes in the morning" (Psalm 30:5).

Father, we thank You for the empty tomb, and for the glorious hope it brings. We thank You that because Jesus conquered the grave, we need not fear death.

AMEN.

Do You Love Me More Than These?

So when they had eaten breakfast, Jesus said to Simon Peter,
"Simon, son of Jonah, do you love Me more than these?"
— JOHN 21:15

After a futile night of fishing, a man on the shore told the disciples to throw the net on the other side of the ship. Immediately the nets were filled; so much so that they could not draw them in. Realizing the man was Jesus, Peter dove in and swam to Him. The other disciples followed in a little boat dragging the net full of fish, and when they got there, they found that Jesus had already prepared breakfast.

Sitting around the fire, Jesus asked Peter, "Do you love Me more than these?"

PUT THE LORD FIRST AND FOREMOST IN YOUR LIFE.

Perhaps Jesus was looking at those fish flopping in the net, probably the largest haul Peter had ever caught. So Jesus may have meant, "Do you love Me more than the pinnacle of success in your career?"

If Jesus looked you straight in the eye and asked, "Do you love Me more than these?" What things in your life vie for your attention and draw your love away from Him? Is it your goals, your career, a relationship, pleasures, television? And what would your answer be?

The Lord longs for your love. He wants to be first and foremost in your life. May God help us that we will be able to respond, "Lord, You know all things; You know that I love You supremely."

Father, so many things fight for our attention. Help us to put You
above everything else. May our love for You exceed
all other loves in our life.

IN JESUS' NAME, AMEN.

POWER

But you shall receive power when the Holy Spirit has come upon you; and you shall be witnesses to Me in Jerusalem, and in all Judea and Samaria, and to the end of the earth.

— ACTS 1:8

In this conversation, just before His ascension, Jesus is declaring to His disciples that they will soon embark on a seemingly impossible task. They are to go into all the world and preach the good news of God to every creature.

They couldn't fulfill this task in their own strength. But Jesus promised that they would receive power. The word in the Greek is *dunamis*, from which we get our English word "dynamic." They would receive dynamic power, which would enable them to be the witnesses God wanted them to be.

THE POWER OF GOD IS THE SAME TODAY AS IT WAS YESTERDAY.

God's power still sets men free. It still brings hope to an otherwise hopeless world. Today, we are the witnesses Jesus sends out. The world is still hopeless, and still hostile. But through us, the love of the Holy Spirit conquers hatred, strife, and bitterness. Through us, the power of the Holy Spirit makes us shine like lights in the darkness.

May your life be a witness for God. I pray that others see Christ shining in you, and that they are drawn by your testimony. May they experience the love of Jesus through your words and your actions, as you walk in the dynamics of the Spirit.

God, help us to receive from You that empowering of Your Spirit in order that we might fulfill the task that You have set before us.

IN JESUS' PRECIOUS NAME, AMEN.

NO OTHER NAME

*Nor is there salvation in any other, for there is no other name
under heaven given among men by which we must be saved.*
— ACTS 4:12

This claim by Peter—made after he healed a lame man in Jesus' name—was first made by Jesus Himself. "I am the way, the truth, and the life," He said. "No one comes to the Father except through Me" (John 14:6). Today we hear people say, "All paths lead to God," but that contradicts what Jesus said. He said, "I am the door of the sheep. All who ever came before Me are thieves and robbers" (John 10:7-8).

These exclusive claims irritate a lot of people. They get upset if you declare that He is the only way. They call you a bigot, or narrow-minded. People would like to think that all roads lead to heaven. They would like to think they can live as they please and abide by their own rules. But God has set the rules for mankind. And the Word of God declares that there is only one way by which a man can be saved.

> YOU CAN'T BE SAVED BY BEING GOOD, RELIGIOUS, OR SINCERE.

You can't be saved by keeping the law. The Bible says, "By the works of the law no flesh shall be justified" (Galatians 2:16).

If the power of the name of Jesus can make a lame man walk, then the power of the name of Jesus can cleanse a person from their sins. No other name under heaven has such power—none but Jesus Christ.

———⋙⋘———

*Father, thank You for Jesus. His name is so sweet and brings such
comfort and hope to us. Thank You that You have
provided salvation through His precious name.*

IN JESUS' NAME, AMEN.

FIGHTING AGAINST GOD

But if it is of God, you cannot overthrow it—lest you even be
found to fight against God.
— ACTS 5:39

Arrested again. The disciples' bold testimony of Jesus had brought them once again before the religious council. Some within the council were so angered that they suggested the disciples be put to death. But then the respected Rabbi Gamaliel spoke up and urged the council to take an easier course of action towards these men. He pointed out that if the disciples' plan was of men, it would come to nothing—but if it was of God, they would be fighting a futile battle.

How foolish to fight against the Lord! Yet how many try to do so—to their own detriment. As Isaiah tells us, "Woe to him who strives with his Maker!" (45:9).

> WHEN YOU FIGHT AGAINST GOD, YOU FIGHT AGAINST YOUR OWN GOOD.

When Gamaliel gave his advice, Saul (later known as Paul) was there in that council. And yet he didn't give heed, because Paul later went out and tried to fight against God. Determined to stamp out the influence of the church, Paul headed for Damascus. And it was there that he encountered the Lord, who asked, "Saul, Saul, why are you persecuting Me?" (Acts 9:4).

No one loves you the way God does. He wants only good things for you. His plan for your life is far superior to yours. If you have been fighting against Him, the wisest thing you could do is surrender. Stop kicking against the goads. Yield yourself to God and let Him begin to work out the beautiful plan He has for your life.

Father, may we never be guilty of fighting against You.
May we always be pliable in Your hands.
AMEN.

THE GOD WHO SEES AND HEARS

I have surely seen the oppression of My people who are in Egypt; I have heard their groaning and have come down to deliver them.
— ACTS 7:34

Standing before the religious council in Jerusalem, Stephen reminds them of the history of their nation, and of how God called Moses to go to the pharaoh to seek the deliverance of the people. God declared to Moses, "I have surely seen the oppression of My people who are in Egypt ... I know their sorrows" (Exodus 3:7).

Sometimes our concept of God puts Him so far out in the universe that we imagine Him to be an impersonal force. We think He is so far removed from man that He really has little concern for His creation. Or we assume that God is unmindful of our pain or our troubles. "Lord, I have cried out, but You didn't hear. You must not be listening." But God is both listening and watching. He is not absent. "I have seen," He assures us.

The Israelites must have wondered why it took God so long to answer their cries for help. We wonder the same thing. We want immediate responses to our prayers, but we must learn what the Israelites learned: What we perceive as late, God perceives as right on time.

> GOD IS NOT IN A HURRY TO ACCOMPLISH HIS WORK. HE IS WAITING FOR THE PERFECT TIME, THE OPPORTUNE MOMENT.

How blessed we are to serve the true and living God, the Creator of the heavens and the earth—the God who sees, the God who hears, and the God who helps in our time of need!

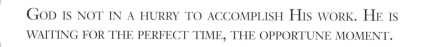

Thank You, Lord, for revealing Yourself to us so that we can know You and serve You.
IN JESUS' NAME, AMEN.

Step by Step

Now an angel of the Lord spoke to Philip, saying, "Arise and go toward the south along the road which goes down from Jerusalem to Gaza." This is desert.

— ACTS 8:26

God was doing a great work in Samaria. Through Philip, multitudes came to the Lord. Many were healed of demons. The lame and the paralyzed were healed. But one day, the angel of the Lord told Philip to leave Samaria and head toward the desert.

That seems like an illogical move. Why would God ask him to leave a place of such tremendous work and go to a desert area, where there was likely no one around? Philip must have wondered what was in God's mind. But Scripture gives us no indication that he questioned God. Instead, Philip obeyed.

GOD WANTS US TO WALK BY FAITH, SO HE DOESN'T EXPLAIN HIS ENTIRE PLAN TO US AT ONCE.

Philip only knew to go, so go he went. Along the road, he encountered a chariot, whose passenger was reading the book of Isaiah. The Holy Spirit told Philip to go near and overtake the chariot, so Philip did so. And once he began talking with the Ethiopian in the chariot, Philip began to understand why God had led him into the desert. The traveler Philip encountered was on a search for God, and Philip was privileged to share Jesus with him.

God leads us step by step, one move of obedience and trust upon another. We don't have to have the whole picture at once. We just have to take the steps He asks us to take.

Trust Him. It will all be clear later.

Father, help us to follow You and trust what You are doing in our lives.

IN JESUS' NAME, AMEN.

HE IS OUR PEACE

The word which God sent to the children of Israel, preaching peace through Jesus Christ—He is Lord of all.

— ACTS 10:36

At the Lord's bidding, Peter delivered this message to Cornelius, who was a Roman centurion … and a Gentile. Cornelius needed to hear that the gift sent to the Jews—peace through Jesus Christ—was sent also to the Gentiles.

In order to have peace within yourself—in order to calm the war inside and rid yourself of turmoil, anxiety, uncertainty, and fear—you must first have peace with God.

ARE YOU IN NEED OF PEACE TODAY? GOD WANTS TO GIVE IT TO YOU THROUGH HIS SON JESUS CHRIST.

Is there turmoil between you and someone else? God wants to establish peace between you and your neighbors, between you and your co-workers, between you and your loved ones. But you will never find peace with your fellow man until you first establish peace between you and your God. And that peace can come only through Jesus.

Jesus said, "Peace I leave with you, My peace I give to you; not as the world gives do I give to you. Let not your heart be troubled, neither let it be afraid" (John 14:27). The psalmist said, "The LORD will bless His people with peace" (Psalm 29:11).

The message of the gospel is the message of peace—the peace that passes understanding, the perfect peace that comes to that man whose mind has become fixed on the Lord because he trusts in Him.

Father, help us come to the end of ourselves so we can surrender to You and accept the peace You want to give us.

IN JESUS' PRECIOUS NAME WE PRAY, AMEN.

WITHSTANDING GOD

If therefore God gave them the same gift as He gave us when we
believed on the Lord Jesus Christ,
who was I that I could withstand God?

— ACTS 11:17

Peter, by a direct commandment from Jesus Christ, had violated the traditions of the Jews by going into the house of a Gentile and eating with the family. The early church council demanded an explanation. Peter said, "Look, God did this. I didn't even touch them. While I was talking, God decided to give them the Holy Spirit. And who am I to stand against God?"

HOW FOOLISH IT IS TO TRY TO LIMIT GOD!

Even today, many try to withstand or stand against the Lord and His work. Some people resist spiritual manifestations of any kind. Others, because of their pre-suppositional stances, have consigned the work of the Holy Spirit to just a certain period of church history. They will tell you after that point in time, the gifts ceased to function. I read not long ago that a certain denomination has begun dismissing some of its churches because they permitted certain gifts of the Spirit to operate.

What a blessing it is to yield fully to God, to let Him work freely in your life, and to receive all He has for you. If tradition has built up barriers in your mind against the gifts or against spiritual manifestations, ask God to remove those barriers to your faith. Don't let tradition rob you of something beautiful God may want to do in and through you.

Father, may we never be guilty of standing against Your work.
Help us to keep ourselves open to You, that we might not miss
a blessing You want to bring us.

IN JESUS' NAME, AMEN.

CLEAVE TO THE LORD

When he came and had seen the grace of God, he was glad, and encouraged them all that with purpose of heart they should continue with the Lord.

— ACTS 11:23

The church in Jerusalem decided to send Barnabas to Antioch in order to get a firsthand report of this move of the Spirit that was taking place in this Gentile city. Once there, Barnabas exhorted them to cleave to the Lord.

Many people start their Christian walk with great zeal and fervor. But as time passes, their love for the Lord begins to wax cold. Their zeal for the things of Christ lessens. And the world starts to take hold of their lives again.

STICKING CLOSELY TO JESUS IS NOT EASY.

As Christians, we find ourselves opposed to the world, to the flesh, and to the devil. The flesh will rebel against some of the demands of the Spirit, and the devil will be there to exploit the weakness of your flesh and to plant doubts in your mind. But the rewards of sticking close to Jesus are so great. Oh, the joy of living in close fellowship with Him, the thrill of seeing Him work in your life and doing for you the things which you recognize you can't even do for yourself!

Cleave closely to God. Don't let anything lure you from His side. You need the strength and the help that He gives. Purpose in your heart that you will stick close to Him—the closer, the better.

Lord, may we commit ourselves this day to obey Your commands and to follow You, no matter where You choose to take us. Keep our zeal burning brightly.

IN JESUS' NAME, AMEN.

WHY?

Now about that time Herod the king stretched out his hand to harass some from the church. Then he killed James the brother of John with the sword.

— ACTS 12:1-2

Why did God miraculously deliver Peter, yet allow Herod to kill James? Why is life so full of sorrow? Why does God allow righteous people to suffer?

God doesn't give us answers to those "whys." And when there is something we don't know, we must rely on what we do know. What we do know is that God is good. We know that God loves us supremely. We know that God is sovereign, that He is on the throne, and that nothing happens without His permission. We know that all things are working together for good to those who love God and are called according to His purpose. We know that God's thoughts towards us are good, not evil; that He is working out an eternal plan for our lives.

WE DON'T ALWAYS UNDERSTAND THE REASON WHY GOD PERMITS SUFFERING.

When pain or trauma comes and we have no answers for why we are suffering, we can hold tightly to the knowledge that "the sufferings of this present time are not worthy to be compared with the glory which shall be revealed in us" (Romans 8:18). Sovereignty is working out an eternal purpose through our circumstances.

We don't always get to know God's reasons for the things that He permits. But we don't need to know why. We need to know Jesus.

Father, even though we don't always know why things are happening to us, we know You. We trust You. We believe in Your goodness and in the great love You have for us. Teach us to trust You more and more.

IN JESUS' NAME, AMEN.

SAVED BY GRACE

*But we believe that through the grace of the Lord Jesus Christ
we shall be saved in the same manner as they.*

— ACTS 15:11

A problem developed in the early church over the subject of salvation. The question at hand was: What does it take to be saved? The Jews believed that salvation was for the Jews only. They believed a Gentile's only hope for salvation was by becoming a Jew, which meant fulfilling the rite of circumcision and baptism.

Those who believed that put a heavy burden on the Gentile believers. So the first church council was established to answer the issue. What does one have to do to be saved? Are we saved by faith alone, or is it a combination of both faith and works?

SALVATION IS THROUGH GRACE—THROUGH JESUS ALONE.

Many today still teach that salvation is through faith and works. Most of the cult groups and even many churches require certain works for salvation. But the Bible teaches that salvation is through faith alone. Works don't save you. Works simply demonstrate the genuineness of your faith. If you truly believe in Jesus Christ, there will be changes in your life. You will no longer practice sin. You'll have a changed attitude and a changed heart. But those good works don't save you. The only one who can save you is Jesus Christ.

Jesus said, "This is the work of God, that you believe in Him whom He sent" (John 6:29). God has made salvation through faith so that no one can glory in what they have done. And that is what the early church concluded. Salvation is through grace—through Jesus Christ alone.

———⋙●⋘———

*Thank You, Father, that the cross was the finished work
for our salvation. Lord, draw us to Your love.*

IN THE NAME OF JESUS, AMEN.

Songs in the Night

But at midnight Paul and Silas were praying and singing hymns to God, and the prisoners were listening to them.

— Acts 16:25

While in Philippi, Paul and Silas were stripped of their clothes, beaten, and put in the stocks in the inner part of the prison. Can you imagine a more dismal plight?

What do you think that you would do under those circumstances? What would your thoughts be? You had only wanted to serve God. You had felt the call to take the gospel to Macedonia, and now your back is throbbing with pain; your hands, feet, and neck are fastened in the stocks. Your future is uncertain. You don't know how serious the charges are, and you don't know how long they are going to keep you in prison.

In this very uncomfortable situation, Paul and Silas did the only thing that made sense to them: they prayed and sang praises to God. Though their bodies were bound, their spirits were free. Instead of moaning and complaining, they turned their dark dungeon into a house of worship. Rejoicing lifted their spirits. The more Paul and Silas focused on the Lord, the smaller their problem became.

> SINGING TAKES OUR THOUGHTS OFF OF OURSELVES AND FOCUSES THEM ON THE LORD.

The next time you find yourself shackled by worry or confusion or pain, look up. Take your eyes off your problem and place them on God. Sing to your Creator—and watch your dark prison change into a house of praise.

Father, we thank You for the songs that You put in our hearts— songs of joy and blessing and rejoicing in Your goodness.

IN THE NAME OF JESUS, AMEN.

THE CURE FOR FEAR

*Now the Lord spoke to Paul in the night by a vision, "Do not be
afraid, but speak, and do not keep silent; for I am with you …"*
— ACTS 18:9-10

Everywhere Paul preached Jesus Christ, the people rose up against him. He
had been beaten, imprisoned, and stoned. In Thessalonica he had to sneak
out of the town at night. Those in Berea drove him out of town. But these were
all fairly civil places. Corinth, however—where Paul now finds himself—was a
rough, wicked city. No doubt Paul felt anxious. No doubt he worried about the
Jews who held his fate in their hands. It was while in this state of fear that Jesus
spoke to Paul in a vision. "Don't be afraid … for I am with you."

THEREIN LIES THE CURE FOR FEAR—THE REALIZATION OF
GOD'S PRESENCE.

Paul wrote to the Romans, "If God is for us, who can be against us?" (Romans
8:31) David said, "The LORD is on my side; I will not fear. What can man do to
me?" (Psalm 118:6). The Lord said to the prophet Isaiah, "Fear not, for I am
with you; be not dismayed, for I am your God. I will strengthen you, yes, I will
help you, I will uphold you with My righteous right hand" (Isaiah 41:10).

Are you going through uncertain times? Are you troubled about the future?
Remember those promises. Remember the One who said, "I will never leave you
nor forsake you" (Hebrews 13:5). You face nothing alone. Your God is with you.

———

*Father, we thank You for the comfort of Your presence with us in
the midst of the dark nights, in the midst of the hours of
discouragement, and in times of fear.*
AMEN.

ACCEPTANCE

So when he would not be persuaded, we ceased, saying,
"The will of the Lord be done."
— ACTS 21:14

Everywhere Paul went, the Holy Spirit warned him that suffering, bonds, and imprisonment awaited him in Jerusalem. Paul's friends, upon hearing these prophecies, cried and begged Paul not to go. But he answered by saying, "I am ready not only to be bound, but also to die at Jerusalem for the name of the Lord Jesus" (Acts 21:13). Seeing his determination, they said, "The will of the Lord be done."

> ACCEPTANCE OF GOD'S WILL IS THE ONLY PATH TO TRUE PEACE. WITHOUT THAT ACCEPTANCE, THERE IS ONLY TURMOIL AND STRUGGLE WITHIN.

Sometimes people are reluctant to commit themselves to God's will because they fear He will make them do something they don't want to do. But that's not how God works. God reveals His will beautifully by aligning the desires of our heart with His.

God's plan for our lives is far superior to anything we could ever devise. He sees beyond our trials to the eternal good He will accomplish through those trials. With God, the end does justify the means. If a little hardship and suffering now will work a good end in our lives, then God will allow the suffering for the moment.

As David said, "I delight to do Your will, O my God" (Psalm 40:8). When we really come to know God, His will becomes our will; His delight becomes our delight.

Father, our tendency is to seek the easier, less painful path. But
You know what is best for us. We offer our desires,
that You would refine them and make them Your own.

IN JESUS' NAME, AMEN.

KNOWING GOD'S WILL

Then he said, "The God of our fathers has chosen you that you
should know His will ..."
— ACTS 22:14

In Jerusalem, Paul told the Jews of his conversion on the Damascus Road, how he was temporarily blinded as the result of the brilliant light, and how he received his sight when Ananias came and laid hands on him. Ananias then told Paul that God had chosen him that he should know the will of God.

This applies to you and me as well. Because He loves you, God has chosen you that you should know His will.

Do you know what God has purposed and planned for you? This should matter to you, because everything you do that is separate from the will of God will pass away.

DO YOU KNOW WHAT THE WILL OF GOD IS FOR YOUR LIFE?

We can get so involved in just getting ourselves through day-to-day living that we don't take eternity into consideration. But you have only one life and it will soon be past; and only what you do for Christ is going to last.

How can you know God's will for your life specifically? You discover God's specific, individual purpose for you by "being transformed by the renewing of your mind, that you may prove what is that good and acceptable and perfect will of God" (Romans 12:2). When you offer your body to God as an instrument willing to be used for His work, when you desire God's plans above your own, then your life will become a progressive manifestation of God's will.

Father, thank You for choosing us to spend eternity with You.
Help us to look at our lives in view of eternity
and always seek to do Your will.

AMEN.

IN THE STORM

But not long after, a tempestuous head wind arose,
called Euroclydon.
— ACTS 27:14

Through no cause of his own, Paul landed right in the midst of a vicious storm. He had warned the captain of the ship not to sail. But the captain didn't listen.

We sometimes wrongly think that because we serve the Lord, we should enjoy smooth sailing all the way. Surely the Lord will calm the seas for us, and send a soft wind to fill our sails. Not so! Jesus does not promise to spare you from the storms, but He has promised to be with you in the storms.

STORMS SERVE A PURPOSE—THEY SERVE GOD'S PURPOSE.

When those storms hit, we wonder if we will survive them. Paul probably wondered the same. But the Lord spoke words of encouragement to Paul as He stood by him in the storm. He told Paul that he would survive, because God had a mission for him.

The real purpose of Paul's storm would not be revealed until later. And that's so often the case in our lives. When our seas are rough, we question the probability of our survival. It is then we need to remember the Lord's words: "Do not be afraid" (Acts 27:24). In other words, "Cheer up. It's not over. I have a plan for you."

He does have a plan. He has not forgotten you—in fact, He is right there with you, riding out the waves. And when the storm is past and the clouds part again, you will see the reason for the storm.

Father, we thank You that You are with us in the storms.
For You promised that You would never leave us nor forsake us.
Use those tempests for Your purposes and Your glory.

IN JESUS' NAME, AMEN.

GOD'S GOOD NEWS

For I am not ashamed of the gospel of Christ, for it is the power of
God to salvation for everyone who believes,
for the Jew first and also for the Greek.
— ROMANS 1:16

In Paul's early years, he was caught up in a religious system where man sought to be justified before God by keeping the law. But the law was never intended to make man righteous before God. The law was intended to show man what a sinner he was, and to make the whole world guilty before God. So when Paul came to know the truth—when he encountered Jesus Christ and found salvation based on His righteousness and not the righteousness of man—Paul happily threw away the false notions of good works, and became eager to share this good news with others.

THE GOSPEL SETS MEN FREE.

"It is the power of God to salvation." What a joy it is to see lives transformed by this good news. It shines light in the darkness and breaks the bondage of sin.

This power, this good news of salvation, is not for the Jews exclusively but is for everyone who believes. It is for the whole world.

Oh, what a glorious message of hope and salvation we have received! May we not keep this news to ourselves; may we never be ashamed of the truth we have received. May we, like Paul, be ready to proclaim the gospel of Jesus Christ to the needy world in which we live.

Father, we thank You for this glorious gospel whereby we have
been cleansed from our sins. We pray for those who do not yet
know this wonderful good news of Your love
and Your offer of forgiveness.
IN JESUS' NAME, AMEN.

SEPTEMBER 7

A MATTER OF THE HEART

For he is not a Jew who is one outwardly, nor is circumcision that which is outward in the flesh; but he is a Jew who is one inwardly; and circumcision is that of the heart, in the Spirit, not in the letter; whose praise is not from men but from God.

— ROMANS 2:28-29

Y ou can say all the right things and still be far from God. That is because God is interested in the heart.

Outwardly, the Jews kept the law. But inwardly, they violated it. God addressed this inconsistency through Isaiah the prophet, who told them, "These people draw near with their mouths and honor Me with their lips, but have removed their hearts far from Me, and their fear toward Me is taught by the commandment of men" (Isaiah 29:13).

IF YOU CONTINUE LIVING AFTER THE FLESH, NO RITUAL CAN SAVE YOU.

What Paul is telling the Jews is that circumcision is worthless if you continue to live after the flesh.

The same is true within the church. Some trust the ritual of baptism for their salvation, rather than a living relationship with Jesus. But baptism is only a symbol of the old life being buried and the new life being raised.

You may go to church, you may sing all the songs, you may know the Word and say an occasional "Amen." But none of that makes you a child of God. He sees your heart. He knows if the two of you are enjoying the relationship of a Parent and child.

—————

Father, help us to have a pure heart and to love You wholeheartedly.

IN JESUS' NAME, AMEN.

SEPTEMBER

KEYS TO FAITH

And not being weak in faith, he did not consider his own body,
already dead.... He did not waver at the promise of God through
unbelief, but was strengthened in faith, giving glory to God,
and being fully convinced that what He had promised
He was also able to perform.
— ROMANS 4:19-21

Whenever the writers of the Bible wanted to give a classic example of a person with faith, they pointed to Abraham. In fact, Abraham is called "the father of the faith."

The first key to Abraham's faith is that he did not consider his or Sarah's age to be an obstacle to God. That is, he did not limit God's ability to override human difficulty. In contrast, that is often the first thing we consider. We often apply our own limitations to God.

Secondly, he did not waver at any of God's promises. Here is a good motto: "If God said it, I believe it." The Bible is so rich with promise that you can always find one that fits your present need. God covers all the bases—and you can trust what He says.

Thirdly, Abraham gave glory to God. He praised God even before seeing any evidence that God would keep His promise. Why? Because faith believes that God is able to perform whatever He has promised.

FAITH BELIEVES AND REJOICES WHILE WAITING.

Though it took a miracle to do so, God did keep His word to Abraham. And He will keep His word to you. One day you will see the fulfillment of His promises to you if you will just follow the keys to faith.

Father, we thank You that what You have promised You are able
to perform. Help us, Lord, that we might truly stand
upon Your promises.
AMEN.

CONSCIOUS OF GRACE

*Moreover the law entered that the offense might abound. But
where sin abounded, grace abounded much more …*

— ROMANS 5:20

At times when I have failed miserably, I have thought, "When will I ever learn? I have blown it again." But it is often in that place of misery and self-condemnation that God chooses to do something outstandingly glorious for me. Conscious of His merciful grace, I can't help but respond with, "Oh Lord, I love You!"

TRUE PRAISE RISES SPONTANEOUSLY FROM THE HEART, RECOGNIZING GOD'S GOODNESS AND GRACE.

Take in the amazing fact that God loves you and has provided forgiveness for your sins. Meditate again on the truth that salvation comes not through your own goodness, your own ability to keep the law, or by earning the favor of God, but by simply believing on His Son, who came to take your guilt and bring you into the family of God.

Because of the obedient sacrifice of Jesus, you can have victory over your flesh. Because of Jesus, you need not fear death. You've been freed from the bondage of sin. You have been redeemed. You have the Holy Spirit—a Protector, a Guide, a Teacher, a Comforter. You have the body of Christ. You have a Father. You have His mercy and forgiveness. You have the promise of an eternal home. And it is all because of His grace.

In light of all that, what is your response today? Don't you feel like praising Him?

*Father, we are amazed at Your forgiveness, love, mercy, and grace.
We thank You that even when we fail miserably, You are there to
pick us up, wash us, and help us start again. We love You, Lord.*

IN JESUS' NAME, AMEN.

WHO SHALL DELIVER ME?

*For the good that I will to do, I do not do; but the evil I will not to
do, that I practice. O wretched man that I am!
Who will deliver me from this body of death?*

— ROMANS 7:19, 24

We have all experienced the struggle Paul describes in this passage. In our hearts we know what's right. We know exactly what we are supposed to do, and exactly what we are not supposed to do. And most of the time we try hard to do what is right, but it is then we find that a perverse law in our flesh is at work against us, and in the end, we don't do the things we know we should. In our minds we serve God, but our flesh keeps coming up short.

> WE NEED TO FIND HELP OUTSIDE OF OURSELVES AND
> LOOK TO JESUS CHRIST.

As Paul is explaining the dilemma, he says, "O wretched man that I am! Who will deliver me?" And with that cry, we see the answer. The answer doesn't lie within us. We can't do it. In this same chapter, Paul says, "In me (that is, in my flesh) nothing good dwells" (7:18). We need to find help outside of ourselves.

Paul then responds to his own question, "Thank God—through Jesus Christ" (7:25).

Recognizing the weakness of our flesh, God provided the answer for us—for you. You can't obey in your own strength. But you can do all things through Jesus Christ, and through the power of the Holy Spirit. With their help, you can be the person God wants you to be.

*Father, we acknowledge our need, and we recognize our inability.
Thank You for empowering us through Your Holy Spirit. May we
abide in You so that we do not fulfill the desires of our flesh.*

IN JESUS' NAME, AMEN.

WHO SHALL CONDEMN US?

*Who is he who condemns? It is Christ who died, and furthermore
is also risen, who is even at the right hand of God,
who also makes intercession for us.*

— ROMANS 8:34

"Who is he who condemns?" Answering his own question, Paul said, "It isn't Jesus Christ; He died for you. In fact, He is at the right hand of the Father making intercession for you." Jesus is doing the opposite of condemning you—He is interceding for you!

When Jesus spoke with Nicodemus, He said, "God did not send His Son into the world to condemn the world, but that the world through Him might be saved. He who believes in Him is not condemned" (John 3:17-18). Romans 8:1 says it again: "There is therefore now no condemnation to those who are in Christ Jesus."

JESUS DOESN'T CONDEMN YOU—HE'S INTERCEDING FOR YOU.

Satan loves to condemn. Every time you stumble, every time you fall, he is there to point an accusing finger at you. He wants to focus your thoughts on your own weaknesses and failures rather than on God's strength. In contrast, the Holy Spirit convicts us. He gently says, "Now, that wasn't right." But that isn't condemning—that is convicting. He wants us to put our thoughts on Jesus, who is ready to hear our confession and wash us of our sin.

God is for you. Jesus is at the right hand of the Father making intercession for you. And the Holy Spirit is dwelling in you to give power to help you overcome your weaknesses. With this divine Trinity on your team, how can you possibly lose?

---

*Father, as we face the temptations and the pressures of the world,
may we discover the power and strength of Your Holy Spirit
to be sufficient for us.*

IN JESUS' NAME, AMEN.

JUST CLAY

*Does not the potter have power over the clay, from the same lump
to make one vessel for honor and another for dishonor?*
— ROMANS 9:21

Clay must be pliable. The only way it can discover what is to become of it is if it yields to the touch of the potter. That lump on the potter's wheel might become a beautiful vase to be set in a prominent place. Or it might become a pot to hold garbage. The clay has no idea what is in the mind of the potter and no business telling the potter what he can form.

We are those lumps of clay. We don't know what God has destined for us, or how He plans to use us. We don't know what we are to become. The only way we can discover it is by surrendering ourselves to Him.

CLAY CAN ONLY YIELD.

The Potter's hands are powerful—powerful enough to mold and shape a life. The wheel spins at a frightening speed. As the whirling begins, questions arise: What is God doing? Why do I feel so out of control? What is to become of me? But if you can silence those questions and trust those hands, if you can accept the pressure and ignore the fear, if you can remind yourself of the goodness of the Potter and the purity of His heart, then faith will replace anxiety. Fear will flee. Peace will surround you.

You might even find yourself enjoying the ride.

---

*Father, as we are whirling on the wheel, confused about what You
might be doing, help us to yield ourselves to Your touch. May we
not resist, and thus become marred in Your hands. Form us into
vessels that will bring You glory and honor.*

IN JESUS' NAME, AMEN.

HOW UNSEARCHABLE ARE HIS WAYS

Oh, the depth of the riches both of the wisdom and knowledge of God! How unsearchable are His judgments and His ways past finding out!

— ROMANS 11:33

As Paul has been sharing with the Romans about God's glorious plan of redemption, and how He has mercy on all, both Jew and Gentile alike, he just has to break forth with praise. He is completely in awe of the wisdom and the knowledge of God in His plan of redemption for man.

ONLY GOD KNOWS THE END FROM THE BEGINNING.

The fact that "His ways" [are] "past finding out" is the cause for much frustration in our Christian walk. We want to find out God's ways. We want to know what He is thinking when He allows certain things to happen. But as God told Isaiah, "My thoughts are not your thoughts, nor are your ways My ways … For as the heavens are higher than the earth, so are My ways higher than your ways, and My thoughts than your thoughts" (Isaiah 55:8-9).

God is working out a plan that we are not privy to. We can only understand His will as it is unveiled day by day. Though at times we don't understand the dark valleys He leads us through, once we reach the mountaintop and look back, we will see the path that led us there. And we will understand what He was doing. We'll understand that we could never have reached the heights if we had not first come through the depths.

Father, You are so rich in goodness, so incomparable in wisdom and kindness. We just want to say that we love You. Lord, help us to commit ourselves to You and trust Your will.

IN JESUS' NAME, AMEN.

REASONABLE SERVICE

*I beseech you therefore, brethren, by the mercies of God, that you
present your bodies a living sacrifice, holy, acceptable to God,
which is your reasonable service.*

— ROMANS 12:1

In writing to the church at Corinth, Paul made a point to tell them to be careful about what they do with their bodies. "Do you not know that your body is the temple of the Holy Spirit ... you are not your own? For you were bought at a price; therefore glorify God in your body and in your spirit, which are God's" (1 Corinthians 6:19-20).

God paid a tremendous price to redeem you, and the very least you can do is present yourself to Him—heart and soul, mind and body—as a living sacrifice. It's your reasonable service. After all, you owe your very existence to your Maker. He's the One who breathed life into you; He's the One who sustains you day by day.

YOU BELONG TO GOD—HEART AND SOUL, MIND AND BODY.

In the name of pleasure, people abuse their bodies with drugs, alcohol, and even perversion. It's bad for anyone, but it is absolutely unthinkable for the Christian. Do not destroy the instrument of your service. It doesn't belong to you anyway. Instead, sanctify yourself unto Him.

Most people use their bodies in the pursuit of pleasures that will pass away—things with no redeeming or eternal value whatsoever. Let's see what we can do for God that will count for eternity. Present your body unto God as a living sacrifice, holy and acceptable to Him, which is not only the least thing that you can do, but also the wisest.

***

*Father, may we devote our time, skills, and energies
to doing those things that will last forever.*

AMEN.

WAKE UP

*And do this, knowing the time, that now it is high time to awake
out of sleep; for now our salvation is nearer
than when we first believed.*

— ROMANS 13:11

What time is it? Paul said, "It's high time to awake out of your sleep." Paul recognized that the church in his day was asleep to the true issues of life. How much more so with the church today! We must be asleep, for there doesn't seem to be an urgency in our hearts about the things of the Lord.

We've slept long enough. The world around us is being ruled by Satan, all while we've napped. We slept through the removal of prayer from our public schools. We slept through the removal of laws that protected us from pushers of pornography. We slept through the opening of the doors for abortion on demand. We have slept through the paganizing of America. It is time to wake up.

> PUT OFF THE WORKS OF DARKNESS AND PUT ON THE LORD JESUS CHRIST.

The Lord's return is close. At the end of each day, we can truthfully say we are one day closer to the return of Jesus Christ than we were yesterday. Our salvation is nearer than when we first believed. Oh, the blessed hope that Jesus Christ is coming soon to deliver us from this present evil world!

It is high time for us to put off the works of darkness and put on the Lord Jesus Christ. It is time for us to live and walk after the Spirit. May God awaken His church and challenge us by His Word to righteous, holy living.

———⋙●⋘———

*We realize, Lord, that we have slept while the world has deterio-
rated around us. We see that the world is on the brink of eternity.
Wake us, Lord. Help us reach the lost.*

IN JESUS' NAME WE PRAY, AMEN.

THE GOD OF HOPE

Now may the God of hope fill you with all joy and peace ...
— ROMANS 15:13

Sociologists, looking for a connection between hope and survival, performed an interesting experiment with Norwegian wharf rats. One group of rats was put in a vat in which water sprinkled down on them continuously so they couldn't roll over and float. These rats survived an average of seventeen minutes before drowning. Those in the second group were removed just before drowning. A few days later, they were put back in the water. This time, the rats survived an average of thirty-six hours. The difference between seventeen minutes and thirty-six hours is hope.

WHEN WE WALK THROUGH DARK OR FEARFUL MOMENTS,
IT IS OUR HOPE FOR THE FUTURE THAT SUSTAINS US.

We gain strength from the knowledge that we will not be here forever, that Jesus will return soon to deliver us from this evil world. Though it is hard to be patient, we wait expectantly for the joy of seeing Him face to face, and the blessing of reigning with Him when He establishes His glorious kingdom upon the earth.

Jesus was sent on a mission by the Father: He came to bring us peace, comfort, and hope. By going to the cross and taking our sins upon Himself, He made peace with God possible. By walking in human flesh, He comforts us with an understanding of our condition. By securing our eternal future, He provides us with the hope of heaven.

Thank You, Father, for that peace that passes human understanding by which our hearts and lives are kept. Help us understand how amazing it is that You loved us that You gave Your Son to bring hope, comfort, and peace.

IN JESUS' NAME, AMEN.

THE MESSAGE OF THE CROSS

For the message of the cross is foolishness to those who are perishing, but to us who are being saved it is the power of God.

— 1 CORINTHIANS 1:18

To the Jew, the notion of their Messiah being arrested, beaten, and crucified on a cross was utterly unthinkable. They expected their Messiah, the descendant of David, to rule over the world in righteousness and peace.

To the Greek, the idea that one man could die for the sins of all men was pure foolishness. None of the many gods the Greeks worshiped would ever have done something that loving. Their gods were selfish. So the idea of a God who was willing to give Himself to save His people was ridiculous.

"The natural man does not receive the things of the Spirit of God, for they are foolishness to him" (1 Corinthians 2:14). Though the world considers the cross to be foolishness, we who are saved see it as the beautiful instrument of our salvation. We are not ashamed of the cross.

IT IS THE POWER OF GOD UNTO SALVATION.

Through the cross, God set us free from the bondage of sin. Through the cross, He conquered death and the grave. Through the cross, He adopted us as His own. Through the cross, He made an end of the war that existed between us. Through the cross, He secured our eternal future.

Let the world think what it wants. We know the truth. And oh, how we love that old rugged cross.

Lord, we thank You that You have set us free—free to love You, free to serve You, free to walk in fellowship with You. Let the message of the cross speak to our hearts today.

IN JESUS' NAME, AMEN.

Natural Man, Spiritual Man

But the natural man does not receive the things of the Spirit of God ... because they are spiritually discerned. But he who is spiritual judges all things ...

— 1 CORINTHIANS 2:14-15

The natural man is one who has not been born again. In fact, the natural man is just as he sounds—he is as natural as the day he was born, with no concept or understanding of God.

The natural man doesn't understand the things of the Spirit, because they are spiritually discerned. Just as a blind man cannot enjoy the brilliance of a sunset, the natural man lacks the faculties by which spiritual things are understood and appreciated.

A WHOLE NEW DIMENSION IS OPENED TO THE SPIRITUAL MAN.

So what is the spiritual man? He is the man whose spirit has been born again so he is alive to the things of the Spirit and understands the things of the Spirit.

And yet Paul said, "He who is spiritual judges all things, yet he himself is rightly judged by no one" (1 Corinthians 2:15). Have you noticed how people often don't understand you as a Christian? You are an enigma to them. "Why do you like going to church so much? Why don't you drink? What do you do for fun?"

The natural man can't understand the joy of living in fellowship with God, but we who are born again by the Spirit know full well the blessing of walking with Jesus—and the peace that comes from being forgiven and cleansed.

Father, thank You for saving us. Thank You that by Your Holy Spirit we can discern Your truth and understand the mysteries of Your Word. May You open the eyes of those who don't yet know You.

IN JESUS' NAME, AMEN.

THE CARNAL CHRISTIAN

And I, brethren, could not speak to you as to spiritual people
but as to carnal, as to babes in Christ.

— 1 CORINTHIANS 3:1

Paul already described the categories of the natural man and the spiritual man, but now he introduces a third category—the carnal man. Paul calls them "babes in Christ." The fact that they are in Christ classifies them as Christians, but tragically, they have not developed spiritually. They are still spiritual infants. Sadly, so many Christians are in this state of arrested development that they are not even a novelty.

The carnal Christian has received Jesus as their Savior but they haven't denied themselves and taken up their cross to follow Him. The flesh still rules in their life. Jesus is Savior, but He's not the Lord of their lives.

ABANDON CARNALITY.

What is the cure for carnal Christianity? The first step is to walk in love. If you walk in love you'll not engage in envy and in strife. If you walk in love you'll not bring division into the body of Christ.

The second cure for Christian carnality is to get into the Word of God. True spiritual growth can only come by feeding on the Word. You need to have a good diet to grow, and the Word of God is the diet that promotes spiritual growth in the believer. Get into the Word, and get the Word in you.

Abandon carnality. Grow up, mature, and develop through the Word of God. Let it feed your soul. Then walk in love and grow in the grace and knowledge of our Lord and Savior, Jesus Christ.

Lord, we desire spiritual maturity. We want to walk in love. May
we come into a deeper, richer understanding of Your Word.

IN JESUS' NAME, AMEN.

FOOLS FOR CHRIST'S SAKE

We are fools for Christ's sake ...
— 1 CORINTHIANS 4:10

People make fools of themselves for all kinds of reasons—because they have been drinking, or they want to make others laugh, or make money, or just to make others think they are clever. And no one seems to think that is odd.

But let someone declare they are a fool for Christ's sake, and the ridicule begins. The world considers it foolish to give up everything for Jesus Christ. Sometimes even our own families mock us. They cannot understand the sacrifices we are willing to make for Jesus.

> WHY IS IT THAT IF YOU GIVE YOUR LIFE FOR THE SERVICE OF YOUR COUNTRY YOU ARE CALLED A HERO, BUT IF YOU GIVE YOUR LIFE FOR THE SERVICE OF CHRIST, YOU ARE CALLED A FOOL?

Paul was beaten, imprisoned, stoned, and ultimately beheaded for the sake of Jesus Christ. The world would say, "He was a fool." But as Paul said, his sufferings were "not worthy to be compared with the glory which shall be revealed in us" (Romans 8:18).

As a teenager, I was greatly inspired by one man who used to say, "Everybody is somebody's fool. You might as well be a fool for Christ." If loving Jesus with all of my heart makes me a fool, then I am a fool. If desiring to serve Jesus with everything I have makes me a fool, then I am a fool. If trusting Jesus for everything makes me a fool, then I am a fool. But I am not ashamed of being a fool for Christ's sake.

———⊰●⊱———

Father, help us to stand against the tide of evil and to speak out for Christ's sake, even at the cost of being considered a fool.
IN JESUS' NAME, AMEN.

CHRIST OUR PASSOVER

Therefore purge out the old leaven, that you may be a new lump,
since you truly are unleavened. For indeed Christ, our Passover,
was sacrificed for us.

— 1 CORINTHIANS 5:7

When leaven is added to bread, gases are released due to fermentation. It is a rotting process. In this way, the bread rises. Just a little bit of leaven can permeate through an entire lump of dough.

Sin is like that too. A little tolerated sin in the church can work its way through the whole body. And it is in this context that Paul addresses the Corinthian church. They had tolerated evil within their fellowship—sin which needed to be purged.

> JUST A LITTLE TOLERATED SIN CAN PERMEATE THROUGH THE WHOLE BODY, ROTTING IT AWAY FROM THE INSIDE OUT.

In the final plague in Egypt, God made provision for His own people. Every household protected by the blood of the sacrificial lamb escaped the plague. But in every household without the protection of the blood, the firstborn was found dead by morning.

In the same way, God has made provision for the forgiveness of our sins so that we don't have to die as the result of them. That provision is in Jesus Christ, our sacrificial Lamb. Through the shedding of His blood, we can have our sins forgiven.

Paul declared that "Christ is our Passover." It was no accident that Jesus was crucified on the day of Passover. God's Lamb fulfilled the foreshadowing of Israel's Passover, purging the sin that defiled our lives, and providing escape from an otherwise inescapable death.

Father, thank You that You sent Your Son to be our Passover. We
receive now the cleansing that He offers. We receive
the forgiveness of our sins.

IN JESUS' NAME, AMEN.

LIMITS TO LIBERTY

All things are lawful for me, but all things are not helpful. All things are lawful for me, but I will not be brought under the power of any.

— 1 CORINTHIANS 6:12

Christians often ask if they can engage in certain activities. What they are really asking is, "How much of the world can I partake in and still be a Christian?"

Just before writing, "All things are lawful for me," Paul gave a pretty specific (though not exhaustive) list of some things that are indeed unlawful: fornication, idolatry, adultery, homosexuality, theft, covetousness, drunkenness, slander, and extortion (1 Corinthians 6:9-10).

> THE MOMENT I COME UNDER THE INFLUENCE OF SOMETHING THEN I AM NO LONGER FREE.

Some would ask, "Is it all right to have a beer with my pizza? As a Christian, can I smoke cigarettes?" Let me ask you—is it possible to come under the influence by drinking beer? Can you become addicted to cigarettes? It may not be a heinous sin, it may not send you to hell, but if it can bring you under its power, then you are sacrificing the glorious liberty you have in Christ. The moment you come under its influence then you're enslaved.

Let's not try to discern if something is right or wrong. As we look at the issues of life, let's ask: Does it impede my walk with the Lord? Would I be apt to find Jesus participating with me? Could it get such a hold on me as to enslave me and rob me of my liberty? Does it build me up in Jesus? Does it make me more like Him?

———✦———

Father, show us those things that tear down rather than build up Christ in us. May we truly reflect our Lord Jesus Christ to the world in which we live.

IN HIS NAME, AMEN.

LIVING IN EXPECTANCY

But this I say, brethren, the time is short …
— 1 CORINTHIANS 7:29

I am convinced that God intended for every generation to believe Jesus is coming in their time. Why? Because He wants us to live in the expectancy of His return.

When we believe His coming is imminent, we feel an urgency to bring the gospel to the world. The realization that time is short motivates us to fulfill the commission Jesus left us.

KEEP YOUR EVERY TOUCH WITH THE WORLD AS LIGHT AS POSSIBLE.

The awareness of His imminent return also gives us the right perspective concerning worldly things. When you know that the curtain on this life could close at any moment, and the curtain to eternity could lift in the blink of an eye, it helps you keep a light touch on worldly things. You are not as apt to put down roots here. You are not as likely to become materialistic.

Anticipating the return of Jesus has a purifying effect on our individual lives and on the church as a whole. When He comes, we don't want to be engaged in an activity that is contrary to His wishes. We want to be busy building up the kingdom, busy using what He's given us for His glory. We don't want to waste our time indulging in sorrow or in pleasure. We don't want to waste time amassing possessions.

Time is short, and the world is passing away. Give yourself, your time, your energies, and your resources to things that are eternal. Live for the kingdom of God, and live forever.

*Lord, guard us from getting so deeply involved in temporal things
that we don't have time for the eternal.
Give us the wisdom to redeem our days.*

IN JESUS' NAME, AMEN.

SEPTEMBER

LOVE THAT BUILDS

We know that we all have knowledge.
Knowledge puffs up, but love edifies.
— 1 CORINTHIANS 8:1

A division had developed in the Corinthian church. Some felt strong convictions against eating meat that had been sacrificed to idols. Others declared their freedom to eat such meat because, as they reasoned, "We know that idols are nothing." Those with freedom looked down on those without as being their inferiors.

There will always be intellectual snobs. There are always those who feel intellectually superior to others and who ridicule them for following "ignorant superstitions." But the prophet Isaiah wrote, "Your wisdom and your knowledge have warped you; you have said in your heart, 'I am right, there is no other opinion'" (Isaiah 47:10 paraphrase). Paul addressed this issue in the Corinthian church with the warning that "knowledge puffs up."

WE ARE TOLD TO WALK IN LOVE.

If we really walk in love, we will seek to build up the weaker brother. I won't try to convince him that he is wrong, nor will I flaunt my liberty before him, and thus cause him to stumble. It is a dangerous thing to encourage someone to do something which violates their conscience, to argue them into doing something they feel is wrong.

"When you thus sin against the brethren, and wound their weak conscience, you sin against Christ. Therefore, if food makes my brother stumble, I will never again eat meat" (1 Corinthians 8:12-13). That is walking in love. Don't go around flaunting your liberty and thus, destroy a weaker brother. Knowledge puffs up, but love builds up.

God, help us to walk in love and build up one another in spiritual matters, not always trying to prove we are right but recognizing that not all feel the same liberties.

IN JESUS' PRECIOUS NAME, AMEN.

The Rock

For they drank of that spiritual Rock that followed them, and that Rock was Christ. Now these things became our examples …
— 1 Corinthians 10:4, 6

The God who brought water from the smitten rock for the thirsty children of Israel is the same God who brought life for us through the body of His smitten Son. The miraculous provision of water they experienced was but a foreshadowing of the miraculous provision of righteousness we have experienced.

> Nothing satisfies man's deep thirst for God except a meaningful relationship with God.

Paul declares, "That Rock was Christ." Jesus spoke of the water of life He would give to those who thirst. In John 4, Jesus told the Samaritan woman, "Whoever drinks of this water will thirst again, but whoever drinks of the water that I shall give him will never thirst. But the water that I shall give him will become in him a fountain of water springing up into everlasting life" (John 4:13-14).

Those who try to quench that thirst with anything else will find that they continue to thirst. But when you go to the Rock, who is Christ, the water He gives you not only satisfies, it overflows like a well of living water.

Are you thirsty today? All you have to do is speak to the Rock. He will cause the water of life to flow forth to you. He will open the floodgates and satisfy your thirst.

Father, we thank You for Jesus Christ, the Rock of ages who was smitten for us. Keep us from going to any other source when we are thirsty. Help us to bring our thirst to You, that we might drink freely and fully and find the satisfaction we long for.

In Jesus' name, amen.

EXAMINE YOURSELF

But let a man examine himself, and so let him
eat of the bread and drink of the cup.
— 1 CORINTHIANS 11:28

Paul had just rebuked those in the church of Corinth for the way many were coming to the Lord's Table and partaking of communion. He warned them that by doing it in a careless, unworthy manner, they became guilty of the body and blood of Jesus. And so he said, "Let a man examine himself."

This is good advice for all of us. It is difficult, but important. You can't deal with an issue until you have first identified and acknowledged it. "If we confess our sins, He is faithful and just to forgive us our sins and to cleanse us from all unrighteousness" (1 John 1:9).

> ONCE WE EXAMINE OURSELVES AND ACKNOWLEDGE OUR SIN, WE CAN THEN BRING IT TO JESUS.

Perhaps there is something in your life that God wants to deal with, some issue you've been trying to hide from Him. Whether you realize it or not, that sin is hindering full fellowship with God. He wants to fix that today. If you will judge yourself, you won't be judged of Him. Let the Holy Spirit search your heart and reveal the truth He knows, and then be sure you respond and react by confessing your sins and receiving His forgiveness.

As David said, "Search me, O God, and know my heart. Try me, and know my anxieties; and see if there is any wicked way in me" (Psalm 139:23-24). It is not what you think about yourself that matters—it is what God thinks.

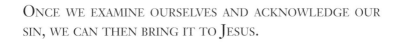

Father, thank You for Your love and mercy towards us.
Lord, as the Spirit reveals the truth to us,
help us to acknowledge and repent.
IN JESUS' NAME WE PRAY, AMEN.

THE GREATEST OF THESE

And now abide faith, hope, love, these three;
but the greatest of these is love.
— 1 CORINTHIANS 13:13

These are the planks upon which Christianity stands:

Faith—When everything else falls apart, faith sustains us—faith that God loves us, faith that God is in control.

Hope—Hope is the anticipation of a good ending. When everything around us looks bleak and hopeless, how is it that Christians can have such a joyful outlook and hope for the future? It's because we have the Guidebook. We know the end of the story.

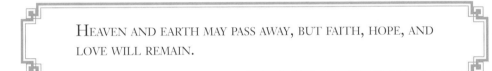

HEAVEN AND EARTH MAY PASS AWAY, BUT FAITH, HOPE, AND LOVE WILL REMAIN.

Love—Paul said, "The greatest of these is love." The heart of the Christian gospel is love. We are called to love God supremely and to love our neighbor as we love ourselves. That is the essence of the Christian message. God wants us to know and to offer the agape love described in this chapter: "Love suffers long and is kind; love does not envy; love does not parade itself, is not puffed up; does not behave rudely, does not seek its own, is not provoked, thinks no evil; does not rejoice in iniquity, but rejoices in the truth; bears all things, believes all things, hopes all things, endures all things. Love never fails" (1 Corinthians 13:4-8).

These are the three planks upon which Christianity rests. Though everything else may cease, these three will abide. In fact, heaven and earth may pass away, but these will remain: faith, hope, and love. But the greatest of these is love.

Father, we ask for faith, that we would believe You. We ask for hope, that we would wait for Your promises. And we ask for love, that we might give to others what You have given us.

IN JESUS' NAME, AMEN.

THE AUTHOR OF PEACE

For God is not the author of confusion but of peace,
as in all the churches of the saints.
— 1 CORINTHIANS 14:33

Things had gotten out of hand in the church of Corinth. They abused the gift of tongues by uttering tongues with no interpretation. They interrupted one another. Sometimes they all spoke in tongues at the same time. Paul rebuked them for conducting their services without order, saying, "Look, God isn't the author of confusion."

All you have to do is look at the universe to see that God is a God of order. And in the descriptions we have of heaven, we can see that worship there is performed in an orderly fashion. So shouldn't worship be orderly in the church?

GOD IS CAPABLE OF BRINGING ORDER OUT OF CHAOS—
EVEN THE CHAOS WE CREATE IN OUR PERSONAL LIVES.

God is not the author of confusion, but of peace. Confusion, disorder, and strife fill our lives when we insist on doing our own thing. But when we follow the rules God established for us in His Word—rules which tell us how we ought to live—then God's peace begins to fill our hearts. Instead of living disorderly lives, we can then live calm, productive, loving lives.

Disorder can make us impatient and touchy. But when God's peace begins to reign in your heart, God is able to help you respond to others in love, in forgiveness, and in peace, and thus, maintaining peace with those around you. It's your choice—you can live in confusion and chaos, or you can live a life marked by peace.

Father, we thank You that we have received Your peace—a peace
that passes human understanding.
IN JESUS' NAME, AMEN.

SEPTEMBER 29

THE GOD OF COMFORT

*Blessed be the God and Father of our Lord Jesus Christ,
the Father of mercies and God of all comfort, who comforts us
in all our tribulation, that we may be able to comfort those who
are in any trouble, with the comfort with which we ourselves
are comforted by God.*

— 2 CORINTHIANS 1:3-4

Paul speaks openly of the tribulation, the suffering, and the affliction he experienced as a follower of Jesus Christ. He was not immune from trouble. Trouble followed Paul wherever he went—all because he proclaimed Jesus.

WHEN SUFFERING COMES, WE HAVE A CHOICE TO MAKE.

SEPTEMBER

Good people do suffer. Scripture affirms it. So when suffering comes—and it will—we have a choice to make. We can disregard God's character and say, "Well, if that is how God is going to treat me, then I don't believe He loves me anymore." Or, we can trust Him and cling to Him even tighter. We can say, "Oh God, I know You really love me. I don't understand what is happening, Lord, but I trust You."

Paul realized that God used his sufferings to give him sympathy so that he could minister to others going through similar experiences. The same is true with us. When we go through trials or tragedies, we understand how others feel when they face their own losses, and we are better able to reach out.

Suffering gives us a history with the Holy Spirit. We learn that He is the Comforter. We learn that He is faithful to strengthen us for the trial. And we, in turn, can share that comfort and strength with others who need it.

*Lord, teach us the value of trusting You completely. May we
accept the ministry of Your Holy Spirit, and share it with others.*

IN JESUS' NAME, AMEN.

Victory in Christ

Now thanks be to God who always leads us in triumph in Christ.
— 2 Corinthians 2:14

The word triumph is a word that presupposes conflict. As children of God, we are in constant conflict. Basically, three forces battle your Christian experience: the world (the world system that is in rebellion against God), our flesh (this corrupt, fallen nature, biological drives that control a person's life), and the devil.

VICTORY COMES AS WE LEARN TO ABIDE IN CHRIST.

Why is it so hard to live a life of victory in Christ? Well, some just don't put up much of a fight. The Scriptures say, "Resist the devil and he will flee from you" (James 4:7). But whenever Satan comes around, some Christians just sort of give up without a fight. They yield without any resistance. Jesus said if you wanted to come after Him you had to deny yourself, take up your cross and follow Him. But, the flesh doesn't like that. It doesn't like to be denied. So some of us don't deny it at all.

Victory comes as we learn to trust in Christ to help us handle the temptations the enemy may throw at us. Victory comes when we ask Him for the strength that we don't have within ourselves, power beyond our own capacities. As Jesus told us, we need to abide in Him and continue abiding in Him, for apart from Him we can do nothing. As we abide in Jesus Christ, and He abides in us, that indwelling presence of His Holy Spirit becomes the secret to constant victory.

Father, how grateful we are for the victory that we have in Christ—for the power You've given us to overcome the world, the flesh, and the devil.
In Jesus' name, amen.

Our Sufficiency

Not that we are sufficient of ourselves to think of anything as
being from ourselves, but our sufficiency is from God …
— 2 Corinthians 3:5

Paul had just told the Corinthians, "You are a living letter; you are known and read by all men." Your life is an example to the world of what God is—His love, His goodness, and His grace. People develop their impressions of God by what they see in you. Like Paul, when you consider this responsibility you may wonder, "Who is sufficient for these things?" But as Paul declares, "Our sufficiency is from God."

No matter how resourceful or strong you might be, you are going to face situations that are beyond your abilities.

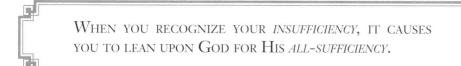

When you recognize your *insufficiency*, it causes you to lean upon God for His *all-sufficiency*.

People often vow to change, only to discover that they don't have the sufficiency within themselves to keep those promises. But when God is your sufficiency, there is no limit to the power available to you. His grace has no measure; His love has no limits; His power has no boundary known to men. For out of His infinite riches in Jesus, He gives and gives and gives again.

With God's help and God's strength, you can overcome any adversity that comes into your life. Acknowledge your limitations. Step out in faith knowing that where you are weak, He is strong, knowing that you can do all things through Christ who strengthens you.

Lord, we thank You that You give strength to the weak. We recognize that You have given us a great responsibility as Your witness to the world, and we recognize that we are not sufficient for the task—but You are. Help us to wait upon You, Lord.

Amen.

OCTOBER

Seeing the Invisible

We do not look at the things which are seen, but at the things which are not seen. For the things which are seen are temporary, but the things which are not seen are eternal.

— 2 Corinthians 4:18

The material world—the world we see and touch—is three-dimensional. But the spiritual world has an untold number of dimensions we are not familiar with. The spiritual world is an invisible world. Though the material world is in a constant process of decay, the spiritual world knows no decay. It is eternal.

> WHEN WE LET OUR VISION BECOME EARTH-BOUND, WE LOSE OUR ETERNAL PERSPECTIVE.

What do we see in this material, three-dimensional world? Perplexities, difficulties, and afflictions. God doesn't promise us heaven on this sin-cursed earth. But when by faith we see the spiritual dimension—the power of God, the hand of God, the love of God—we gain strength to endure. Having glanced at Him and observing His majestic power, we stop fearing the mountains before us, because we are confident that He will bring us through.

It is tragic that so many people trade in the world they could have for the world they know. They mindlessly sacrifice God's eternal kingdom for some temporal pleasure, excitement, or possession—a pleasure, excitement or possession that will eventually pass away. When we have a worldly perspective, we lose sight of eternity. We can't afford to lose that eternal perspective; it is the key to endurance. We need to look beyond our problems to the eternal God who is our refuge and our strength, and behold the eternal rewards awaiting those who live a godly life.

Father, the material world is so attractive and so alluring at times. Correct our perspective, Lord. Help us to give ourselves over to things that are eternal.

In Jesus' name, amen.

OCTOBER 3

PERFECTING HOLINESS

... I will receive you. I will be a Father to you, and you shall
be My sons and daughters ... Therefore, having these promises,
beloved, let us cleanse ourselves from all filthiness of the flesh
and spirit, perfecting holiness in the fear of God.
— 2 CORINTHIANS 6:17-18; 7:1

In light of the great promises God gives in these verses, what should be our response?

First, we need to cleanse ourselves from all the filth that clings to us while we are out trying to fulfill the flesh. It is the filth we have planted in our minds—the thoughts, attitudes and desires that don't belong in the mind of God's child. How do you do this? You replace the wrong things with the right things. You fill your mind with the Word of God. As the psalmist said, "How can a young man cleanse his way? By taking heed according to Your word" (Psalm 119:9).

WHAT AN AMAZING TRUTH: YOU ARE A CHILD OF GOD.

Second, we need to separate ourselves from the unbelieving world around us. God wants His people to be holy. The Lord says, "Come out from among them and be separate. Do not touch what is unclean" (2 Corinthians 6:17). Because of the great love God has shown us, and the great lengths He went to adopt us and call us His own, our response should be holiness. Since God desires that in His children, we should determine to live separate lives from those around us and walk in purity before God.

Through Jesus, God has received you and called you His own. Does that motivate you to bless Him?

God, help me to be pure in thought, in heart, and in mind.
Make me pure, as You are pure.
IN JESUS' NAME, AMEN.

OCTOBER

THE RICHES OF HIS GRACE

For you know the grace of our Lord Jesus Christ, that though He
was rich, yet for your sakes He became poor,
that you through His poverty might become rich.

— 2 CORINTHIANS 8:9

Who could possibly estimate the riches of God? In Psalm 50:10, He tells us, "Every beast of the forest is Mine, and the cattle on a thousand hills." But that is just to give us a picture we can understand. The truth is, the whole universe and everything in it belongs to Him. And if that weren't enough, He is able to speak a billion more universes into existence, just by His word.

Jesus prayed, "Father, glorify Me together with Yourself, with the glory which I had with You before the world was" (John 17:5). All God's riches are shared with His Son, and yet, for your sake, He became poor. He left the place of glory, where He was exalted and adored, and allowed Himself to be born in a stable, born to poor parents, born in obscurity. He came knowing He would wander the earth as an adult, owning nothing, though it all technically belonged to Him.

> THE RICHES JESUS DESIRES TO SHARE WITH YOU ARE ETERNAL RICHES, WHICH CANNOT BE MEASURED BY TEMPORAL THINGS LIKE GOLD OR SILVER.

Peter describes these riches as "an inheritance incorruptible and undefiled and that does not fade away, reserved in heaven for you, who are kept by the power of God through faith" (1 Peter 1:4-5).

Some riches are waiting for us in heaven. Some are available today: abundant joy, unending mercy, the peace of Christ, righteousness, hope, and love.

Thank You, Father, for the beautiful riches we experience
each day as we walk in love with You.

IN JESUS' NAME, AMEN.

SPIRITUAL WARFARE

For though we walk in the flesh,
we do not war according to the flesh.
— 2 CORINTHIANS 10:3

It is possible that those times when we feel disturbed, upset, discouraged, despondent or depressed for no apparent reason, a spiritual force is to blame. We are all in a spiritual battle, whether we are aware of it or not. And in this spiritual battle, it is important that we use the right weapons.

One of the best weapons for spiritual warfare is God's Word. "For the Word of God is living and powerful, and sharper than any two-edged sword" (Hebrews 4:12). Every time Satan tempted Jesus, He responded with the Word of God. God's Word becomes a powerful weapon in your life against the temptations the enemy places before you.

> KNOWING HOW FIERCE THE BATTLE WOULD BE, GOD WAS CAREFUL TO EQUIP US TO FIGHT EFFECTIVELY.

Prayer is another important weapon, but strangely, people often reserve prayer as a last resort. How might our thinking about prayer change if we realized how hard Satan fights against it? He knows what we apparently do not—that prayer is the deciding factor in a spiritual battle.

God was careful to equip us to fight effectively. We have His Holy Spirit. We have the Word of God. We have the power of prayer. Let us use these mighty weapons to stand against the wiles of the devil who is seeking to destroy us and take us captive. May we use these weapons to claim the victory that Jesus has already accomplished through the cross.

Father, forgive us for relying upon our own devices.
May we begin to fight this battle with the advantage
that You have given to us in the things of the Spirit.

IN JESUS' NAME, AMEN.

ALL-SUFFICIENT GRACE

And He said to me, "My grace is sufficient for you,
for My strength is made perfect in weakness."
Therefore most gladly I will rather boast in my infirmities,
that the power of Christ may rest upon me.

— 2 CORINTHIANS 12:9

Paul had what he called "a thorn in the flesh." Three times he asked the Lord to remove it, and this passage of Scripture is God's response. "My grace is sufficient for you."

Life is filled with sorrow, pain, tragedy, disappointment, and grief, and God does not promise us immunity from these things. The difference between the Christian and the non-Christian is that for the child of God, these experiences come through God's filter. They only happen as God allows them to happen.

AFFLICTION OFTEN RESULTS IN OUR GREATEST SPIRITUAL GROWTH.

Suffering develops a deep relationship with God that seems unable to develop apart from affliction. Paul learned through the thorn in the flesh to praise God. The day came when Paul actually began to rejoice and thank God for that thorn in the flesh. And he wrote, "For I reckon that the present sufferings are not worthy to be compared with the glory that shall be revealed." It changed his attitude completely. He no longer saw that thorn as a curse but as a blessing.

It is so important that we come to know and experience this all-sufficient grace, because it will lead us through the darkest nights, and help us smile through our disappointments. It's this grace that will sustain us when everything else fails. It is this grace that turns your cross into a crown.

Father, we thank You for Your all-sufficient grace which sustains
us. May we rest in that grace when we need it most.

IN JESUS' NAME, AMEN.

GRACE AND PEACE

*Grace to you and peace from God the Father
and our Lord Jesus Christ.*

— GALATIANS 1:3

Paul took the Greek greeting *charis*, "grace," and combined it with the Hebrew greeting *shalom* or "peace." "Grace and peace." This greeting is used seventeen times in the New Testament, always in this order, "grace and peace." I think that this was by design, because I have discovered in my own life that I didn't know the peace of God until I understood the grace of God.

I grew up being taught that I had to earn God's blessings. If I worked hard or kept my commitments, God would bless me. But if I failed, He wouldn't. I was trying to deserve something that can't be deserved. Grace means "undeserved, unmerited, unearned favor." If we could earn it, then it would no longer be grace—it would be payment.

> GOD'S BLESSINGS ARE NOT DEPENDENT ON OUR FAITHFUL-NESS OR OUR HARD WORK BUT ARE PREDICATED UPON HIS NATURE OF LOVE.

Now that I have a better understanding of grace, I have learned to expect God to bless me even though I am fully aware I don't deserve it.

Paul tells us that God has manifested His grace towards us through sending His Son who gave Himself for our sins. "All we like sheep have gone astray; we have turned, every one, to his own way; and the LORD has laid on Him the iniquity of us all" (Isaiah 53:6). While we were yet sinners Christ died—not for the good people, not for the righteous people, but for the ungodly.

That is grace.

*Thank You, Lord, for the wonderful peace and understanding in
which our hearts and minds are kept because of Your grace.*

IN JESUS' NAME, AMEN.

BEAUTIFUL DELIVERANCE

*I have been crucified with Christ; it is no longer I who live, but
Christ lives in me; and the life which I now live in the flesh I live
by faith in the Son of God, who loved me and gave Himself for me.*

— GALATIANS 2:20

God wants to give us victory over sin. He knows we are tempted at every turn, and He wants to free us from both the temptation and the consequences of sin. His solution is for us to put the flesh life to death. Paul wrote, "Knowing this, that our old man was crucified with Him, that the body of sin might be done away with, that we should no longer be slaves of sin" (Romans 6:6). "Therefore do not let sin reign in your mortal body, that you should obey it in its lusts. And do not present your members as instruments of unrighteousness.... For sin shall not have dominion over you" (Romans 6:12-14).

THE OLD, SINFUL NATURE DOESN'T HAVE TO RULE US ANYMORE.

When temptation arises, we can reckon that old nature to be crucified with Christ. When we fall, we can bring that sin right back to the cross and say, "I have been crucified—that sin cannot have dominion over me; I won't be ruled by that." And gradually, slowly, the Lord will begin to deliver us from that sin until it is no longer attractive to us.

How beautiful it is when God does for us what we could not do for ourselves—deliver us.

⟶⟶◆⟵⟵

*Father, we thank You for the victory that we have through Jesus
Christ over the power that sin once held over us. Help us, Lord, to
grasp these truths and to live in righteousness and peace.*

IN JESUS' NAME, AMEN.

THE CURSE OF SIN

Christ has redeemed us from the curse of the law,
having become a curse for us (for it is written,
"Cursed is everyone who hangs on a tree") …
— GALATIANS 3:13

The law God gave the children of Israel was for their benefit, for their blessing. But the law is harsh. The law carries a curse, which says those who would not obey the law must die. As James pointed out, "Whoever shall keep the whole law, and yet stumble in one point, he is guilty of all" (James 2:10). If you are trying to be righteous before God by keeping the law and yet you violate one point, then you come under the curse of the law.

So we are guilty. We are deserving of death. Yet Jesus took our sins and died in our place. Not only does that mean we don't have to suffer the curse of the law, it also means that we are blessed. His sacrifice brought us the blessings of Abraham. For we read, "That the blessing of Abraham might come upon the Gentiles in Christ Jesus, that we might receive the promise of the Spirit through faith" (Galatians 3:14).

> THROUGH HIS DEATH ON THE TREE, JESUS BROUGHT US FREEDOM, DELIVERANCE, FORGIVENESS, RIGHTEOUSNESS, AND HOPE.

OCTOBER

Oh, the blessings of God that have come upon me through Jesus Christ! How good He is, and how loved we are, that He would become the curse for us, that He would endure so much shame, so much pain, that we might be freed from the curse of the law!

Father, how grateful we are that You sent Your Son to redeem us
from the curse of the law. How grateful we are for
Your love and mercy.

IN JESUS' NAME, AMEN.

ABBA, FATHER

*And because you are sons, God has sent forth the Spirit of His Son
into your hearts, crying out, "Abba, Father!"*
— GALATIANS 4:6

 am not a son of God by natural birth; I am a son of God by a new birth, being born again by His Spirit. "For as many as are led by the Spirit of God, these are the sons of God. For you did not receive the spirit of bondage again to fear, but you received the Spirit of adoption by whom we cry out, 'Abba, Father'" (Romans 8:14-15).

Abba is the Hebrew word for father, but it is more like our English word daddy. It has an endearing, intimate quality to it.

WE NEED TO BELIEVE THAT GOD IS *OUR* ABBA, FATHER.

Some people profess that because God is so awesome, we should not even say His name. Others, though, get too chummy, too casual with God. They refer to Him as "The Big Daddy upstairs."

We need a balance between the two. We need to know that God is our Father, that He is our Abba. We need to understand that we can have that kind of beautiful intimacy with Him. But it is also important that we have the deepest reverence and respect for Him, that we never get to a place where we think of Him casually.

May we, as His children, call upon our Abba, Father, and realize the benefits of this glorious inheritance that we have in Jesus Christ, the blessings that are ours by being a child of God.

---

*Father, we thank You for the provision through Jesus, that we
who were once foreigners can now be called Your children.
Thank You, Abba, Father, for the riches that are ours
in and through Christ Jesus.*

WORK VERSUS FRUIT

But the fruit of the Spirit is love ...
— GALATIANS 5:22

Paul had been talking about the works of the flesh, and then in verse 22 he begins, "But the fruit of the Spirit." The word "but" is a disassociative conjunction. It ties together two contrasting ideas. The contrast is between the works of the flesh and the fruit of the Spirit.

Whenever you talk about works, you are talking about a fleshly effort. We all fall into that disappointing trap from time to time. We promise God we will do better next time. Somehow, in spite of the sincerity of my heart, I can't keep the vows I made. If I endeavor to please God with my works, I already have an impossible situation, because, "by the works of the law no flesh shall be justified" (Galatians 2:16).

> IF YOU HAVE THE AGAPE LOVE OF THE SPIRIT, FRUIT WILL COME FORTH FROM YOUR LIFE.

Whenever you speak of fruit, you're speaking of a relationship. "As the branch cannot bear fruit of itself, unless it abides in the vine," Jesus said, "neither can you, unless you abide in Me" (John 15:4). If you have that right relationship with God through Jesus Christ, the natural consequence will be fruit. I cannot bring forth the kind of fruit that God wants, except by abiding in Jesus.

The fruit of the Spirit is agape love. You can't be in a relationship with God without this love coming forth from you—it happens naturally as you abide in Him.

Is the fruit of the Spirit coming forth from your life? Abide in Him and let His words abide in you. Hang in there, and God's love will begin to develop and be perfected in your life.

Father, help us to leave that positive mark of Your love upon others.

IN JESUS' NAME, AMEN.

OCTOBER

My Glory, the Cross

*But God forbid that I should boast except in the cross
of our Lord Jesus Christ ...*

— GALATIANS 6:14

If you possess anything of value, God gave it to you. Sometimes people waste the gifts God has entrusted to them, using them for their own glory instead of for His. And people often boast of their talent, as if they had given it to themselves. But you can't boast in something that has been given to you.

BOAST AND GLORY IN THE CROSS. IT SAYS HOW MUCH JESUS CHRIST LOVES YOU AND ME.

Why then are we told to glory in the cross of Jesus Christ? First of all, we boast in the cross because it speaks to us of the extent of God's love for us. It reminds us of how far God was willing to go—and did go—in order to help us, to save us, and to bless us. We glory in the cross because it was on the cross that Jesus conquered Satan and freed us from sin so that we could enjoy fellowship with God. It is through the cross that we have victory over the flesh and the grave.

So we glory in the cross of Jesus Christ for bringing us deliverance, an abundant life, and the hope of eternal life in heaven.

God forbid that I should glory in anything except the cross of Jesus! There is no other name by which we have been saved; no other name which has brought us such great freedom and victory.

---

*Father, we give thanks that You loved us so much You sent Your
Son who redeemed us from the bondage of corruption that we
might know You and live in eternal fellowship with You.*

IN JESUS' NAME, AMEN.

KNOWING GOD

That the God of our Lord Jesus Christ, the Father of glory, may give to
you the spirit of wisdom and revelation in the knowledge of Him …
— EPHESIANS 1:17

The natural man cannot understand the deep things of God except by His Spirit. "But the natural man does not receive the things of the Spirit of God; nor can he know them, because they are spiritually discerned" (1 Corinthians 2:14). Without the Holy Spirit, we can know nothing of God except that He is.

We know that God exists, in part, because His creation testifies of Him. "The heavens declare the glory of God; and the earth shows His handiwork. Day after day they utter their speech, night after night reveals knowledge" (Psalm 19:1-2). Because He is so clearly revealed in nature, men are without excuse when it comes to knowing that God exists.

But more than just knowing He exists, we can know God's character by looking at Jesus. He came to reveal God to man. "God has in these last days spoken to us by His Son" (Hebrews 1:1-2). Jesus said, "If you have seen Me you have seen the Father" (John 14:9).

We know of God's mercy, grace, compassion, kindness, and love because we see those things in Jesus. He is God in the flesh.

Through nature, through the Word, and through Jesus, we can come to a saving knowledge of God the Father.

> AS WE BEGIN TO WALK WITH JESUS, THE HOLY SPIRIT THEN TEACHES US THE DEEP TRUTHS OF GOD.

How blessed we are to know God!

———◦◦———

Father, thank You for revealing Yourself to us,
that we might know the joy of living in fellowship
with You and have the hope of eternal life.

IN JESUS' NAME, AMEN.

OCTOBER

His Workmanship

We are His workmanship, created in Christ Jesus for good works,
which God prepared beforehand that we should walk in them.
— EPHESIANS 2:10

God has your future all mapped out—every second of every moment, every hour of every day. He knows exactly what He wants you to do in this world for His glory, and He knows exactly what He needs to work out in your life today to prepare you for tomorrow's tasks. What a comfort to know that before we drew our first breath, God had a design in mind for us and already knew every step He would take in order to work out His sovereign plan for us.

> GOD IS WORKING IN YOU BECAUSE YOU ARE HIS WORKMAN-
> SHIP. MAY WE YIELD TO HIS TOUCH.

Many of the things God does, or allows, don't seem very pleasant at the moment. In fact, sometimes those things are very unpleasant. Because we are not able to see the bigger picture—the completed picture—we don't understand how those unpleasant lessons are working together to complete the puzzle. Sometimes God's decisions confuse or unsettle us. Nothing seems right; nothing seems like a right fit. But in the end, we will see that every single part was necessary to create the life God wanted to build in us.

Those times of preparation are not easy, but they are necessary. God is working in you because you are His workmanship. May we yield ourselves to His touch that He might mold and shape us according to His purposes. May we use our every breath to bring Him glory and honor.

Father, thank You for that work that You have done and are doing
in our lives today. We want to be vessels that glorify You. Have
Your perfect way with us, Lord. Train us for Your use.
IN JESUS' NAME, AMEN.

HE IS ABLE

*Now to Him who is able to do exceedingly abundantly above all
that we ask or think, according to the power that works in us …*
— EPHESIANS 3:20

We have a tendency to measure the obstacles before us by our own ability
to climb them. And that is reasonable if we are the ones who have to do
the hiking. But that is the wrong measuring stick if God is the One who is going
to handle that mountain for us. Difficulty must be measured by the capacity of
the agent handling the task. If God is the One tackling the mountain, the word
"difficulty" has no place in the equation. As He said, "Behold, I am the LORD. Is
there anything too hard for Me?" (Jeremiah 32:27).

WE MUST LEARN TO LOOK AT SITUATIONS NOT IN THE
LIGHT OF OUR STRENGTH BUT IN THE LIGHT OF GOD'S
STRENGTH.

When the doctor says, "We are sorry, there is no hope. We have done all
that we can possibly do," we despair. Why? Because men have done all they can.
We reach the end of that sentence and conclude that there is no hope, without
ever taking God into account. But the moment you factor God into the problem, despair flees. When you remember God, hope returns.

We must remember that God is able to deliver from the fiery furnace, and
the den of lions. He is able to deliver you from sin and from death—and from
any present trouble causing you distress.

Are you facing a mountain today? Ask God for help. Ask the able One to
show Himself mighty on your behalf—and then believe that He will.

*Father, thank You for loving us. Help us to get our eyes off of the
circumstances and on Your great ability.*

AMEN.

OCTOBER

Built up in Love

*But, speaking the truth in love, may [we] grow up in all things
into Him who is the head—Christ—from whom the whole body,
joined and knit together by what every joint supplies, according
to the effective working by which every part does its share, causes
growth of the body for the edifying of itself in love.*

— Ephesians 4:15-16

Walking out of church one day, a little boy turned to his dad and said,
"Looks like God is mad at us again." That is a sad commentary on a sad
truth. Although the church has been called to speak the truth in a loving way, so
that the body of Christ would grow and mature in His image, the truth is not
always spoken lovingly. Sometimes the message He's entrusted to us is shared in
anger or frustration.

LOVE MUST BE THE COVERING FOR ALL WE DO.

If we minister to others in love, build them up and encourage them with our
words and help them find their place of service to the Lord, the people will be
loved to maturity—and the body of Christ will increase mightily.

Each of us has a special calling in the body of Christ. If we don't fill that
place, we leave a gap. The body is weakened, and the church can't be all that it
could be. May God help you find your special service, and may He use you to
nurture others—strengthening them, encouraging them, and loving them … for
His sake, and for His glory.

---

*Father, we want to become everything You would have us to be.
May we show Your love and be built up in that love as we
encourage and strengthen one another through the Spirit.*

Amen.

The Believer's Walk

See then that you walk circumspectly, not as fools but as wise …
— Ephesians 5:15

The fool kills time. He wastes the precious moments God has given him, passing through life with little or no thought to what he is doing with the time entrusted to him. But the wise man walks circumspectly. He redeems the time.

The wise man wants to know God's will for His life, for this is the most important knowledge that you can ever attain. The fool stumbles through life blindly, never knowing why he exists and never really caring. He just lives for the moment with no thought of eternity.

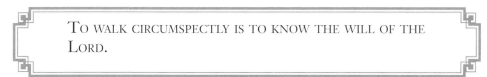

To walk circumspectly is to know the will of the Lord.

To walk circumspectly is to be filled with the Spirit. The foolish man clouds his mind with wine, dulling and numbing himself to the things that matter. But the wise man is filled with the Spirit, which sharpens his mind on the things of the Spirit. His desire is to walk according to the will of the Lord; to have his life follow precisely the plan and purpose for which God created him.

God's will is for us to give thanks always and for all things (1 Thessalonians 5:18). But I can only give thanks to God in all things if I understand and realize that all things are working together for good.

Knowing His will and being filled with His Spirit helps us walk in the way He has called us to walk—circumspectly, wisely, always giving thanks in every circumstance, making the most of every opportunity—all to His glory.

OCTOBER

———⋙●⋘———

*Father, help us to consider what You have done and who You are,
and give thanks unto You continually for all things
through Your Son, Jesus Christ.*

Amen.

THE POWER OF PRAYER

Praying always with all prayer and supplication in the Spirit,
being watchful to this end with all perseverance and supplication
for all the saints …
— EPHESIANS 6:18

e are familiar with the spiritual armor Paul describes in the sixth chapter of Ephesians—the breastplate of righteousness, the shield of faith, the helmet of salvation, the sword of the Spirit, prayer. Without this armor, you wouldn't be able to stand. Spiritual warfare calls for spiritual weapons.

I suggest to you that of all the weapons at your disposal, prayer is the most vital. It must be, for Satan tries everything he can to keep us from praying. He doesn't want you inviting God into the battle. He would like to keep it just between the two of you.

PRAYER IS THE DECISIVE WEAPON.

In the garden, Jesus prayed while Peter slept. When Jesus awoke him, He said, "Peter, are you asleep? … Watch and pray, lest you enter into temptation" (Mark 14:37-38). When Jesus faced the actual conflict, He was victorious because He won the victory in prayer. Peter faced a conflict that night too, but he was defeated. Perhaps if he had prayed instead of slept, he would have been victorious. I wonder how often we are defeated because we fail to pray.

By prayer, we take power from the enemy. When we pray, Satan must yield to the name of Jesus Christ.

May God help us to use the weapons He has given us—all the weapons. And may He move us to pray, waiting upon God and persevering until we see God's will wrought in this earth.

Father, we thank You for the powerful weapon of prayer whereby
we can pull down the strongholds Satan has in lives of those
around us. Teach us to pray, Lord.

IN JESUS' NAME WE PRAY, AMEN.

NO FEAR IN DEATH

For to me, to live is Christ, and to die is gain.
— PHILIPPIANS 1:21

The Bible tells us that it is appointed unto man once to die. That means you have an appointment with God—an inescapable appointment. How does that make you feel? Are you fearful of that appointment? Man has a natural fear of death, but that is because we are not sure what to expect. We fear the unknown.

> BECAUSE OF JESUS, THE CHILD OF GOD NEED NEVER FEAR DEATH.

The truth is, if unbelievers knew the reality of what awaits them after death, they would be more terrified than they are now. But if believers knew the truth of what awaits them after death, they would lose all fear. Paul, who was given just a small glimpse of heaven (2 Corinthians 12:2-7), said that the choice between living and dying was hard, because he knew that while in the body he could glorify God, but that he would rather be absent from the body in order to be present with the Lord (2 Corinthians 5:8).

Because of Jesus, the child of God need never fear death. He came to save us from sin and remove the sting of death. With the sting gone, we no longer need to fear death. And so we have a win-win situation.

"For me to live is Christ, and to die is gain." If I live, I live my life for the Lord and in fellowship with the Lord. I live to do His will. I have the opportunity to lay up more treasures in heaven. And when I die, I will live in His presence, in the fullness of joy everlasting.

Father, how grateful we are that the future is not unknown or uncertain for us but it is secure in Christ Jesus.

IN JESUS' NAME, AMEN.

OCTOBER

Be Anxious for Nothing

Be anxious for nothing, but in everything by prayer and supplica-
tion, with thanksgiving, let your requests be made known to God;
and the peace of God, which surpasses all understanding, will
guard your hearts and minds through Christ Jesus.

— Philippians 4:6-7

The Bible doesn't just give a command and then leave you to see how you will figure it out. It always gives you steps to obey. When Paul told us not to worry—to be "anxious for nothing"—he also gave us the antidote for worry. "But in everything by prayer and supplication with thanksgiving, let your requests be made known to God." In other words, take the things that are worrying you and let them become the subjects of your prayer life. Rather than worrying about them, pray about them.

Turn your cares into prayers.

Paul makes a distinction between prayer and supplication. Prayer is communion with God. It is talking with Him, worshiping Him, and simply loving Him for who He is. Supplication is making a request. It is when the conversation between you and God gets down to your present need. Paul instructs us to make our requests known to God, but we need to start with first things first—loving worship and prayer. Prayer should always precede our requests.

When we handle our worrisome issues in this way—coming to God through prayer, supplication, and thanksgiving—the end result is that we gain peace that passes all understanding. Though the outward problems have not yet been taken care of (and may even be getting worse), you still find that you are experiencing an incredible peace.

Father, thank You for who You are and all that You do for us.
Bless us with Your peace as we seek You.

In Jesus' name, amen.

PAUL'S PRAYER

*… to ask that you may be filled with the knowledge of His will in
all wisdom and spiritual understanding; that you may walk
worthy of the Lord, fully pleasing Him, being fruitful in every
good work and increasing in the knowledge of God …*

— COLOSSIANS 1:9-10

From the time he first heard of their faith in Jesus, Paul prayed continuously for the believers in Colossi.

First, he prayed that they might be filled with the knowledge of His will, and he asked that this knowledge come through wisdom and spiritual understanding. That's the key to knowing God's will for you. Your flesh might pull you in one direction or another, but God's Spirit in you will guide you in fulfilling God's specific, individual, sovereign purpose.

IT IS ONLY AS WE WALK IN THE STRENGTH AND THE POWER
OF THE SPIRIT OF GOD THAT WE COULD EVER HOPE TO WALK
WORTHY OF THE LORD.

Then Paul prayed that they might walk worthy of the Lord. Is this possible in our own strength? Not even remotely. As His adopted children, we must live according to the code of the royal family. To walk worthy is to walk in love, purity, and peace. It is to walk in faith.

Paul's next petition for them was that they might be fruitful in every good work. Our good works result from our relationship with Jesus. As His life flows into us, it naturally produces fruit.

Lastly, Paul asked that they increase in their knowledge of God. All we need to know about God has been revealed to us in His Word.

What a beautiful prayer—and it's for you too.

*Father, teach us Your ways and guide us in Your truth,
that our lives will be a reflection of Jesus.*

AMEN.

OCTOBER

TRIUMPH

*Having disarmed principalities and powers, He made a public
spectacle of them, triumphing over them in it.*

— COLOSSIANS 2:15

Jesus won a decisive battle on the cross. Through His obedience, He defeated Satan and opened our prison doors. So great was that victory, that even today, two thousand years later, Satan is still defeated, still conquered. Today, if any man wishes to change his allegiance from the kingdom of darkness (where Satan rules) to the kingdom of light (where Jesus rules), Satan has to release his grip. The cross opened the door wide—and Satan is powerless to shut it.

JESUS MADE PROVISION FOR OUR VICTORY.

We don't have to submit to Satan. We don't have to yield to dark impulses or fleshly rebellion. The victory won on Golgotha means we can have a new life. We can receive the Victor as our Lord and Savior, and serve Him with gladness. The powers and principalities of darkness are stubborn, but they can't dominate you unless you let them. Through Jesus, you can conquer those dark powers and force them to retreat.

In those six hours on the cross, Jesus made provision for our cleansing. He made provision for our strengthening. He made a way for us to conquer our captors. He breached the gap between God and man so that we could draw near to Him and know Him as Father.

His victory means we can know victory. Though Satan will never stop trying to tempt you away from God, you can stand against that temptation and know the glorious victory of Jesus Christ.

*Father, for those struggling with the flesh today, we pray that You
bring them to a realization of what You have done. Open their
eyes to the victory they can have through Your Son.*

IN HIS NAME, AMEN.

HIDDEN WITH CHRIST

*If then you were raised with Christ, seek those things which are
above, where Christ is, sitting at the right hand of God. Set your
mind on things above, not on things on the earth. For you died,
and your life is hidden with Christ in God.*

— COLOSSIANS 3:1-3

To be a Christian means that you are a new creation, born again, living after the Spirit. The logical conclusion of your being risen with Christ is that you will now seek those things that are above where Christ sits on the right hand of God. Because I am a Christian, because I am a new creature, because my spirit is now alive, I am interested in spiritual things, those things that are above.

> YOU ARE DEAD TO THAT OLD LIFE OF THE FLESH, OF THE
> MATERIAL THINGS.

Paul makes the point in this passage that we, as Christians, need to seek the things that are spiritual rather than material, things that are eternal rather than temporal. John said, "Love not the world, neither the things that are in the world, for he that hath the love of the world in his heart hath not the love of the Father" (1 John 2:15).

You are dead to that life that was devoid of God—that life that was in love with the world and the things of the world. Now your life is hidden with Christ in God.

May our lives, our thoughts, and our hearts be on the things that are above— that the Lord will somehow lift us above the corruption of this world and we might walk after the Spirit and invest our lives in that which is eternal.

Father, we thank You for the future that You have promised to us.
IN JESUS' NAME, AMEN.

CONTINUE IN PRAYER

Continue earnestly in prayer,
being vigilant in it with thanksgiving …
— COLOSSIANS 4:2

Because they were about to be judged for their sin, the Israelites said to Samuel, "Pray for us that we don't die." And Samuel said, "God forbid that I should sin against the Lord by ceasing to pray for you." He saw that not to pray would actually be a sin against the Lord. I wonder how many of us are guilty of the sin of prayerlessness, or how many give up prematurely because those prayers aren't answered in our timing.

WE ARE NOT TO GIVE UP.

But you might ask, "Why should I continue in prayer? If God plans to do it, isn't He going to do it anyhow? Can't I just pray once and then let it be?" First of all, prayer should never be thought of as changing the mind of God. That would put me in the driver's seat. God is not a genie who answers my every wish, and we are not trying to change the mind of God through prayer.

Sometimes God delays the answers to our prayers in order that He might bring us into harmony with His purposes. Sometimes God delays in order that He might give us much more, that He might be glorified. But either way, we are to continue in prayer.

May we give ourselves to continual prayer, and may we be thankful. "Oh, that men would give thanks to the LORD for His goodness, and for His wonderful works to the children of men!" (Psalm 107:8).

Father, we do give thanks to You today for life, for strength,
and for all of Your provisions for us.
Help us not to give up but to continue in prayer.
IN JESUS' NAME, AMEN.

KNOWN FOR LOVE

Remembering without ceasing your work of faith, labor of love, and patience of hope in our Lord Jesus Christ in the sight of our God and Father ...

— 1 THESSALONIANS 1:3

Paul commended the Thessalonians for a few things. First of all, he talks about their work of faith. They didn't work out of a sense of obligation or fear, but as a response to the love and grace of God. Good works should be a manifestation of our faith.

Next he notes their labor of love. Love, I believe, is the strongest motivator in the world. Nothing inspires a man like love. The labor of love is never a burden. It is always a joy. How important that the love of Christ so fills our hearts that it motivates us in our service for Him.

MAY WE BE KNOWN BY THE LOVE OF JESUS IN US.

The third characteristic that marked this church was the patience of hope—the hope of Jesus' return. Hope, as Paul pointed out in Romans 8:24, is not something we see—it is something we anticipate with pleasure. It is something we believe and rely on.

How are you doing in these three areas? Are you accomplishing the works of faith? Are you laboring in love for your Savior? And are you resting in the hope of His soon return? May we be known by these traits. May we be known for the love of Jesus Christ working in our hearts—love for Him, for His Word, for one another, and for the lost world in which we live.

Father, thank You for the faith You give and for the privilege of laboring for You. We wait for that day when Your will is done here on this earth even as it is done in heaven.

IN JESUS' NAME, AMEN.

OCTOBER

GOD'S POWERFUL WORD

For this reason we also thank God without ceasing, because when you received the word of God which you heard from us, you welcomed it not as the word of men, but as it is in truth, the word of God, which also effectively works in you who believe.

— 1 THESSALONIANS 2:13

If the Bible was the invention of man, you must confess that they had to be the smartest men who ever lived. Forty-four different authors wrote over the span of 1,500 years, and yet, it is one unified story that has stood the test of time and extreme critical analysis. No other book has had such a profound influence for good in the world than the Bible. It has been likened unto an anvil that has been hammered upon for centuries by skeptics and doubters. The hammers wore away and have been discarded, but the Anvil still stands.

THE BIBLE IS UNIQUE IN ITS PROPHETIC ASPECTS, AS IT SPEAKS OF THINGS YEARS—EVEN THOUSANDS OF YEARS, IN SOME INSTANCES—BEFORE THEY TAKE PLACE.

Paul described the Word as that "which effectually works in you that believe." It is so beautiful to see the effect of the Word on the lives of those who were nearly destroyed by sin. Once they are cleansed, redeemed, and set free, their lives become meaningful. God's Word brings change—not only to those in the church in Thessalonica 2,000 years ago, but to those in the church today.

Father, thank You for the power of Your Word and for the way You use it to change and restore lives. And Lord, how thankful we are that You are the same yesterday, today, and forever. Help us that we might receive and then share Your truth.

IN JESUS' NAME, AMEN.

Perfecting an Immature Faith

*... we rejoice ... night and day praying exceedingly that we may
see your face and perfect what is lacking in your faith.*

— 1 Thessalonians 3:9-10

So many people today are lacking in their faith. It is manifested by the way they live. They profess faith, but they live after the flesh. Rather than hating evil, they are actually attracted to it. If they truly believed the Bible they couldn't do the things they do. If they truly believed the gospel, they wouldn't settle for a halfhearted commitment to their Savior. But these are they who manifest Jesus only when it is convenient for them, only if it doesn't interfere with their plans.

Is there hope for someone with such an incomplete, immature faith? Yes. Bring them to God's Word.

Complete faith in God's Word emboldens our witness. It sends fear fleeing. It banishes anxiety. But those whose faith is immature lack both boldness and confidence. They can't testify of Jesus because they don't fully trust Him.

Is there hope for someone with an immature faith? And if so, how do you perfect such a faith? It is accomplished by bringing them to a greater understanding and knowledge of God and by teaching God's Word, which is God's revelation of Himself. And as you study the Scriptures and read of the accounts of those who have put their faith in God and how God has delivered them, it increases your faith—for faith comes by hearing and hearing by the Word of God.

We all lack faith in certain areas, so our prayer must be, "Lord, increase my faith." May we spend time in His Word so that He can perfect that which is lacking in us.

*Father, increase our faith. Bring us to a full, complete faith
in You, in Your Word, and in Your promises.*

In Jesus' name, amen.

OCTOBER

SNATCHED AWAY

For the Lord Himself will descend from heaven with a shout, with the voice of an archangel, and with the trumpet of God. And the dead in Christ will rise first. Then we who are alive and remain shall be caught up together with them in the clouds to meet the Lord in the air. And thus we shall always be with the Lord.

— 1 THESSALONIANS 4:16-17

One day Jesus is coming for His church; He's going to catch us up. He is going to take us by force out of this world.

This "snatching away" is known as the rapture. Some people ignorantly argue against the idea of the rapture, declaring that the actual word "rapture" doesn't even appear in the Bible. But the Greek word *harpazo* is translated in the King James Version as "caught up." The word means "to be taken away by force or by power." In translating from Greek into Latin, the Latin Vulgate version uses the word *raptus*, and the word rapture is a transliteration of that word.

> GOD WANTS US TO LIVE IN CONSTANT, MINUTE-BY-MINUTE READINESS FOR HIS RETURN.

When the rapture happens, it is going to take us by surprise. "Therefore you also be ready, for the Son of Man is coming at an hour you do not expect" (Luke 12:40). The day is coming soon. With a shout, He will say, "Come on up!" And we who are alive and remain will be caught up, snatched up, taken by force out of this sin-cursed world.

Are you ready for this magnificent event?

Father, thank You for the glorious hope of the blessed appearing of our great God and Savior Jesus Christ. Help us to live in such a way that we are ready when the moment comes.

AMEN.

WATCH

Therefore let us not sleep, as others do,
but let us watch and be sober.
— 1 THESSALONIANS 5:6

In His letter to the church of Sardis, Jesus said, "Therefore if you will not watch, I will come upon you as a thief, and you will not know what hour I will come upon you" (Revelation 3:3). We must be watching for the return of Christ. Over and over, when Jesus spoke to His disciples about His coming, He said, "Watch."

If you watch for the return of Jesus Christ, it will not take you as a thief in the night, coming to spoil your goods. The world around us is in darkness. It is not even aware of the signs of His return. Ignorant of the things of God and of the Word of God, the world goes on, business as usual.

WE CAN'T AFFORD TO BE BLIND OR IGNORANT.

As children of God we must walk in the light. That means we need to recognize the times in which we live and walk circumspectly—not in darkness or in ignorance of the close return of our Lord. As God's children, we must not be caught sleeping, but must be watching for His return with eagerness.

We are to be watching for signs, and we won't recognize those signs if we are not aware of what is happening around us. Jesus said, "When these things [calamities, violence, wars, moral breakdown, social disorder] begin to happen, look up and lift up your heads, because your redemption draws near" (Luke 21:28). It is time today to be looking up, to be watching, to be sober—for Jesus is coming soon for His church.

Father, in these days of darkness, may we be sustained by the hope
of Your coming. Come quickly, Lord.

AMEN.

OCTOBER

GIVE THANKS

*In everything give thanks; for this is the will of God
in Christ Jesus for you.*
— 1 THESSALONIANS 5:18

There are certain aspects of the will of God that we can know with certainty. For instance, it is God's will that we confess Jesus Christ as our Lord; it is His will that we should walk in love; it is His will that we treat each other kindly; it is His will that we forgive those who have offended us. Whenever Scripture tells us to do a thing, we can be certain that it is God's will for us.

In this passage, Paul tells us that it is the will of God that, "In everything we give thanks; for this is the will of God in Christ Jesus concerning us." Notice that He didn't say, "In some things give thanks...." He said "in everything."

IF WE ARE TO GIVE THANKS IN EVERYTHING, WE MUST UNDERSTAND SOME BASIC TRUTHS ABOUT GOD.

We must understand that God is in control of all of life's circumstances, and that those circumstances are working for our good. And we must grasp the amazing fact that God loves us supremely.

God doesn't promise us that we are not going to suffer. He doesn't promise that we won't have pain in our lives, but we are told that in that suffering or pain, we are to give thanks—because God has allowed it. And if God has allowed it, we can trust He has a good purpose for it.

---

*Father, help us to have the right perspective about pain, loss, disappointment, and all the other difficult circumstances that try to steal our faith. When those hard moments come,
remind us, Lord, to give thanks.*
IN JESUS' NAME, AMEN.

RIGHTEOUS JUDGMENT

It is a righteous thing with God to repay with tribulation those who trouble you, and to give you who are troubled rest with us when the Lord Jesus is revealed from heaven with His mighty angels …

— 2 THESSALONIANS 1:6-7

While ministering in Thessalonica, men sought to kill Paul, so he had to flee for his life. This frustrated Paul's would-be killers, who then turned their rage on the Thessalonian church. Paul wrote this letter to comfort them.

It seems that people always come against those trying to live a godly life. They mock you, cheat you, and lie against you, and it makes you wonder, "Lord, why do You allow these evil people to torture and torment those who are serving You?" The Thessalonian believers must have wondered that. So Paul wrote to encourage them that when the Lord returns, His first order of business will be to deal with their persecutors.

SCRIPTURE REPEATEDLY WARNS THAT GOD WILL JUDGE HIS ENEMIES.

The righteousness of God will be manifested in His judgments against those who persecuted the church. The tribulation will not be for the church; it will be for those who troubled the church. Because God is just, fair, and righteous, we can be sure that His judgments will be just, fair, and righteous.

The day of the Lord is a two-fold event. It begins with judgment and ends with the glorious establishment of the kingdom of God on the earth. I believe that the world today is ripe for the judgment of God. May we be accounted worthy to live in peace and rest with Him.

Father, help us to stand for Jesus Christ and to stand against the tide of evil. Lord, let us live in a way that pleases You.

AMEN.

The Mystery of Lawlessness

For the mystery of lawlessness is already at work; only He who
now restrains will do so until He is taken out of the way.

— 2 Thessalonians 2:7

Paul wrote to the Thessalonians to assure them that despite the persecution they were suffering, they were not in the great tribulation. Two things would happen before that day came: a falling away would occur in the church, and the man of sin would be revealed.

Lawlessness had already begun in Paul's day. And it has only increased. Why are people drawn toward lawlessness when it always results in calamity? Therein lies the mystery.

EVERY DAY, MEN REJECT JESUS CHRIST—THE ONE TRUE WAY TO HEAVEN.

It is inconceivable that people could willfully choose evil over good—even knowing that their choice could kill them. Yet they do. It began in the garden of Eden, when Adam and Eve chose to eat of the tree that God had declared would kill them. It's a mystery that men would choose a path that leads to death rather than the path that leads to life—a path that will bring them only misery and destruction. Yet they do.

"Come now, and let us reason together," the Lord invited in Isaiah 1:18. Obedience is reasonable. Accepting the salvation Jesus offers is reasonable. Yet men continue to cast reason aside, all because they love darkness more than light, all because lawlessness is more appealing to them than obedience.

Search your heart today. Ask God to show you if you are choosing lawlessness over obedience. And if you find you are, repent.

———✦———

Father, help us to heed Your Word that we would not be deceived.
May we surrender our hearts and our lives
to Jesus Christ, the living Lord.

Amen.

HIS MISSION TO SAVE

This is a faithful saying and worthy of all acceptance, that Christ
Jesus came into the world to save sinners, of whom I am chief.
— 1 TIMOTHY 1:15

One day, while Jesus was dining with tax collectors and other sinners, He overheard the scribes and Pharisees questioning His choice of dinner companions. "When Jesus heard it, He said to them, 'Those who are well have no need of a physician, but those who are sick. I did not come to call the righteous, but sinners, to repentance'" (Mark 2:17).

NO MAN IS BEYOND THE REACH OF GOD'S LOVE.

If you are well, you avoid the doctor. But when you are sick, you know you need help. Man was sick. He had chosen a deadly path, a path that led to sickness, misery, and destruction. God saw man's plight and had mercy on him by sending His Son, the Great Physician. He didn't send Jesus to condemn the world. That wasn't necessary, for the world was already condemned. He sent Jesus "that the world through Him might be saved" (John 3:17).

Note that Paul calls himself the chief of sinners. He knew who he was. Paul made no excuses for his past life. The point he was making was that if Jesus could save him—after he blasphemed Jesus, approved of crimes against Christians, and even hunted and killed them—then the rest of us have no worries. Jesus will forgive and save us too. He who reached down to the lowest depths and saved the worst of the violators can reach you in the pit of your sin and bring you into His light. No man is beyond the reach of God's love.

Father, thank You for sending Your Son into the world
to forgive and save those sickened by sin.
IN JESUS' NAME, AMEN.

ONE MEDIATOR

For there is one God and one Mediator between God and men, the
Man Christ Jesus, who gave Himself a ransom for all,
to be testified in due time …
— 1 TIMOTHY 2:5-6

It is both arrogant and audacious for finite, sinful man to think we can come brazenly before the eternal, holy God. He is infinitely pure; we are marred by sin. He is light; we dwell in darkness. So how can sinful man ever hope to stand in God's presence?

There is a way, but only one. Job cried out for a Mediator, a bridge, who could lay His hand on both God and man. And we have that Mediator in Jesus. He who was God became man that He might stand in the gap between God and us.

NO SAINT CAN SAVE YOU—ONLY JESUS CAN SAVE YOU.

No saint can stand in the gap for you. Mary can't do that for you. No matter how holy or how righteous that saint was in his or her lifetime, he was just a man; she was just a woman. You can pray all day long to a dead saint, and that saint will remain helpless to cross the chasm between you and God. Only Jesus can do that for you, because He alone can touch both you and God. He is the one true Mediator God sent to bring us to Himself.

Through the death and resurrection of Jesus Christ, the way has been made possible for us to approach the infinite, eternal, holy, pure, and majestic Father. We stand righteous before Him because of the righteousness of our Mediator.

Praise God for His Son!

Father, thank You for providing that which Job was crying for, a
mediator who would touch us both.
Thank You for that hope of eternal life.
IN JESUS' NAME, AMEN.

THE MYSTERY

*… great is the mystery of godliness: God was manifested in the
flesh, justified in the Spirit, seen by angels, preached among the
Gentiles, believed on in the world, received up in glory.*

— 1 TIMOTHY 3:16

There is a tremendous mystery to godliness—to the fact that man becomes like his god. In speaking of the mute, deaf, blind, immobile idols of the heathen, the psalmist declares that, "Those who make them are like them; so is everyone who trusts in them" (Psalm 115:8). It is a basic psychological truth that a man becomes like his god. If your god is loving, then you become loving. If your god is good, you become good. If your god is hateful and bitter, then you become hateful and bitter.

> WE WHO FOLLOW GOD ARE BEING CHANGED TO BE LIKE HIM DAY BY DAY.

The Bible tells us that, "We are children of God; and it has not yet been revealed what we shall be, but we know that when He is revealed, we shall be like Him, for we shall see Him as He is" (1 John 3:2).

How I love to see this mystery unfolding in my own life, to see the changes He makes day by day as I follow and serve Him.

David said, "I will be satisfied when I awake in Your likeness." And one day I will wake and find I am in heaven, and I will be just like Him. That is the mystery of godliness: the transformed life made into His image.

*Father, thank You for the power of Your Spirit to transform
a person's life and conform them into Your image. Work in our
hearts and lives this day. Help us to yield to Your touch,
never resisting what You want to do in us.*

IN JESUS' NAME, AMEN.

BE AN EXAMPLE

Let no one despise your youth, but be an example to the believers
in word, in conduct, in love, in spirit, in faith, in purity.
— 1 TIMOTHY 4:12

Because Timothy was young, some in the church looked down on him and refused to receive from him. So Paul wrote to Timothy, saying, "Look, just be an example." Paul outlined six areas where Timothy should be an example to the believers:

In word—This could be interpreted two ways. First, Paul may have meant, "Be an example in your language." But he could also have meant, "Be an example in your knowledge and understanding of the Scriptures—be a man of the Word." Both are important.

In conduct—Let your lifestyle be an example of what a believer is. Model Christ in your actions and your attitudes.

In love—The love that Paul described in 1 Corinthians 13 is the love that should emanate from the life of every believer.

In spirit—Some people have a sweet spirit; others are just mean-spirited. There is no place for mean-spiritedness among believers.

In faith—This also could mean one of two things. Either we are to be an example in our trust in God, or in our own trustworthiness—or both.

In purity—Timothy was young, not married, and living in a corrupt, pagan society. Paul urged him to live a life of purity, a life above reproach.

PAUL'S MESSAGE IS FOR EVERY AGE. WE ARE TO MODEL CHRIST BOTH TO THE CHURCH AND TO A WORLD WONDERING ABOUT CHRISTIANITY.

Father, help us to be a godly example to the world,
that we may bring You glory.
AMEN.

THE SIN OF PREJUDICE

I charge you before God and the Lord Jesus Christ and the elect
angels that you observe these things without prejudice,
doing nothing with partiality.

— 1 TIMOTHY 5:21

Paul has been instructing Timothy on such matters as taking care of the widows, his relationship with the church elders, rules for the young women, and so forth. Then he said, "Timothy, you are not to show preferential treatment or partiality. See that you observe these things without preferring one above another."

Throughout the Bible we are told that God is not a respecter of persons. But unfortunately, we often do show partiality. We are prone to honor the rich and sort of shuttle the poor aside, but God isn't like that. He is just as concerned in saving the soul of the poorest man on the face of the earth as He is the richest. Social standing means nothing to God; we all exist on the same level and on the same plane.

> IF WE CALL OURSELVES BY HIS NAME, WE NEED TO DEVELOP HIS PERSPECTIVE ON PREJUDICE.

It doesn't matter how much success you have accomplished, how much wealth you have accumulated, or who you are in terms of the world's ranking. It doesn't matter if you dwell in a mansion or a shack. Regardless of how anyone else views you, you matter to Jesus.

We must find a way to dissolve the differences between us. How can we reach a lost world if we don't view them the way Jesus does? We need to learn to love as He loved, and to value others because they matter so much to Him.

Father, thank You for Your great love for us. Help us to love with
Your love—without preference or partiality.

IN JESUS' NAME, AMEN.

NOVEMBER

TRUE RICHES

Now godliness with contentment is great gain.
— 1 TIMOTHY 6:6

People often say, "Oh, if only I won the lottery!" But you might be surprised. Studies have shown that quite frequently, those giant jackpots mess up the winners' lives. They go from being happy-go-lucky to being anxious. Though they thought the money would bring them great happiness, in many cases it only brought sorrow.

Men scrape and sweat to build their wealth, but in the day of judgment those riches will be of no value, because you can't buy God off. True riches, however, are eternal. They last forever; nothing can diminish them. You can be poor in this world and yet be an heir of the kingdom of God.

EARTHLY RICHES ARE A COMPLETE SHAM.

Jeremiah said, "Thus says the LORD: 'Let not the wise man glory in his wisdom, let not the mighty man glory in his might, nor let the rich man glory in his riches; but let him who glories glory in this, that he understands and knows Me, that I am the LORD, exercising lovingkindness, judgment, and righteousness in the earth. For in these I delight'" (Jeremiah 9:23-24).

"I have learned in whatever state I am, to be content," Paul said. "I know how to be abased, and I know how to abound. Everywhere and in all things I have learned both to be full and to be hungry, both to abound and to suffer need" (Philippians 4:11-12).

Instead of striving to accumulate more, let's learn the value of contentment.

Father, we thank You that You have offered us such vast riches.
Teach us what it is to be content with what You have given us.
IN JESUS' NAME, AMEN.

DEATH IS ABOLISHED

*… our Savior Jesus Christ, who has abolished death and brought
life and immortality to light through the gospel …*
— 2 TIMOTHY 1:10

One thing you can say about death is that it is certain. Thus far, the statistics have been impressive: 100 out of every 100 have died. But here is an interesting phenomenon: if you are born once, you will die twice; if you have been born twice, you will only die once.

At our physical death, we will be changed. We will undergo a metamorphosis. That is necessary, because right now we exist in corruptible bodies. But in order to exist in heaven, we need incorruptible bodies. And when these tents are dissolved, when our bodies go back to dust, we will enter our eternal existence with God. What a glorious promise! What a blessed hope!

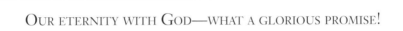

OUR ETERNITY WITH GOD—WHAT A GLORIOUS PROMISE!

One of these days you may pick up a paper and read, "Chuck Smith, pastor of Calvary Chapel, has died." Don't you believe it! If you see that, know with certainty that I didn't die—I simply moved out of an old, worn out tent and into a beautiful mansion, "a building from God, a house not made with hands, eternal in the heavens" (2 Corinthians 5:1). So please don't weep for me, because you know I won't be weeping. "In His presence is fullness of joy; at His right hand are pleasures for evermore" (Psalm 16.11).

God wants to have fellowship with you, and He sent His Son to abolish death in order that you might have eternal life and immortality through Him. And that's the gospel truth.

*Father, thank You for that life and immortality that is ours
through Jesus Christ. We pray for those who don't know You
and ask that You will speak to their hearts.*

IN JESUS' NAME, AMEN.

VESSELS OF HONOR

Therefore if anyone cleanses himself from the latter, he will be a vessel for honor, sanctified and useful for the Master, prepared for every good work.

— 2 TIMOTHY 2:21

Vessels were quite common in Bible days. Some, made of gold or silver, were used for decorative purposes. Others were made of clay and used for anything from carrying water to holding garbage or wastewater. Thus, some were called vessels of honor, and some vessels of dishonor.

Take a moment and ask yourself, "What are the contents of my life?" Are the things filling your life pure, or are they wastewater?

YOU HAVE BEEN MADE TO CONTAIN GOD.

God has chosen to fill a clay pot—you—with the most valuable thing in existence—Himself. He wants to fill you with Himself so that you overflow His grace, mercy, and love to a thirsty world.

Paul wrote to Timothy about men in the church who were subverting the people with faulty teaching. These men had become vessels of dishonor. God could not use them; their doctrine was impure. They taught their own concepts rather than the truths of God, and in this way, they tainted the contents of their lives with their own flavor.

How easy it is to become a vessel of dishonor! All one must do is to stop cleansing their mind each day. But if you want to be a vessel of honor, fit for the Master's use, then you need to flee the lust of the flesh. You have to commune with God at the end of every day and ask Him to cleanse you anew.

God, make us vessels of honor, that we would pour forth Your grace to the world around us. Cleanse us and use us, Lord.

AMEN.

Inspired by God

All Scripture is given by inspiration of God, and is profitable for doctrine, for reproof, for correction, for instruction in righteousness …

— 2 Timothy 3:16

The Bible tells of the eternal God who created the universe, the God who exists outside of time and space. It tells us that this God, who created all things, loves man and desires to live in fellowship with him, that man might receive the blessings of knowing Him. The Scriptures are God's Word to man.

Because the Bible is inspired by God, it is infallible and inerrant.

Through prophecies, God proves that He is outside of time. Only He knows the end from the beginning. Only He can foretell a thing before it comes to pass. By prophesying things that are yet future, He proves that He is indeed the Author of this Book, which is about eighty-percent prophecy.

When Jesus was talking to His disciples about His death and resurrection, He said, "I am going away and coming back to you. I am going to the Father. And now I have told you before it comes, that when it does come to pass, you may believe" (John 14:28-29). He told them in advance of the things to come so that they could see that He is indeed who He claimed to be—the Son of God.

God has given us His Word so that we understand His nature, His plan of redemption, and the path to spiritual growth. The truths it contains will build our faith. May we study it daily, being doers of the Word and not hearers only.

Thank You, Father, for Your Word, a light unto our path which guides us in Your truth.

In Jesus' name we pray, amen.

NOVEMBER

THE LORD STOOD WITH ME

But the Lord stood with me and strengthened me, so that the
message might be preached fully through me,
and that all the Gentiles might hear.
— 2 TIMOTHY 4:17

At Paul's first trial before Nero, things looked so dark that all of his companions forsook him. "At my first defense no one stood with me," he said, "but all forsook me" (2 Timothy 4:16).

How horrible it feels to be abandoned. The Bible says that "a friend loves at all times" (Proverbs 17:17), but too often we discover that what we thought to be true friends were really only acquaintances. Though all others may leave you, Jesus will always stand with you. The Lord will not forsake His people. As David said, "Though I walk through the valley of the shadow of death, I will fear no evil; for You are with me" (Psalm 23:4).

> AS LONG AS I KNOW THE LORD IS STANDING WITH ME, I CAN FACE THE TRIALS OF TOMORROW AND THE UNCERTAINTIES OF THE FUTURE.

Today you might feel like Paul—deserted, standing alone, and facing an unknown future. On this dark night, you can be certain that Jesus stands with you. "Lo, I am with you always, even to the end of the age" (Matthew 28:20). He said, "I will never leave you nor forsake you" (Hebrews 13:5).

As someone once said, "I don't know what tomorrow holds, but I know Who holds tomorrow, and I know Who holds my hand." He will stand with me and see me through.

Father, we thank You that we have such wonderful assurance that
You will be with us. Hold us up, Lord, when we think we can't
take any more. Hold us with Your right hand.

IN JESUS' NAME, AMEN.

PROFESSION VS. PRACTICE

They profess to know God, but in works they deny Him, being
abominable, disobedient, and disqualified for every good work.

— TITUS 1:16

A lot of people think that because they say, "Now I lay me down to sleep, I pray the Lord my soul to keep," then that means they know God. But that is a false sense of security if you are not living the way you should be. As Jesus said, "Why do you call Me 'Lord, Lord,' and not do the things which I say?" (Luke 6:46).

Which do you think God is most interested in—profession or practice? John the Baptist said, "Bear fruits worthy of repentance" (Luke 3:8). In other words, "Let your life be consistent with your words."

IT IS ONE THING TO KNOW *OF* GOD, AND QUITE ANOTHER THING TO *KNOW* GOD.

To say that you believe in God is not enough; you must follow your words with a life that is consistent with God. Words are meaningless. You can say anything at all. But how are you living?

Paul encourages us to examine ourselves, for he said, "If we would judge ourselves, we would not be judged" (1 Corinthians 11:31). Is it possible that you are one of those who Paul was speaking about—those who are in the church and who profess to know God, but who actually deny Him by their works? Have you allowed other gods to supersede your love for Him? Is He really first in your life?

Don't just profess your faith—practice it as well.

⎯⎯⎯◦⟐◦⎯⎯⎯

Lord, show me if in my work I am denying You. Show me if there
is an inconsistency between my profession and my practice.
Help me, Lord, to know and serve You in truth.

IN JESUS' NAME, AMEN.

The Blessed Hope

Looking for the blessed hope and glorious appearing of our great
God and Savior Jesus Christ …

— Titus 2:13

The believer's hope is eternal life with God. For us, death is not the end; it is simply a metamorphosis. It is merely a change of body. But if your hope isn't in Jesus Christ for eternal life, then as Paul said, you are "without Christ … having no hope and without God in the world" (Ephesians 2:12).

> IF YOU DON'T HAVE CHRIST, THEN YOU DON'T HAVE GOD … AND YOU DON'T HAVE HOPE.

We believers hope not only for eternal life, but we also look for the glorious appearing of Jesus Christ. He promised that He would come again. He said to His disciples, "Let not your heart be troubled; you believe in God, believe also in Me. In My Father's house are many mansions; if it were not so, I would have told you. I go to prepare a place for you. And if I go and prepare a place for you, I will come again and receive you to Myself, that where I am, there you may be also" (John 14:1-3). And so we wait in hope for the glorious appearing of our Lord Jesus Christ.

Jesus gave us many signs of His return, things we could watch for so we knew it was close. Our hopes rise as we look around the world today and see that all those conditions are present—everything the Bible said would take place prior to that day. The darker the world becomes, the brighter the hope is for the child of God.

Father, we thank You that in a world darkened by despair and
hopelessness, we have a glorious hope that sustains us.

IN JESUS' NAME, AMEN.

JUSTIFIED

That having been justified by His grace we should become heirs according to the hope of eternal life.

— TITUS 3:7

Through mercy God forgives you of your sins. But by grace He justifies you, and that means He has dismissed the charges against you. He has wiped the slate clean. "There is therefore now no condemnation to those who are in Christ Jesus" (Romans 8:1). Because you have received Jesus Christ as your Lord, as God looks at you today He sees you as absolutely innocent. So where justice is getting what we deserve, and mercy is not getting what we deserve, grace is getting what we don't deserve.

BEING JUSTIFIED BY HIS GRACE, I AM NOW GOD'S CHILD.

I don't deserve God's love. I don't deserve the total blotting out of my sins, or eternal life in His kingdom. But those are things that God gives to me because of the justification that came through His grace. I deserve death; through grace God gives me life. I deserve hell; through grace God opens heaven's doors to me.

As His child, I become an heir of God. The world has many millionaires, and even billionaires. But the wealth accumulated by those people is absolutely nothing compared with God's riches. We who belong to God are richer than the richest people on earth, because the eternal glory of God's kingdom belongs to us. In the endless ages to come, we who are God's children will enjoy the riches of the kingdom, the beauty of His presence, the majesty of His love, and the comfort of His grace and mercy—forever.

Father, thank You that by Your grace You have wiped the slate clean. Oh, how happy we are because of Your grace towards us!

IN JESUS' NAME, AMEN.

Charge it to Me

But if he has wronged you or owes anything,
put that on my account.

— PHILEMON 18

T he book of Philemon is actually a letter Paul wrote to intercede on behalf of Onesimus, a runaway slave. Evidently, when he left, Onesimus stole some money from Philemon who lived in Colossi. Using the money, he made his way to Rome—no doubt hoping to be lost in the crowd. But Onesimus was arrested and placed into prison, where he met Paul the apostle. Paul began to witness to him of the saving grace of Jesus Christ, and Onesimus was born again. In time, Paul discovered he was a runaway slave. Paul knew his master Philemon because he had led him to the Lord as well. So Paul wrote this letter to Philemon asking that he receive Onesimus as he would receive Paul himself. He appealed to Philemon to set his slave free, so Onesimus could come back and serve with him in the work of the gospel.

OUR DEBT HAS BEEN PAID IN FULL BY JESUS CHRIST.

Paul wrote, "If he owes you anything, charge it to me." Paul is willing to pay Onesimus' debt, which is exactly what Jesus Christ has done for us. He paid the debt that we owed.

We were all like Onesimus, running from our Master. We were runaway slaves, owing a debt we couldn't pay. But just like Onesimus, we too have an Advocate, a Mediator, an Intercessor. We have the Lord Jesus Christ, who intercedes on our behalf. "And the LORD has laid on Him the iniquity of us all" (Isaiah 53:6).

The debt has been paid in full. We owe nothing now—except our life and our gratitude.

Lord, how thankful we are that You have paid our debt in full!
IN JESUS' NAME, AMEN.

THE MESSAGE

*God, who at various times and in various ways spoke in time past
to the fathers by the prophets, has in these last days spoken to us by
His Son …*
— HEBREWS 1:1-2

God has been speaking to man from the beginning of time. He speaks through nature, through His prophets, through His Word, through visions, and through dreams. He speaks through the still small, inner voice. Sometimes He speaks in an audible voice. God is still speaking to us; the problem is that we do not always listen.

In the Bible, we see that man distorted God's messages by trying to interpret His laws in their own way. Man had become so confused, they no longer knew the truth about God. So God sent His Son into the world to reveal the truth to man.

GOD IS STILL SPEAKING TODAY. LISTEN.

What is the basic message God gave us through His Son? First of all, Jesus taught us that God is love. "God so loved the world that He gave His only begotten Son, that whoever believes in Him should not perish but have everlasting life." He taught that God is merciful, gracious, compassionate, and forgiving. He taught that God is light. Jesus also taught that God wants us to love one another, even as He loves us.

May we hear God's voice clearly as He speaks to us about life, love, our relationship to Him, and our relationships with one another. May God help us to really listen. May we obey His voice and love others as He would have us to love.

*God, give us an ear to hear what You are saying to us through
Your Word and Your Holy Spirit.*

IN HIS NAME, amen.

DRIFTING

*Therefore we must give the more earnest heed to the things
we have heard, lest we drift away.*

— HEBREWS 2:1

Hebrews was written to warn those Jews drifting back into Judaism that the old ways were not the answer, because now we have God's final revelation through His Son.

The word "therefore" refers back to the previous chapter which discussed how in times past, God spoke to the fathers by the prophets. The writer then said that in these last days God spoke through a more direct revelation—He spoke through His Son, Jesus. So we must heed the things we have heard from the lips of Jesus.

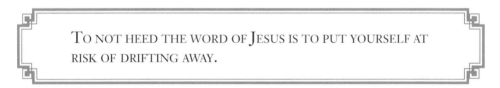

TO NOT HEED THE WORD OF JESUS IS TO PUT YOURSELF AT RISK OF DRIFTING AWAY.

What did Jesus say? He said, "If you want to enter heaven, you must be born again" (John 3:3). He said, "I am the way, the truth, and the life; no man can come to the Father, but by Me" (John 14:6). He said that He "did not come into this world to condemn the world; but that the world through Him might be saved" (John 3:17). He said, "For God so loved the world, that He gave His only begotten Son that whoever would believe in Him would not perish but have everlasting life" (John 3:16).

Drifting is a slow, imperceptive process. The only way to know you are drifting is to have a stationary frame of reference. As you see yourself moving from that stationary point, you then realize you are drifting.

Keep your eyes on the Anchor, Jesus Christ. Heed His words. He will be your stationary reference. He will keep you from drifting.

***

*Father, we are prone to wander from You.
Keep us close. Anchor us in Your truth.*

IN JESUS' NAME, AMEN.

ENTERING GOD'S REST

So I swore in My wrath, "They shall not enter My rest."
— HEBREWS 3:11

The writer of Hebrews is quoting from Psalm 95 concerning the day when the people failed to enter the Promised Land, failed to experience the peace and abundance God wanted to give them.

God has promised us rest. Jesus said, "Come to Me, all you who labor and are heavy laden, and I will give you rest" (Matthew 11:28). When you receive Jesus as your Savior, one of the first experiences you have is deep peace. Having surrendered, you are no longer fighting against God.

> UNBELIEF CAN KEEP YOU FROM ENJOYING THE RICH, FULL LIFE THAT GOD WANTS YOU TO EXPERIENCE IN CHRIST.

God wants you to have a beautiful, placid, unperturbed life—a life of peace and rest. Yet, how few of God's people really know and experience that perfect peace that passes human understanding. Perhaps that is because we don't believe His promise. Like the children of Israel, we let the giants in life keep us from taking all that God wants to give us.

Many of you are still in the wilderness in your Christian experience; you still struggle with the flesh and you're not gaining ground or conquering anything. You are not living a victorious Christian life.

In our unbelief, we don't trust Him to do the things He promised He would do. God is saying, "You have been in the wilderness long enough. It's time to move into the Promised Land. It is time to go in and conquer the land." Take the victories that God has for you and begin to experience the richness and the fullness of life in Jesus Christ. Experience His rest.

NOVEMBER

Lord, may we follow You into that place of victory.
IN JESUS' NAME, AMEN.

THE DECEITFULNESS OF SIN

But exhort one another daily, while it is called "Today," lest any of you be hardened through the deceitfulness of sin.

— HEBREWS 3:13

Sin is deceitful—wickedly deceitful. On the surface, sin looks to be pleasurable, but the Bible warns us that, "There is a way that seems right to man, but its end is the way of death" (Proverbs 16:25). Sin justifies itself. You have heard those justifications. "Times have changed; everyone is doing it." "I'm only human." "Just one time can't hurt you." "I can't help it, God made me this way."

> BEING HARDENED BY SIN, YOU FIND YOURSELF DOING THINGS THAT YOU ONCE SWORE YOU WOULD NEVER DO.

Sin deceives you by hardening you. If you embrace anything long enough, you begin to accept it.

The solution to sin's deceitfulness is to surround yourself with other believers, true friends who will warn you when you are going astray. "Faithful are the wounds of a friend, but the kisses of an enemy are deceitful" (Proverbs 27:6). Peer pressure can be a positive thing when those peers love the Lord and are intent on serving Him.

If the Spirit of God has been speaking to your heart about a sin you have allowed in your life, it is so important that you let it go this moment. Don't wait until tomorrow or next week. Don't wait for a more convenient time. Remember: sin is deceitful. If you let it, sin will harden your heart against God.

Father, help us to listen to Your Word and heed it, lest our hearts be hardened through sin's deceitfulness. Help us to forsake the path of sin and to walk in the ways of righteousness.

AMEN.

LIVING AND POWERFUL

The Word of God is living and powerful ...
— HEBREWS 4:12A

Seeds are alive. Because of the unique DNA embedded within seeds, each one is capable of reproducing itself, whether it be from a tree, a vine, or a plant. In Luke 8, when Jesus gave the parable of a man who sowed seed on four different types of soil, He said, "Now the seed is the Word of God." This means that when you take in the Word of God, it plants itself in your heart and begins to transform you.

> GOD'S WORD BEGINS TO CHANGE YOU—FROM THE INSIDE OUT—INTO THE IMAGE OF JESUS.

Then the writer of Hebrews said, "It is powerful." And it is. The power of God's Word is awesome. In Psalm 33:6 we read, "By the word of the LORD the heavens were made, and all of the host of them by the breath of His mouth." Think of that—the whole, vast universe was made by the word of the Lord, by just the breath of His mouth. We read in Genesis, "Then God said, 'Let there be light'; and there was light." God created all we see and know by the power of His Word.

The power of God's Word is evident in the lives it has transformed. People who were once society's castoffs—men and women who were looked upon as hopeless and worthless—have been changed and healed by the power of God's Word. By simply taking it in and meditating on the truths of Scripture, depression has been lifted, hearts have been mended, minds have been transformed, and lives have been changed—forever.

Lord, move us to study Your powerful, living Word that it might work in us a glorious transformation.

AMEN.

NOVEMBER

The Power of the Word

The Word of God is living and powerful, and sharper than any
two-edged sword, piercing even to the division of soul and spirit,
and of joints and marrow, and is a discerner
of the thoughts and intents of the heart.

— Hebrews 4:12

U p until the Romans developed the two-edged sword, they had fought all their battles with a single-edged sword. Two edges enabled them to swing both ways and cut from both directions. With this secret weapon, the Roman legions were able to conquer the world.

It is through the Word of God that I gain truth about God—and about myself.

The Word of God is sharper than a two-edged sword, sharp enough to cut between the soul and the spirit. Man is a three-fold being—body, soul and spirit—yet we are so integrated that it is next to impossible to thoroughly separate the three. Many people go to church and have a highly emotional experience, but it doesn't touch their spirit, and they leave unchanged. Experience doesn't change a man nor does it minister to his spirit. It takes the Word of God to do that.

The Word of God is a discerner of the thoughts and intents of the heart. So often we ourselves don't know our own heart. Why did I do that? What were my real intentions? Motives are often disguised. What may appear to be a wonderful gesture may have an improper motive behind it—the motive of self-glory or recognition. That is why the Word of God is so important to us, because it reveals the true motives of our hearts.

Father, we thank You for Your Word.
Give us a hunger to read it and meditate upon it.
Amen.

Lessons in Suffering

Though He was a Son, yet He learned obedience
by the things which He suffered.

— Hebrews 5:8

Jesus learned obedience, and His obedience caused Him suffering. His death on the cross was unbelievably horrific. But His suffering served to work out the eternal purpose of God. We can learn much from Him, "Who for the joy that was set before Him endured the cross, despising the shame" (Hebrews 12:2).

Unlike Jesus, we often learn obedience the hard way. Usually, we disobey and then learn that obedience would have been much better. We learn obedience through the suffering we receive as a consequence of our disobedience.

SUFFERING IS A DIVINE INSTRUMENT.

All God's children will suffer. Believing in Jesus Christ as our Lord and great High Priest does not grant us immunity from suffering. We would like to believe that because we belong to God, He will protect us from any kind of pain whatsoever. But are we greater than our Lord? If Jesus suffered and learned obedience through that suffering, how much more do we need to learn the lesson?

God uses suffering to work out His eternal purposes. He uses it also to teach us obedience, dependence, faith, grace, and patience. We can trust that God will never allow us to suffer needlessly, just as He did not allow His Son to suffer needlessly.

Whatever challenge God places before you, obey with gladness. You don't know how God might use that suffering for your benefit and for His glory.

Father, we rest in the fact that Your thoughts toward us are good,
not evil; that You have a glorious future for us.
Help us to obey joyfully.

IN JESUS' NAME, AMEN.

NOVEMBER

Our Anchor

This hope we have as an anchor of the soul, both sure and stead-
fast, and which enters the Presence behind the veil ...
— HEBREWS 6:19

Unless you are moored to something solid, it is very easy to drift away. You may not notice any movement at first, but over time, that slow drift can take you far away. You wake up one morning and are shocked to see how far you have gone.

As the psalmist said, "He brought me out of a horrible pit, out of the miry clay, and set my feet upon a rock."

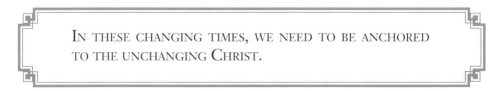

IN THESE CHANGING TIMES, WE NEED TO BE ANCHORED TO THE UNCHANGING CHRIST.

After describing the anchor of our soul—which is the hope of Christ's return—the author of Hebrews mentions the Presence behind the veil. The veil referred to is the thick separation between the Holy Place in the temple and the Holy of Holies—the most holy place. Before Jesus, no one but the high priest could enter that holy place, where God's presence dwelt. But when Jesus was crucified, it is recorded that the veil of the temple was ripped from the top to the bottom.

That is the only way the separation could be breached—from top (heaven) to bottom (earth). God issued an invitation in that breach. The door is open, and because of the sacrifice of His Son, you can have access to God at any time. "Let us therefore come boldly to the throne of grace, that we may obtain mercy and find grace to help in time of need" (Hebrews 4:16).

———

Lord, we are so grateful for the cross, through which You have
provided the hope of eternity and the right to enter into
Your presence. May we cling to the Anchor, which is Jesus.
AMEN.

To the Uttermost

Therefore He is also able to save to the uttermost those who come to God through Him, since He always lives to make intercession for them.

— Hebrews 7:25

The phrase "He is able to save to the uttermost" carries some broad ramifications, and tells us much about the length and breadth of God's power. We learn that:

He saves from all people groups—God's salvation is inclusive. He is able to save people of all nations, races, and ethnic groups. No matter who you are or where you are from, you can be saved through our great High Priest, Jesus Christ.

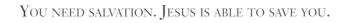

You need salvation. Jesus is able to save you.

He saves the worst of sinners—no matter how horrible your life has been or how evil your behavior, you are not beyond the reach of God's forgiveness and grace. Little sinner, big sinner, it doesn't matter. He is big enough to save you.

He saves from extreme circumstances—whether you find yourself tossed in a lion's den, thrown into a fiery furnace, abandoned in prison, floating in the ocean, hauled before hostile magistrates, or exiled on an island—God is able to deliver you. He may have you in that circumstance for a specific reason; He may choose to leave you in that situation for a time. But don't ever doubt His ability to rescue you. He is the God who has the power to shut the lion's mouth, walk with you in the furnace, spring open the prison door, snatch you from the deep, conquer your enemies, and deliver you from exile.

He is the God who saves from the uttermost.

Father, we acknowledge Your majesty—Your power, strength, wisdom, and justice. We are so grateful that we belong to You. Thank You that You went the uttermost distance to save us.

Amen.

NOT WRITTEN ON STONE

For this is the covenant that I will make with the house of Israel
after those days, says the LORD: I will put My laws in their mind
and write them on their hearts; and I will be their God,
and they shall be My people.

— HEBREWS 8:10

Because He desired a relationship with His people, God established a covenant with the children of Israel. It was a wonderful, rich covenant—and it failed. God kept His part of the bargain, but man did not keep his. So it became necessary for God to establish a new covenant, which He brought through His Son.

GOD GIVES US A NEW COVENANT—A WILL THAT DESIRES
TO PLEASE HIM, TO SERVE HIM, AND TO OBEY HIM.

At the Last Supper with His disciples there in the upper room, Jesus "took bread, gave thanks and broke it, and gave it to them, saying, 'This is My body which is given for you; do this in remembrance of Me.' Likewise He also took the cup after supper, saying, 'This cup is the new covenant in My blood, which is shed for you'" (Luke 22:19-20).

The rules of this new covenant, given in that upper room, are not written externally on tables of stone; they are written in our heart.

What a blessed covenant, what a magnificent truth: God writes His laws on our hearts, and then motivates and empowers us to keep them. How great is our God!

Father, keep us completely dependent upon You for the strength
and the desire to obey Your laws. We thank You that the covenant
between us is not dependent upon us, but upon You.
We love You, Lord.

AMEN.

An Inescapable Appointment

And as it is appointed for men to die once,
but after this the judgment …
— Hebrews 9:27

Even as death is inescapable, so is the judgment of God. When we cease to live in this body and we meet God at our death, our eternal destiny will be determined at that time. He is a holy, righteous, and true God, and only those who are holy and righteous will be allowed to share eternity with Him.

Men would like to live as though no judgment awaited them.

The unbeliever would like to think he will never be required to answer to God for the way he lived his life. But those who believe such things will be surprised. Because life is unfair, we need a future judgment. Evil men often prosper in this life, while the righteous suffer persecution. Many people have gotten away with their evil deeds. For there to be equity, there must be a future justice in which these people pay for the evil they have done.

John said, "These things I have written to you who believe in the name of the Son of God, that you may know that you have eternal life, and that you may continue to believe in the name of the Son of God" (1 John 5:13). Are you ready for your appointment with God? Do you know for certain that you will spend eternity in the kingdom of heaven?

Lord, we pray for those today who are living in uncertainty about
the future. We ask that Your Spirit will grab hold of their hearts
and cause them to be ready when that appointment arrives.

In Jesus' name, amen.

SACRIFICE OF PRAISE

*Therefore by Him let us continually offer the sacrifice of praise to
God, that is, the fruit of our lips, giving thanks to His name.
But do not forget to do good and to share,
for with such sacrifices God is well pleased.*

— HEBREWS 13:15-16

Sacrifice means giving something of value. I may sacrifice of my time to come over and help you with a project. I may sacrifice the seat I am occupying so that someone else can sit down.

Scripture talks a great deal about the sacrifices we are to offer to God. We are encouraged to offer Him the sacrifice of praise, the fruit of our lips. This implies that sometimes we won't feel like praising God, but we need to do it anyway. Other times, our praise is a spontaneous response to God's goodness. I find myself breaking out in spontaneous praise whenever I contemplate all that God has done. I think of the blessings in my life, I think of you, and I think of this work that God has done. And my heart just bursts forth in praise.

We are also told to sacrifice of our material goods. God is pleased whenever we care for one another, whenever we see a brother in need and give to cover that need. He is blessed when we see others with His eyes—when we consider the poor and reach out to help them.

> AS YOU OFFER SACRIFICES OF PRAISE AND GOOD WORKS TO YOUR FATHER, MAY YOU OVERFLOW WITH THE JOY AND FULFILLMENT OF BLESSING YOUR GOD.

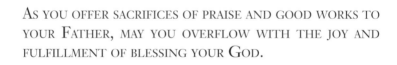

*Father, we ask that Your Holy Spirit would prompt us to offer You
praise, and that You will give us many opportunities
to sacrifice for those in need.*

IN JESUS' NAME WE PRAY, AMEN.

THE TESTING OF OUR FAITH

My brethren, count it all joy when you fall into various trials,
knowing that the testing of your faith produces patience.
— JAMES 1:2-3

When the space shuttle was being built, NASA knew that as it re-entered the earth's atmosphere, it would be exposed to extreme heat and pressure. To withstand that stress, they designed special heat-resistant tiles to protect the shuttle, but they couldn't send the shuttle off without first putting the tiles through extreme tests. Those tests were not designed to destroy the tiles but to prove their strength.

In the same way, God designs tests for us—tests that prove His strength, His faithfulness. Each test demonstrates God's character more clearly for us.

EACH TEST HELPS US TO RELY ON JESUS JUST A LITTLE BIT MORE.

It is not easy to feel joyful during a trial, but this Scripture tells us we need to do so. The joy comes from looking beyond the testing to the fruit it will bear. Paul said, "We also glory in tribulations, knowing that tribulation produces perseverance; and perseverance, character; and character, hope" (Romans 5:3-4).

God wants to bring you into a spiritual maturity and into a deeper relationship with Himself. So the next time you find yourself going through a heavy testing, count it all joy. Realize you are getting closer to the purposes of God being accomplished in you.

Father, we pray that You will help us to rejoice in our tribulations.
Lord, help us to look beyond the present adverse circumstances to the
fruit of righteousness that will come in our lives
as the result of our being proved faithful.

IN JESUS' NAME, AMEN.

FAITH AND WORKS

*What does it profit, my brethren, if someone says he has faith but
does not have works? Can faith save him?*
— JAMES 2:14

It takes two oars to row a boat. If you have only one, all you will do is row yourself in circles. But with two oars, you can row anywhere you want to.

Faith and works are companions that work together. Faith produces the works; works demonstrate the genuineness of the faith. Whatever you believe will show itself in the things you do. For example, if someone goes forward and receives Jesus Christ, his life will be changed. If someone says they went forward, but they leave and go right back into the sin they knew before, you can tell they didn't really receive Christ. Their words meant nothing.

TRUE FAITH SHOWS ITSELF IN ACTION.

James tells us that, "Faith by itself, if it does not have works, is dead" (James 2:17). He then gives the example of a brother or sister in need. If you simply wish them well, but do not help feed or clothe them, your well wishes are meaningless. You've not demonstrated true faith.

True faith produces works of love, kindness, and goodness. You are not saved by those works of righteousness; they simply demonstrate that you are saved.

The faith that will save you will bring forth the fruit of righteousness in your life. Remember what Jesus said in Matthew 7:16: "You will know them by their fruits."

Is your life bearing good fruit—fruit that proves your faith?

*Father, may our actions always prove our words. Help us abide in
You, that the faith we have will produce good works through us,
works that demonstrate the genuineness
of our commitment to Jesus Christ.*

IN HIS NAME, AMEN.

THE TONGUE

Even so the tongue is a little member and boasts great things.
See how great a forest a little fire kindles!

— JAMES 3:5

O h, the damage the tongue can do! Such a little thing, and yet it can cause so much heartache. James tells us that when given over to a destructive purpose, the tongue can be "set on fire from hell" (3:6). He further tells us that an endless number of beasts can be tamed, but "no man can tame the tongue. It is an unruly evil, full of deadly poison" (3:8). How many wars have begun because of the tongue? How many people have had their reputation destroyed because of gossip? How many hearts have been broken?

HOW MANY LIVES HAVE BEEN SHATTERED—ALL BECAUSE OF THE TONGUE?

It is wrong to use the tongue for purposes other than what God intended, and it is wrong to use the tongue inconsistently—to use the same mouth to bless God and curse our brothers who were made in the likeness of God.

There is so much potential for harm in the tongue. Yet conversely, the tongue can also bring much hope and comfort. It can encourage, strengthen, and reassure. It can remind others that they matter to God. It can share the gospel of Jesus Christ with a dying world. If you use the tongue in the way God intended, you can build others up and spur them on to good works. You can bring salvation to the lost.

May God help us to use our tongues in ways that bring Him much glory.

⟶⟼⟻⟵

Father, help us to guard our tongue, and use our words to bless
and not curse, to build up and not destroy.

IN JESUS' NAME, AMEN.

LOOKING FOR HIS COMING

Therefore be patient, brethren, until the coming of the Lord.
— JAMES 5:7

Jesus is coming again—not as a babe in a manger, but as the King of kings and the Lord of lords. He is coming to reign in righteousness over the earth. And He's coming quickly. Three times in the last chapter of the Bible, Jesus used the word "quickly" to describe His coming.

"Quickly." That is what He said. But 2,000 years have passed and He hasn't yet come. For that reason, people often scoff at talk of His return. Peter wrote about those scoffers in chapter 3 of his second book, and then explained, "But, beloved, do not forget this one thing, that with the Lord one day is as a thousand years, and a thousand years as one day. The Lord is not slack concerning His promise, as some count slackness, but is longsuffering toward us, not willing that any should perish" (2 Peter 3:8-9).

> THE LORD HAS A GOOD REASON FOR DELAYING HIS RETURN.

James tells us that God is waiting for the perfect fruit of harvest and has long patience towards it. I was hoping that the Lord would come back in 1978, but I am very glad He didn't. Just think where some of you would be today if He had. He is waiting for more.

I imagine that He is as anxious to take us home as we are to go, but He is giving others an opportunity to become a part of His family. Wait patiently and establish your heart, because the Lord is coming quickly.

Father, thank You for the glorious hope of the coming again of Jesus Christ. In the meantime, please give us patience as we wait.
IN JESUS' NAME, AMEN.

DECEMBER 2

MORE PRECIOUS THAN GOLD

*In this you greatly rejoice, though now for a little while, if need
be, you have been grieved by various trials, that the genuineness
of your faith, being much more precious than gold that perishes,
though it is tested by fire, may be found to praise, honor, and glory
at the revelation of Jesus Christ ...*

— 1 PETER 1:6-7

When we are going through trials, God does not deny us our natural emotions. For a season, we grieve. For a short time, we experience the heaviness of our disappointment, our sorrow. But when that season of mourning is over, we do something odd in the eyes of the world: we rejoice. We can do so only because we have the glorious promises of God. Even though we feel burdened, even though we have suffered loss or experienced pain, our souls are able to rejoice.

> GOD WILL CONTINUE TO REMOVE THE IMPERFECTIONS WITH-
> IN US UNTIL HE CAN LOOK AT US AND SEE HIS REFLECTION.

Peter wrote that the genuineness of your faith is much more precious than gold. Gold is known as one of the precious metals, but it is going to perish eventually. And just as the goldsmith heats the gold until all the dross is burned away and it becomes so pure he can see his reflection, so too, God lights a fire under our faith. He allows trials to break the dross in our life and cause it to come to the surface. That is the point at which we will be purified.

Remember: trials mature our faith. May we not resist the purifying work of God, but rejoice.

*Father, thank You for the testing of our faith, and for the fiery
trials which You bring to mature and purify us.*

IN JESUS' NAME, AMEN.

FROM DARKNESS TO LIGHT

But you are a chosen generation, a royal priesthood, a holy nation,
His own special people, that you may proclaim the praises of Him
who called you out of darkness into His marvelous light …

— 1 PETER 2:9

God intended that Israel would be an example to the world of the blessings He would bestow upon those who made Him their God. He chose Israel to be His light to the world. But the Jews forsook God's ways and followed after other gods. They did not bring the light of God to the world but rather, gloried in the fact that God had chosen them.

The blessings God offered Israel have now been offered to you, the church. We are His royal priesthood, and just as the priest's job was to bring the people to God and God to the people, our job is to represent God to the world.

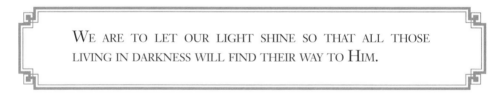

WE ARE TO LET OUR LIGHT SHINE SO THAT ALL THOSE LIVING IN DARKNESS WILL FIND THEIR WAY TO HIM.

God has called us out of darkness and into the light, so we are to declare His praises to those watching our lives and wondering about our strength, our hope, our joy. Jesus declared Himself to be "the light of the world" (John 8:12). And He has made us to be "the light of the world" (Matthew 5:14). We are to be His ambassadors and His witnesses.

What a blessing it is to belong to the Father of lights! And what a privilege it is to testify of His goodness to a world so desperate for love and forgiveness.

Father, may we indeed let our light so shine that when men see
the good works You produce in us, they will glorify You.

AMEN.

THE GOOD LIFE

He who would love life and see good days, let him refrain his tongue from evil, and his lips from speaking deceit. Let him turn away from evil and do good; let him seek peace and pursue it.

— 1 PETER 3:10-11

According to Peter, if you want the good life, here are the rules:

Rule number one: keep your tongue from evil. Gossip is pure evil. There is nothing loving or productive about gossip. It brings only harm.

Rule number two: keep your lips from speaking guile. In other words, don't be deceitful in your speech. Deceitful speech twists or omits the truth. It is speech which exploits terminology. Those who are deceitful in their speech soon lose credibility and trust.

> OBEY GOD AND HE WILL SHOWER YOU WITH JOY, HAPPINESS, PEACE, AND PROSPERITY.

Rule number three: flee that which is evil. Not only must we avoid evil, we need to seek that which is good. As Paul wrote to the Ephesians, "Put off … the old man which grows corrupt according to the deceitful lusts … put on the new man which was created according to God, in true righteousness and holiness" (Ephesians 4:22, 24). Paul then gave specific examples. They weren't just to stop lying, they were to start telling the truth. They weren't just to stop stealing, they were to get jobs so they could help those in need. They weren't just to stop slandering, they were to edify one another with their words. Avoiding evil means choosing what is good.

And what is the result of following these rules? Only blessing.

Father, we thank You for loving us so much that You desire to bless us. Help us to obey the rules You have established for good living.

IN JESUS' NAME, AMEN.

GLORY TO GOD

... that in all things God may be glorified through Jesus Christ,
to whom belong the glory and the dominion forever and ever.
Amen.

— 1 PETER 4:11

As an expression of His great and generous love, God has given each of us gifts. To some He has given the gift of mercy, to others He has given the gift of exhortation, to others the gift of wisdom or prophecy, teaching or giving. Each of us can be sure that we've been given at least one gift—one area in which we are supernaturally adept.

> THE GIFTS WE HAVE BEEN GIVEN ARE NOT FOR OUR OWN GLORY, BUT FOR GOD'S.

It is sad when people try to gain notoriety or adoration from God's gifts. But it is beautiful when someone gives God credit for their abilities. One of the world's greatest composers, Johann Sebastian Bach, used to write on every composition, "To the glory of God."

As Paul said, "What do you have that you did not receive? Now if you did indeed receive it, why do you boast as if you had not received it?" (1 Corinthians 4:7). Every gift will find its highest and greatest value when it is used to minister God's grace to others.

Do you know what your spiritual gift is? It is important that we discover the gift (or gifts) God has given to us and use them to serve others and glorify God. Are you doing that? Are you blessing God by giving Him back the gifts He gave to you?

———

Father, we are so awed by Your generosity and Your love.
Help us, Lord, to use the gifts which You have entrusted into
our care for Your benefit and for Your glory.

IN JESUS' NAME, AMEN.

He Cares for You

Casting all your care upon Him, for He cares for you.
— 1 Peter 5:7

Hannah, as the Old Testament tells us, was tormented by her inability to conceive a child. When she tried to talk to her husband about the issue, it only caused a rift in their marriage. To make matters worse, her husband's other wife, Peninnah, taunted and teased her until the pressure became so great that Hannah had lost her appetite and couldn't stop weeping. When she traveled with her husband to Shiloh for one of the feast days, she cast her cares unto the Lord. She told Eli the priest, "I am a woman with a sorrowful heart and I poured out my soul to the Lord." And Eli said to her, "Go your way, and may the Lord grant your request."

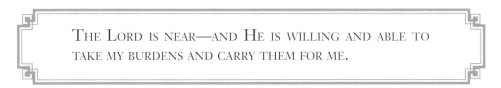

THE LORD IS NEAR—AND HE IS WILLING AND ABLE TO TAKE MY BURDENS AND CARRY THEM FOR ME.

Her husband had not helped her with her sorrow, but when Hannah brought her burden to God, she received assurance that He would take care of it.

Satan wants you to believe that you are all alone in your issue. He wants to deceive you into believing that nobody understands and nobody really cares. But God understands. God cares. And because He cares so much, He tells you to cast all your cares on Him.

Though I may fail again and again, though I may bring trouble into my life, God has promised that He would never leave me nor forsake me. Oh, how that thought encourages me! I am not alone.

Father, may we be quick to give You all of those concerns
and cares that have been weighing us down.
Thank You for lifting our heavy load.
Amen.

Conformed into His Image

*His divine power has given to us all things that pertain to life and
godliness, through the knowledge of Him who called us
by glory and virtue …*
— 2 Peter 1:3

God desires that we be as He is. "Be holy, for I am holy" (1 Peter 1:16). So it should be the goal and desire of every believer to be conformed into the image of Jesus Christ—to be holy as He is holy, pure as He is pure, perfect (or complete, mature) as He is perfect and complete.

In Genesis, we read that God created man in His image. But when man sinned and fell from the image of God, his spirit died. It is God's desire to restore man back into His image. And according to this passage of Scripture, God has provided everything we need to live a life of glorious virtue.

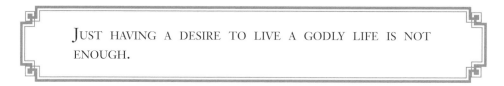

> JUST HAVING A DESIRE TO LIVE A GODLY LIFE IS NOT ENOUGH.

Apart from the empowering of God, it's impossible to live a godly life. It is through the relationship we have with Jesus that we become like Him. And it is by the power of the Word, planted deep in the fertile soil of our hearts, that we become transformed into the image of Jesus Christ.

One day the Word of God and the Spirit of God will have completed their work in us and we will once again be in the image of God. "Being confident of this very thing, that He who has begun a good work in you will complete it until the day of Jesus Christ" (Philippians 1:6).

*Father, teach us to walk closely to You and to love Your Word,
that we would be conformed again into Your image.*
IN JESUS' NAME, AMEN.

HOW SHOULD WE THEN LIVE?

Therefore, since all these things will be dissolved, what manner of persons ought you to be in holy conduct and godliness…?
— 2 PETER 3:11

In light of the fact that the material universe will one day pass away completely, how should I then live? Only a fool would put all of their time, value, and energy into things that are purely material, things destined to burn. Paul wrote, "We don't look at the things which we can see because those are temporal, but we look at the things which we cannot see because they are eternal." If I count my wealth and my treasure by my material possessions, when all of these things are destroyed, I will have absolutely nothing.

So what manner of persons ought we to be? In verse 14, Peter says, "Therefore, beloved, looking forward to these things, be diligent to be found by Him in peace, without spot and blameless." We're to live a life devoted to the things of the Spirit. We are to be diligent in our walk with the Lord, living in harmony and peace with the will of God, living without spot, and blameless.

> IF THE LORD SHOULD COME TODAY, WOULD YOU BE READY TO MEET HIM?

Amos cried out, "Prepare to meet your God, O Israel!" (Amos 4:12). Take stock of your life. Are you at peace with God, living in harmony with Him, busy about the work of the kingdom? Have you resolved the issues in your life? If you can't answer yes to these questions, start today. Ready your heart.

Father, we thank You for the hope of the kingdom of God. We pray that when You come, You will find us as faithful servants, doing Your will.

IN JESUS' NAME, AMEN.

No Darkness

This is the message which we have heard from Him and declare to you, that God is light and in Him is no darkness at all.

— 1 JOHN 1:5

No one has actually seen the sun. You see the brightness shining from the sun, but you haven't actually seen the sun itself. In fact, it is because of that brightness that you can't see the source of the light. In the same way, "No one has seen God at any time. The only begotten Son, who is in the bosom of the Father, He has declared Him" (John 1:18). Jesus is the outshining of the Father.

LIGHT AND DARKNESS ARE MUTUALLY EXCLUSIVE.

It is either light or it is dark, but you can't have a light-dark day existing at the same moment because light always dispels darkness. And because God is light, His presence dispels the darkness. In Him there is no darkness at all. As Paul asked, "What communion has light with darkness?" (2 Corinthians 6:14).

The darkness of sin alienates man from God. God loves you and longs for fellowship with you. But don't be deceived. If you are walking in darkness you cannot be in fellowship with God. "If we say that we have fellowship with Him, and walk in darkness, we lie and do not practice the truth. But if we walk in the light as He is in the light, we have fellowship with one another" (1 John 1:6-7).

Walk with Him today. Renounce sin's darkness; choose the Light.

Father, how grateful we are that the light of the gospel has shined unto us, that we may walk in the light, as You are in the light, and enjoy fellowship with You.

IN JESUS' NAME, AMEN.

THE LIFE THAT OVERCOMES

I have written to you, young men, because you are strong, and the
word of God abides in you, and you have overcome the wicked one.

— 1 JOHN 2:14

Make no mistake about it: if you are a Christian, you are in a battle. The battle is for mastery of your mind, and thus your life. God wants to rule your life so He can bless you and have fellowship with you. Satan wants to rule in your life so he can destroy it. Using lies and the promises of immediate fulfillment, he tries to lure you after the lust of your flesh. But whatever gain he gives you, it is just a temporary pleasure.

GOD WANTS YOU TO OVERCOME THE TEMPTATIONS OF SATAN.

God wants you to know victory. But you cannot know victory on your own strength. You overcome only through Jesus Christ, who can empower you to stand against the wiles of the devil.

What is the secret to victory? Today's passage says that the strength of the young men came from the Word of God abiding in them. As David said, "Your word I have hidden in my heart, that I might not sin against You" (Psalm 119:11). Jesus overcame the enticements of Satan with Scripture, as He responded to every tempting lie with a truth from God's Word. If God's Word is in our hearts, then we will not be vulnerable to the lies of Satan. When he brings temptation, we will have within us the strength we need to counteract his lies with the blessed truths of our Father.

Father, thank You that we can overcome by following in
Your steps—by living a life that is pleasing,
a life that is governed by Your Spirit.

IN JESUS' NAME, AMEN.

CHILDREN OF GOD

*Beloved, now we are children of God; and it has not yet been
revealed what we shall be, but we know that when He is revealed,
we shall be like Him, for we shall see Him as He is.*

— 1 JOHN 3:2

Because we are His children, God has a glorious future in store for us. As His Word tells us, "Eye has not seen, nor ear heard, nor have entered into the heart of man the things which God has prepared for those who love Him" (1 Corinthians 2:9).

Jesus prayed that we would share His kingdom with Him. "Father, I desire that they also whom You gave Me may be with Me where I am, that they may behold My glory which You have given Me" (John 17:24).

> ONE DAY WE'LL PASS THROUGH THAT VEIL CALLED DEATH
> AND WE WILL SEE THE FACE OF OUR SAVIOR.

When we leave this body and begin our life with God, He will reveal to us the depths, the riches, the fullness of His love—a love so great it will take all of eternity to comprehend. And even then, I don't believe we will be able to fully fathom the totality of His love.

We will dwell in the glorious light of His presence and live forever in His kingdom, discovering day-by-day, year-by-year, aeon-by-aeon, the richness of His love and grace and mercy towards us.

"Behold, what manner of love the Father has bestowed upon us, that we should be called children of God!" (1 John 3:1). How blessed we are to be His!

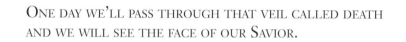

*Father, we look forward to that eternal kingdom when You will
reveal to us the exceeding richness of Your grace and love and
mercy through Jesus Christ.*

IN HIS NAME WE PRAY, AMEN.

WHY DID HE COME?

*For this purpose the Son of God was manifested, that He might
destroy the works of the devil.*

— 1 JOHN 3:8

W hat are the works of the devil? They are those works that separated the man
of the tombs (Mark 5:2) from his family and from the rest of the society,
and so tormented him that he cut himself with stones. The works of the devil are
those demons which filled the boy in Mark chapter 9 and made him gnash his
teeth, convulse, and foam at the mouth—those spirits that threw him repeatedly
into both fire and water, trying to kill him.

JESUS CAME TO DESTROY THE WORKS OF THE DEVIL.

Make no mistake about it; Satan hates you and wants to destroy you. He will
try in every way possible to deceive you onto a path that leads to death—a path
of rebellion against God. Jesus warned us that the devil has come to "steal, and
to kill, and destroy" (John 10:10). He will rob you of a blessed life. He will kill
your relationship with God and with others. He will destroy your reputation,
and ultimately, your life. Though his recruiting strategies are tempting, those
who join forces with him will share his destiny.

One of those works of the devil is the power of death. But Jesus destroyed
that power by bringing us eternal life. In contrast to Satan's destructive goals
for you, Jesus came "that they may have life, and that they may have it more
abundantly" (John 10:10).

*Father, we are so grateful for Your love. Thank You for sending Your
Son into the world to destroy the works of the devil, for sending Jesus
into the world to give us life eternal in Your Kingdom.*

AMEN.

GOD'S LOVE

And we have known and believed the love that God has for us.
— 1 JOHN 4:16

As vast as God's love is, some refuse to believe that He loves them. Despite all the evidence He has given of His great love, some people deny that love because they say He has failed them. "I have prayed and asked for certain things," they say, "but God didn't answer those prayers." For these people, the proof of God's love—and in some cases, God's very existence—would be not just answered prayer, but prayer answered according to their wishes.

How foolish to base your acceptance of God's love for you on that one test. Do we give our children everything they ask for? Of course we don't. Sometimes they ask for things that aren't good for them. Prayer is not a test of God's love. Prayer is not a means by which you get your own will accomplished. Prayer is a means by which God accomplishes His own will.

So if prayer is not the test of God's love, what is? How can we know we are loved? John gave us the answer to those questions in the previous chapter. "By this we know love, because He laid down His life for us" (1 John 3:16).

THE PROOF OF GOD'S LOVE IS JESUS.

The proof is the Son of God walking willfully to the cross, taking on the sins of mankind, and dying to redeem us. When you know Jesus, you have come to know Love itself, and you can say with John, "We have known and believed the love that God has for us."

Father, thank You for Your great love for us. May Your love be
perfected in our lives, dispelling all fears.
AMEN.

TRUTH

*I rejoiced greatly that I have found some of your children walking
in truth, as we received commandment from the Father.*

— 2 JOHN 4

What is truth? Today's philosophy says that "since truth is relative," then anything you believe to be true is true. But those who follow this thinking have rejected genuine truth. Paul said that God had clearly revealed Himself to man through creation, but man "exchanged the truth of God for the lie, and worshiped and served the creature rather than the Creator" (Romans 1:25).

GOD IS TRUTH; HE IS THE FINAL AUTHORITY FOR TRUTH.

God is not discovered through intellectual quest, but through written revelation—through the Bible. The Bible is God's Word, and therefore God's truth. When praying for the disciples, Jesus said, "Sanctify them by Your truth. Your Word is truth" (John 17:17).

What is truth? The truth is that you have been created by an all-wise Creator. You didn't evolve through a long process of accidental circumstances, but were created for a specific purpose. The truth is that the eternal almighty God who created you loves you and wants what is best for you, so He provided a means for your salvation—His Son, Jesus Christ—and a means for abundant life—His rules for living, the Bible. And if you will submit your life to God's Son and follow God's rules, you will experience joyful life on earth, and eternal life in heaven.

*Father, how thankful we are that You have given Your Word,
whereby we can know Your truth—the only truth. Give us a love
for Your Word and a desire to submit ourselves to it.*

IN JESUS' NAME, AMEN.

IMITATE JESUS

Beloved, do not imitate what is evil, but what is good. He who
does good is of God, but he who does evil has not seen God.
— 3 JOHN 11

This exhortation of John falls in between the illustrations of an evil man, Diotrephes, and a good man, Demetrius. In comparing the two, John exhorts us to imitate that which is good, not that which is evil.

John says of Diotrephes that, "He loves to have the preeminence." Jesus had said, "The kings of the Gentiles exercise lordship over them.... But not so among you; on the contrary, he who is greatest among you, let him be as the younger, and he who governs as he who serves" (Luke 22:25-26). If God has given you a position of authority within the church, then that means God has actually placed you as a servant to the church.

> WHETHER YOU LIKE IT OR NOT, YOU ARE AN INFLUENCE TO SOMEONE—FOR GOOD OR FOR BAD.

No matter where you are, someone is looking to you as a role model, and following your example. Your child is learning how to be a parent from what they observe in you. Younger Christians are learning what it means to follow Christ from watching you. How important it is that we take this responsibility seriously. What are people seeing in you?

If you don't like your answer, you can begin changing it today. "Be an example to the believers in word, in conduct, in love, in spirit, in faith, in purity" (1 Timothy 4:12).

Father, help us to imitate the good examples we see in Your Word,
learn from the bad, and live consciously and mindfully, aware that
others are watching and learning from us.
IN JESUS' NAME, AMEN.

KEEP YOURSELF IN THE LOVE OF GOD

Keep yourselves in the love of God …
— JUDE 21

Does Jude mean I am to keep myself so sweet and wonderful that God won't have any other choice but to love me? If that were the case, I would be in big trouble. Thankfully, that is not what Jude meant. He meant that we are to keep ourselves in a place of blessing—a place where God can do all the things He longs to do for us.

The giants within the Promised Land frightened the children of Israel so much that they refused to cross over. Though they had been delivered out of Egypt, they perished in the wilderness because of unbelief. They stopped short of the full blessings God had for them.

> THE BEST WAY TO KEEP YOURSELF IN THE LOVE OF GOD IS TO REALIZE THAT JESUS IS COMING SOON.

Many of you have been delivered out of the bondage of sin, but you are living in the wilderness. You haven't entered in to that full, rich life in Jesus because you are still clinging to the world.

Jesus is coming soon. Something about that thought loosens your grip on the things of this world. It makes you want to reach for heaven. It makes you want to purify yourself and change your priorities. It gives you an urgency to share the message of the gospel to a dying world.

Keep yourself in the love of God. Believe His promises, submit to Him, and obey everything He asks you to do. Then prepare yourself for all the blessings He'll bring.

———

Father, we pray that You will help us keep ourselves in that place of blessing, remembering that You are coming soon.

IN JESUS' NAME, AMEN.

Jesus is Coming Again

Behold, He is coming with clouds, and every eye will see Him,
even they who pierced Him. And all the tribes of the earth will
mourn because of Him. Even so, Amen.

— REVELATION 1:7

"Behold, He is coming," John said. Although many verses in Scripture foretell the rapture of the church—that event that will happen in a twinkling of an eye—this prophecy is not speaking of the rapture. This prophecy foretells the second coming of Jesus Christ. Those two events—the rapture and the second coming—are separate, distinct events. One must not be confused with the other.

The rapture is for the church. It is that time when Jesus will come to gather His bride unto Himself. No one knows when that will happen; all we know is that every sign Jesus gave to prepare us for that event has already occurred.

> ALL THE SIGNS HAVE BEEN FULFILLED, WHICH MEANS THAT THE RAPTURE COULD HAPPEN AT ANY MOMENT. IT COULD BE THIS VERY DAY.

Some seven years after the rapture, Jesus will return with His church to judge the earth and to establish God's kingdom. This is the second coming of Jesus. It will follow a time of great tribulation such as the world has never seen— a time of terror and devastation.

You don't want to be here when God's judgment falls. The beautiful thing is that you don't have to be here. Jesus is coming first to receive His church unto Himself. If the rapture should happen this day—and it very well could—are you ready?

><>

Lord, we want to be ready when You come. Help us that we might
take advantage of every opportunity to grow close to You.
Keep us looking up, watching for You.

AMEN.

First Love

Nevertheless I have this against you,
that you have left your first love.

— REVELATION 2:4

From outward appearances, Ephesus was one fine, well-organized church. But a vital ingredient was missing—their first love.

How important is that first love? It's more important than all of our works put together. Yet tragically, many churches today have forgotten this. Like Ephesus, they have become so organized that they can function without the presence of the Lord. But God is not interested in the works that you might do out of a sense of obligation. He wants your service to flow out of a heart of love for Him.

> WHAT IS THE MOTIVE BEHIND YOUR WORKS? ARE YOU WORKING OUT OF HABIT? TRADITION? THE DESIRE TO MAKE A NAME FOR YOURSELF? OR IS YOUR MOTIVE LOVE FOR YOUR SAVIOR?

"Remember therefore from where you have fallen; repent and do the first works" (Revelation 2:5). This was the word of the Lord to the church of Ephesus. And it's His word to you if you have lost your first love. "Remember," He said. Remember the love you felt when Jesus first lifted that heavy guilt of sin off your life. Remember the reckless abandonment you felt because you loved Him so much. Then He said, "Repent." Godly sorrow, the Bible tells us, leads to repentance. And repentance involves a change. And lastly, Jesus said, "Repeat." Go back and do your first works over—reading, worshiping, fellowshiping regularly.

If you do those things—remember, repent, repeat—your love for God will be rekindled. You will find your passion for Jesus once again.

———

Father, forgive us for moving away from our first love. Draw us
again by Your Holy Spirit, that we may do the first works over.

IN JESUS' NAME, AMEN.

THE PURPOSE OF LIFE

You are worthy, O Lord,
To receive glory and honor and power;
For You created all things,
And by Your will they exist and were created.

— REVELATION 4:11

Why am I here? What is the purpose of my existence?

If the evolutionary theory is true, those questions are moot. If there is no God, and no specific plan or purpose for our existence; if life is truly about "survival of the fittest," then life is completely meaningless.

People set a lot of goals for themselves hoping that if those goals are achieved, they will fill the void within and find happiness. But if there *is* a God and we have been put on this earth to bring Him pleasure, then we will never find fulfillment until we set ourselves to fulfilling our purpose.

WHEN YOU LIVE TO PLEASE GOD, YOU FULFILL THE PURPOSE FOR YOUR EXISTENCE.

Paul wrote, "For it is God who works in you both to will and to do for His good pleasure" (Philippians 2:13). That is good news. It tells us that God did indeed create us for His pleasure—and that He will enable us to fulfill that purpose. If you yield to Him, God will plant His desires within you. If you offer Him your whole self—heart, soul, and mind—He will give you the capacity to do those things that will honor Him.

When you live to please God, you fulfill the purpose for your existence. Instead of seeing your life as a random accident or a meaningless journey, you see it as an adventure. You view every day as an opportunity to see the work of God and the hand of God in your life.

———

Father, help us to learn what pleases You, and set ourselves to
doing those things. May our thoughts, our conversations,
and our actions bring You pleasure.

AMEN.

WHO IS WORTHY?

Then I saw a strong angel proclaiming with a loud voice,
"Who is worthy to open the scroll and to loose its seals?"

— REVELATION 5:2

I n the Old Testament, God established certain laws concerning redemption. If you owed a debt you couldn't pay, you could be sold as a slave in order to pay off that debt. If you had a sympathetic relative, they could pay the debt for you and set you free. Such a relative was called the "goel," or the "kinsman redeemer." The same law held true for property issues. If you needed to sell your field, the "goel" could redeem the field for you.

When John recognizes that no one has been found worthy to redeem the earth back from Satan's clutches, he begins to sob. But then an elder tells him, "Do not weep. Behold, the Lion of the tribe of Judah, the Root of David, has prevailed to open the scroll and to loose its seven seals" (Revelation 5:5). Jesus was worthy to take the scroll. He paid the price to redeem us from our sin, and to redeem the world from the powers of darkness.

IT WON'T BE LONG BEFORE THIS SCENE PLAYS OUT IN HEAVEN.

It is just a matter of time before this redemption comes due, and Jesus will step forth to loose the seals and to declare that "the kingdoms of this world have become the kingdoms of our Lord and of His Christ, and He shall reign forever and ever!" (Revelation 11:15).

Father, we thank You for the glorious salvation that Jesus Christ
purchased for us at such a great price; that as a result of this
redemption we have hope for Your coming kingdom.

IN JESUS' NAME WE PRAY, AMEN.

THE MAN OF SIN

*And I looked, and behold, a white horse. He who sat on it had a
bow; and a crown was given to him,
and he went out conquering and to conquer.*

— REVELATION 6:2

hen the Antichrist comes to power, he will be a pawn in Satan's hands. Through this false Christ, Satan will have complete control of the world. Using Satan's power, the Antichrist will win the world's trust and admiration through miraculous signs and wonders. And the false prophet who accompanies this man of sin will cause the world to worship the Antichrist—the "beast" (Revelation 13:12-13).

> JESUS WARNED THAT IN THE LAST DAYS, MANY WOULD BE DECEIVED.

Israel today is ripe for that deception. They are waiting for their Messiah. If you ask them, "How will you know your Messiah?" Their stock answer is, "He will lead us in the rebuilding of the temple." That is an open door for deception. All the Antichrist has to do is make a treaty that enables the Jews to rebuild their temple—and they will believe he is their Messiah.

Scripture tells us that after three-and-a-half years, the Antichrist will brazenly enter the Holy of Holies and demand to be worshiped as God. The Jews will flee to the wilderness where God will preserve them through the last three-and-a-half years, as the Antichrist goes to make war against the remnant of Israel.

Thankfully, we—the bride of Christ—won't be here to see or experience this time of terror. But those who reject the Lord and despise the truth will indeed suffer the consequences of their choice.

---

*Father, we pray for those sitting on the fence right now—those
who have not yet committed their lives to You.
May You reach them by Your Holy Spirit.*

AMEN.

THE FRAGRANCE OF PRAYER

Then another angel, having a golden censer, came and stood at the
altar. He was given much incense, that he should offer it with
the prayers of all the saints upon the golden altar
which was before the throne.

— REVELATION 8:3

What an awesome gift prayer is. To think that the Creator of the universe has granted us an audience with Himself is almost unbelievable. Prayer is a privilege. And we are told that God values our prayers so much, they rise to Him as a sweet fragrance.

Prayer is worship. It is sitting at God's feet, loving Him, adoring Him, opening your heart, and letting Him open His heart to you. I believe this kind of worshipful prayer—communing with God friend to Friend—is the highest form of prayer.

ARE YOU USING THE GIFT GOD GAVE YOU?

Probably the most common form of prayer is petition. This is where we seek God's help, provision, or guidance for our lives. We all have needs, and it is perfectly proper to bring those needs to God.

Prayer is also intercession. It is going beyond our own needs to lift up the needs of others.

Prayer is a dialogue. It is God speaking to you, as well as you speaking to God. It's important to hear from God as well as to speak to Him.

Are you worshiping through prayer, petitioning through prayer, interceding through prayer, and hearing God through prayer?

Are you offering God the sweet fragrance of prayer?

Father, forgive us for wasting so much time in pursuit of worthless
things. Let our hearts be attuned to the things of the Spirit as we lift
our voices, express our praise, and spend time with You.

IN JESUS' NAME, AMEN.

HARDENED HEARTS

But the rest of mankind, who were not killed by these plagues, did
not repent of the works of their hands.... And they did not repent
of their murders or their sorceries or
their sexual immorality or their thefts.

— REVELATION 9:20-21

evelation 9 tells of the fifth and sixth trumpet judgments in which hell is opened and demonic forces invade the earth, killing one-third of the earth's inhabitants. You would think that the remainder of the people would be on their faces crying out to God for mercy, repenting of their sin. But such is not the case. They actually blaspheme God, and refuse to repent of their worship of Satan.

TODAY, THE SAME IDOLS IN THE BIBLE ARE WORSHIPED.

It is easy to shake our heads at those in Bible times who foolishly worshiped false idols, but Revelation makes it clear that men will continue to worship idols all the way through the tribulation period. Those same idols are still worshiped today.

If you worship your intellect, you are worshiping Baal, the god of the intellect. If you worship pleasure, then you are worshiping Molech, the god of pleasure. If you are worshiping power—the drive to reach the top, even if it means crushing other people beneath you—then you are worshiping Mammon, the god of power. If you are worshiping sex, then you are worshiping Ashtoreth, the goddess of sex.

How do you know if you are worshiping any of those gods? You can tell by what absorbs your time, your thoughts, your energy—your life.

Search your heart. What are you worshiping?

Lord, may we be quick to repent and to call upon You for the for-
giveness that You have so wonderfully provided through
Your Son and our Lord Jesus Christ.

IN HIS NAME WE PRAY, AMEN.

OVERCOMING THE ENEMY

*And war broke out in heaven: Michael and his angels fought with
the dragon; and the dragon and his angels fought,
but they did not prevail …*

— REVELATION 12:7-8

The enemy we face is one of the most powerful of all of God's created beings. Note, however, that he is merely a created being. People sometimes consider Satan to be God's opposite, equal opponent. That is not true. Satan is in opposition to God, he is opposed to the people of God and the things of God, but he is *not* the opposite of God.

> THOUGH OUR ENEMY IS POWERFUL, HE IS NOT INVINCIBLE.

In today's passage, we see him being overcome by Michael, the archangel of God, who has been at war with Satan through the centuries. We read that "the dragon and his angels fought, but they did not prevail." And Satan will not prevail against you either if you belong to God. As Jesus promised Peter, "On this rock I will build My church, and the gates of hades shall not prevail against it " (Matthew 16:18)

Though Satan strategizes against you, though he works tirelessly and relentlessly to try to arouse your fleshly nature and pull you away from God, he can't prevail against you if you arm yourself with Christ. You're no match for Satan on your own strength. You dare not try to face him on your own. But you can stand in the strength of the Lord. You can overcome through the cross of Jesus Christ, which gives us victory over the powers of darkness.

*Lord, we are so thankful that because we dwell in You, we are
shielded from the enemy; the wicked one cannot touch us.
Thank You for the victory You provided on the cross.*

IN JESUS' NAME, AMEN.

GREAT AND MARVELOUS ARE HIS WORKS

"Great and marvelous are Your works, Lord God Almighty!
Just and true are Your ways, O King of the saints!
Who shall not fear You, O Lord, and glorify Your name?
For You alone are holy.
For all nations shall come and worship before You,
For Your judgments have been manifested."
— REVELATION 15:3-4

It is very likely that every one of the singers of this song had been martyred for their faith. By the time John sees and hears them in this heavenly scene, these faithful believers had stood firm against the Antichrist—who ordered everyone on earth to receive a mark on either the right hand or the forehead—and had lost their life because of their refusal to obey. But though they experienced death, they escaped the judgments to come upon the earth. And now here they are in heaven, standing before the throne of God and offering Him praise.

The song these martyrs sing is a song of victory. Though Satan had raged against them, God gave them victory over the powers of darkness, and the beautiful lyrics that spring forth are lyrics motivated by awe and gratitude. "Great and marvelous are Your works, Lord God Almighty. Just and true are Your ways, O King of the saints!" How worthy He is to receive our worship!

THE SONG OF THE LAMB—A BEAUTIFUL SONG OF THANKS-GIVING AND PRAISE FOR THE ONE WHO SHOWS MERCY AND GRACE TO THE LOST.

Lord, we are so grateful that we have come to know You and to experience Your love and compassion. May we be faithful in our service to You always.

IN JESUS' NAME, AMEN.

THE LAMB WILL OVERCOME THEM

*These are of one mind, and they will give their power and authority
to the beast. These will make war with the Lamb, and the Lamb
will overcome them, for He is Lord of lords and King of kings ...*

— REVELATION 17:13-14

Who would be so foolish as to make war against Jesus Christ? Yet we read that during the tribulation, the leaders of the world will try that very thing. But even when all the powers of the world unite with one strength, one mind, and one purpose—to make war with the Lamb of God—those godless forces will fail.

"And the Lamb will overcome them," our text tells us. The final victory belongs to the Lord. "He who sits in the heavens shall laugh; the Lord shall hold them in derision" (Psalm 2:4).

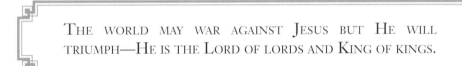

THE WORLD MAY WAR AGAINST JESUS BUT HE WILL TRIUMPH—HE IS THE LORD OF LORDS AND KING OF KINGS.

Nebuchadnezzar—the first world ruler—sought to battle against the Lord and against His word. He too was soundly defeated. After he came to his senses, he wrote these words: "And at the end of the time I, Nebuchadnezzar, lifted my eyes to heaven, and my understanding returned to me; and I blessed the Most High and praised and honored Him who lives forever: for His dominion is an everlasting dominion, and His kingdom is from generation to generation" (Daniel 4:34).

It may appear that the world is winning the battle, but never forget that the ultimate victory belongs to the Lamb.

Father, we wait for that day when You will subdue the powers of darkness that rebel against You and establish Your righteous kingdom upon this earth. May that day come soon.

AMEN.

GONE FOREVER

The fruit that your soul longed for has gone from you, and all the
things which are rich and splendid have gone from you,
and you shall find them no more at all.

— REVELATION 18:14

What fruit does this verse refer to? What were these people lusting after? The fruit is commercialism, and the people lusted after "merchandise of gold and silver, precious stones and pearls" (expensive jewelry), "fine linen and purple, silk and scarlet" (extravagant clothes), and "… ivory … precious wood, bronze, iron, and marble" (Revelation 18:12). Does that sound familiar? How many people today lust after the fruit of commercialism, spending money they don't have to fill their closets with clothes and their homes with expensive furniture and decorations? How many years do they spend trying to pay off the credit cards they used to satisfy this lust?

GOD HATES ANYTHING THAT ENSLAVES HIS PEOPLE.

Commercialism is a system that can enslave you. How foolish to put yourself under the domination of something so fleeting and insignificant. We are here for such a short time, but eternity is forever. Is it wise to put everything into this life, and nothing in the life to come?

Jesus said, "One's life does not consist in the abundance of the things he possesses" (Luke 12:15). Our lives consist in a relationship with God through Jesus Christ. I would much rather be poor in this world and rich in faith, than rich in this world and poor in faith. The riches that we have in Christ are lasting—they are eternal.

Father, we realize that the god of this world has deluded men.
We pray that You would open the eyes of those who have been
blinded by Satan's deceptive powers.

IN JESUS' NAME, AMEN.

THE BRIDE OF CHRIST

Let us be glad and rejoice and give Him glory, for the marriage of the Lamb has come, and His wife has made herself ready.

— REVELATION 19:7

In his second letter to the Corinthians, Paul said, "For I am jealous for you with godly jealousy. For I have betrothed you to one husband, that I may present you as a chaste virgin to Christ" (2 Corinthians 11:2).

In those days, marriages were arranged because parents felt the decision was too important for a child to make. Paul, speaking as a father to the Corinthian church, tells them the arrangement has already been made. They are betrothed to Christ.

Revelation chapter 19 describes the marriage of the Lamb to His bride, the church. "His wife has made herself ready." In this heavenly scene, the espousal period is over, and the time has come for the marriage ceremony. Every wedding has a bride. We read here that the bride of Christ is "arrayed in fine linen, clean and bright." And we are told that the fine linen "is the righteous acts of the saints."

> THE BRIDE OF CHRIST WILL BE DRESSED IN RIGHTEOUSNESS.

Isaiah said regarding our self-righteousness: "But we are all like an unclean thing, and all our righteousnesses are like filthy rags" (Isaiah 64:6). When we present ourselves to Jesus, we can either wear our own filthy rags—which represents our best efforts at righteousness—or we can wear the beautiful, clean, white garments of a bride—the righteousness of Jesus Christ through faith.

What will you choose to wear when you meet your Groom? Are you dressed in your own righteousness today, or His?

Father, we thank You that we can be clothed in Your righteousness, and that through Christ, we can stand before You, holy, pure, and clean.

IN JESUS' NAME, AMEN.

THE GREAT WHITE THRONE

*Then I saw a great white throne and Him who sat on it, from
whose face the earth and the heaven fled away.*

— REVELATION 20:11

People often think they are getting away with their sin because no one seems to know. But God knows. He sees it all—every thought, every action, every secret deed. And as the Bible tells us, "God will bring every work into judgment, including every secret thing, whether good or evil" (Ecclesiastes 12:14). In that day, the books will be opened, and each man will be judged by the things written in those books—even the secret things he has said and done.

But there is another book called the Book of Life, and that is the one you want your name recorded in. For those whose names are not found in the Book of Life will be cast into the lake of fire. But those who put their faith and trust in Jesus Christ and received Him as their Lord and Savior will be saved.

> WHEN WE STAND AT THAT GREAT WHITE THRONE JUDG-
> MENT OF GOD AND HEAR OUR NAMES CALLED, WE NEED NOT
> FEAR.

The Word tells us that, "We have an Advocate with the Father, Jesus Christ the righteous" (1 John 2:1). On that day, Jesus will step forward and say, "Father, this one belongs to Me. Charge this child's sin to My account." And in that moment, each of us who belong to Jesus will be declared justified. Our names will be found in the Book of Life, we will be welcomed into heaven, and our eternity with our Savior will begin.

*Thank You, Father, for the wonderful work of Jesus Christ on our
behalf. May we live to bring You glory.*

IN JESUS' NAME, AMEN.

THE TRUE AND FAITHFUL WORD OF GOD

Then He who sat on the throne said,
"Behold, I make all things new." And He said to me,
"Write, for these words are true and faithful."
— REVELATION 21:5

Sometimes the things God prophesies are so amazing, He finds it necessary to confirm that His Word is true.

In Ezekiel chapter 36 God prophesied the redevelopment of the land of Israel. He described how the bare mountains would be covered again with trees, and how the fields would again bring forth their fruit for the people. After making these amazing predictions, God said, "I have spoken it and I will do it." It took Him almost 2,500 years to do it, but He has done it. This little land, smaller than New Jersey, is the fourth largest exporter of fruit and vegetables in the world.

PROPHECIES ARE BEING FULFILLED BEFORE OUR VERY EYES.

As Jesus told His disciples of the things that would transpire at the end of the age, He said, "Heaven and earth will pass away, but My words will by no means pass away" (Matthew 24:35).

Week after week, newspaper headlines chronicle the fact that God keeps His word.

What is God affirming to be true here in the twenty-first chapter of Revelation? "It is done! I am the Alpha and the Omega, the Beginning and the End. I will give of the fountain of the water of life freely to him who thirsts. He who overcomes shall inherit all things, and I will be his God, and he shall be My son" (21:6-7).

Father, thank You for Your glorious promises, whereby we are made
partakers of eternal life in Your kingdom.
IN THE PRECIOUS NAME OF JESUS, AMEN.

GOD'S INVITATION

*And the Spirit and the bride say, "Come!" And let him who hears
say, "Come!" And let him who thirsts come.
Whoever desires, let him take the water of life freely.*

— REVELATION 22:17

This marvelous book—God's very Word—ends with an invitation. "Let him that hears say, 'Come!'"

Once you have heard the message of God's love and received His forgiveness, once you've experienced the wonder and the joy of walking in fellowship with Him, then you also find yourself wanting to give the invitation to others.

"And let him who thirsts come." John tells us that at the Feast of Tabernacles Jesus stood and cried, "If anyone thirsts, let him come to Me and drink" (John 7:37). The thirst Jesus spoke about was not physical. He spoke of that universal thirst that lies deep within the spirit of man. It is the thirst that David spoke about when he said, "As the deer pants for the water brooks, so pants my soul for You, O God" (Psalm 42:1). It's the thirst for God.

Man's problem is that he tries to satisfy the thirst for God with physical and emotional experiences or possessions. But temporary things cannot satisfy that thirst. God is freely offering to fill that void in your life. He wants you to have intimate fellowship with Him so that His living water fills you to overflowing. Only then will that thirst in you be quenched.

GOD IS INVITING YOU TO A RICH, ABUNDANT LIFE—A LIFE WITH HIM. WILL YOU ACCEPT THE INVITATION? WILL YOU COME?

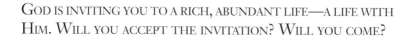

*Lord, thank You for being the God who pursues. Help us to
respond to Your invitation and enter into a deeper, more intimate
relationship with You. We acknowledge, Lord,
that only You can satisfy our thirst.*

AMEN.